HENRY BLACK

HENRY BLACK

On Stage in Meiji Japan

IAN McARTHUR

MONASH University
Publishing

Monash University Publishing

Building 4, Monash University
Clayton, Victoria 3800, Australia
www.publishing.monash.edu

Monash University Publishing brings to the world publications which advance the best traditions of humane and enlightened thought. Monash University Publishing titles pass through a rigorous process of independent peer review.

www.publishing.monash.edu/books/hb-9781921867507.html

Design: Les Thomas; cover image: from *East of Asia Magazine* vol. 1, 1902.

The Monash Asia Series

Henry Black: On Stage in Meiji Japan is published as part of the Monash Asia Series.

The Monash Asia Series comprises works that make a significant contribution to our understanding of one or more Asian nations or regions. The individual works that make up this multi-disciplinary series are selected on the basis of their contemporary relevance.

The Monash Asia Series of the Monash Asia Institute replaces Monash University's MAI Press imprint, which, from the early 1970s, has demonstrated this University's strong interest and expertise in Asian studies.

National Library of Australia Cataloguing-in-Publication entry:

Author: McArthur, Ian 1950.

Title: Henry Black : on stage in Meiji Japan / Ian McArthur.

ISBN: 9781921867507 (paperback)

Series: Monash Asia series.

Notes: Includes bibliographical references and index.

Subjects: Black, Henry James, 1858–1923; Rakugo--Biography; Storytellers--Japan--Biography; *Kabuki*--Biography; Japan--Social life and customs--1868–1912; Japan--Social life and customs--1912–1945.

Dewey Number: 808.5430952

Printed in Australia by Griffin Press an Accredited ISO AS/NZS 14001:2004 Environmental Management System printer. The paper this book is printed on is certified by the Programme for the Endorsement of Forest Certification scheme. Griffin Press holds PEFC chain of custody SGS - PEFC/COC-0594. PEFC promotes environmentally responsible, socially beneficial and economically viable management of the world's forests.

Contents

List of illustrations

Acknowledgements

This book had its beginnings in an encounter with Henry Black in the pages of the scholarly journal *Monumenta Nipponica* during a ride on a train on Tokyo's Ginza Line in 1983. I had just bought my copy of the journal at a bookshop in Nihonbashi and opened it to find, to my astonishment, a photo of Henry Black dressed for a female role in a *kabuki* play. I was surprised to learn that Black had been born in Australia and that his father had been a journalist in Japan. As I was a correspondent for a number of Australian newspapers at the time, I contacted the authors of the article in the journal, Sasaki Miyoko and Morioka Heinz. I later interviewed them for a feature article about Black and, with them, attended the first graveside ceremony commemorating Black's death at the Yokohama Foreigners' Cemetery. Some years later, after my return to Australia, I had the opportunity, under the expert supervision of Dr Elise Tipton, to write a doctoral thesis at the University of Sydney about Black's contribution to the modernity debate in Meiji-era Japan. This book includes the findings of my research for that thesis. It is the end result of that first encounter on the Ginza Line. In particular, I would like to acknowledge the pioneering research efforts of Sasaki Miyoko and Morioka Heinz as well as the researcher Asaoka Kunio. The book would not have been possible without their enthusiasm for the project and their willingness to share their research findings. Others to whom I owe similar debts are San'yūtei Enraku and San'yūtei Tonraku, who freely supplied me with support and information about the life of a *rakugoka*. I also acknowledge a special debt of gratitude to: the team at Monash University Publishing; Rachel Salmond for her tireless attempts to ensure accuracy in the text; my parents Jim and Beres McArthur, who kept asking me when I would complete the book; my parents-in-law Kiyofumi and Kazuko Minami, who supplied me with accommodation and encouragement on research trips to Japan; my wife Mari Minami and our daughter Hillary Minami McArthur for their support and patience.

Author's note

Japanese personal names in this book follow Japanese convention, with the surname given first. In some cases, I refer to *rakugoka* by the name by which they are best known, while I refer to some authors by their pen names.

With the names of non-Japanese nationals of Japanese ancestry, I have placed the surname last. I have used the revised Hepburn system for romanisation of Japanese words, with macrons for long vowels in Japanese words. Exceptions are for a limited number of commonly accepted spellings of names of places, companies or persons.

Unless otherwise indicated, translations of original Japanese are mine.

Introduction

'The first foreigner on the Japanese boards'

As the audience at the Haruki Theatre in Tokyo held their collective breath, the actor they had come to see emerged from the palanquin into the full glare of the new electric lighting. In spite of the *kabuki* makeup and fluent Japanese, the actor was unmistakably a European whose eyes and prominent nose betrayed Scottish ancestry. Before them stood the image of Banzuiin Chōbee, leader of a band of demoralised town vigilantes known as *machiyakko* who fights a group of troublesome *samurai* suppressing local townspeople. This Banzuiin Chōbee stamped his feet in the right manner and assumed the correct bombastic *aragoto*-style *kabuki* poses. The newspaper review of his August 1892 appearance described it as an accomplished performance whose minor departures from the traditional staging were even welcomed with supportive applause from an enthusiastic audience. The actor was a professional storyteller with the stage name of Kairakutei Burakku and the naturalised Japanese name of Ishii Burakku, but who had been born to British parents as Henry James Black 34 years before in North Adelaide, in the British colony of South Australia. Henry Black's stage performances were a source of embarrassment to family members, but were extremely popular with Japanese audiences. To his admirers, Henry Black's Banzuiin Chōbee had added cachet because he claimed to have trained for the part under the great *kabuki* master, Ichikawa Danjūrō IX (1839–1903). As this was Danjūrō's signature role, he would not have taken lightly the task of training someone for it. Henry Black's performance that day represented the triumphal end-point of a decades-long journey across time and worlds from a distant British colony to the spiritual heart of Japan's theatre culture. It was a journey that began with the shedding of a Victorian-era British–Australian identity and the creation of a new one as a celebrated storyteller on the stages of Japanese towns and cities. The storyteller profession to which he belonged was in the words of the British correspondent of *The Times*, Captain F. Brinkley, 'without parallel in any other country' (Brinkley 1904:105).

In a globalised age, the story of how Henry Black used a career on the stage to negotiate a new identity in his adopted country is as relevant today as then. Born British in colonial Australia in December 1858, Henry Black became a naturalised Japanese citizen, but lies buried in a foreigners' graveyard in Yokohama. Henry Black spent most of his life between 1865 and 1923 as an oral storyteller in theatres in Japan. During those years, his accomplishments included performances of *kabuki* and hypnotism, the management of a Western-style band, and the recording of his own narrations on the first disc-shaped records ever made in Japan. He also underwent an arranged marriage with a Japanese woman while maintaining a same-sex relationship with a Japanese man, adopted a Japanese boy, attempted suicide, drank heavily, and was frequently in debt.

By any benchmark, Henry Black led an extraordinary life. But this is not merely an account of his life. It is the story of how his popular adaptations of European detective fiction helped Japanese audiences come to terms with rapid social change in what is known as the Meiji era, the turbulent years between 1868 and 1912. On the Japanese calendar these years delineate the reign of Emperor Meiji. In the minds of most Japanese today, the era is associated with the country's irreversible transformation from an Asian backwater to a prosperous nation capable of defeating Russia in battle. The great reform experiment of those years opened Japan to new ideas, but also brought far-reaching changes that affected everyone from prime minister down to night-soil carrier. The changes produced a radically new Japan, which has since served as a template for modernisation in other Asian countries.

Henry Black was one of many agents of change in Japan during those years. His main strength was his adaptation of European detective novels and the retelling of them in theatres for Japanese audiences. Because they depicted life in the modern industrialising European and North American democracies, his stories served as Meiji-era templates for a new Japan. They introduced to his audiences new concepts such as trial by jury, a woman's right to inheritance, and the use of science to uncover crime. They were also replete with prescient warnings about the dangers of class division and poverty in the newly industrialising capitalist economies upon which Japanese leaders modeled their nation. In Henry Black's stories, characters had Japanese names and lived hybrid lives amid liminal landscapes containing familiar landmarks such as Tokyo's famous bridges, Eitai bashi and Nihon bashi. They also read *The Times* and rode in horsedrawn coaches that crossed those same bridges on their way to the Paris Opera. They wore top hats and brandished polished walking sticks. They returned home by fast train from stations by the Thames to dine on rice and *miso* soup. In the process, European concepts of modernity made the leap across geographic and cultural boundaries to find an appreciative mass audience in Japan.

The times served Henry Black well. In the 1880s and 1890s, audiences in Japan were eager for information about the West. They crowded into theatres to listen to his adaptations of European detective and sensation fiction writers, including Mary Braddon, Fortuné du Boisgobey, and Charles Dickens.

Henry Black's life followed a trajectory from his arrival in Yokohama in 1865, through early involvement with the pro-democracy movement and a career in theatre to his decline as an all-but-forgotten narrator for silent films in the 1920s. He died within three weeks of the 1923 Great Kanto earthquake, which destroyed much of Yokohama and Tokyo. That disaster put an end to his career by destroying Tokyo's theatres. Vaudeville never fully recovered after the advent of cinema.

Henry Black's story demonstrates how audacity and persistence enabled a young boy, brought from a struggling British colony at the age of six, to take advantage of the opportunities provided by the drive for reform in 19th-century Japan by forging an unconventional career, free of Victorian-era constraints on morality and imagination. His life is testimony to the human qualities of plasticity, adaptability, determination and inventiveness. In an era when unrelenting reform forced every Japanese to confront change, Henry Black was able to leverage his European heritage to show his Japanese audiences where the future lay. His capacity to adapt meant that in many ways he was the consummate Meiji man.

Chapter 1

In the beginning

> These days, things are peaceful in this country but it was not always like that. Foreigners such as myself used to live in fear for our lives. Once when my family took a carriage to a party in the foreign quarter we were suddenly approached by a drunken samurai wielding a sword and threatening our lives. It wasn't till a distinguished Japanese gentleman came up and spoke in a calm manner that he calmed down and left us in peace. In those days we used to have to say our prayers whenever we ventured out. (Henry Black reminiscing about pre-Meiji era dangers in the preamble to his narration *Eikoku Rondon gekijō miyage* [Eikokujin 1891:2]).

In the years just before and after Henry Black arrived in Yokohama, images of Japan received in the West were of petite and pliant women in kimonos, of tiny wooden and paper houses, of excessively polite people who bowed, or of fearless *samurai* who cut down all in their path with the sharpest of swords. Many of the images were inaccurate and contributed to misunderstanding. Globetrotting, wealthy Britons came and went and wrote travelogues about the Japanese, perpetuating myths about quaintness by writing admiringly of 'miniature' villages, the beauty of the women, and the delicacy of the landscapes. Some of them complained about the fleas in the inns. One of the Englishmen whom Henry Black hosted on a tour of Tokyo in the 1890s even wrote about the Japanese as 'amiable seals' because the custom of bowing reminded him of the bobbing head of a seal. One man's politeness is another man's bobbing seal. Japanese artisans were happy to cater to the demand for exotica, complicit in this conspiracy to conjure up a fine-quality porcelain fairyland with blue willow trees in tidy villages of thatched houses and water-wheels. You can't see the fleas in a painting on porcelain.

These were years when the French naval officer Pierre Loti wrote semi-anecdotal kiss-and-tell about his dalliances with the doll-like temporary wives of Nagasaki, inspiring Puccini to compose an opera called *Madama*

Butterfly. In these same years, tourists snapped up the woodblock prints artists mass-produced at cheap rates serving as the equivalent of today's postcards from Tokyo and Yokohama. Some were used as wrapping for porcelain exported to Europe. In Paris, van Gogh and other impressionists haunted the stalls to collect these prints, which inspired in them new notions of colour and perspective. Thus, intrigued by the mystique of Japan, the Greek-born Irish vagabond journalist Lafcadio Hearn arrived to settle, marry and reproduce the country's ghost stories for grateful foreign consumption. Hearn's writings perpetuated the notion that Japan was an exotic place and compounded the Western appetite for japonaiserie.

Believing Japan to be an exotic land of flimsy paper houses, English entrepreneur JH Brooke brought his own tents when he arrived in Yokohama in 1862 'with an amount of luggage that set Yokohama society talking for years'.[1] Unsure of what to expect, even for his horses, Brooke also brought hay. Brooke had edited a small weekly in Lincolnshire, England before becoming a lecturer at London Polytechnic, then going to Australia where he was a cabinet minister in the Victorian state government for a week. He moved to Japan following election defeat. Aside from raising eyebrows by the sheer number of belongings he brought, Brooke was also responsible for 'an event that considerably stirred life in Yokohama' (Williams 1958:161) This was the arrival of the 'first foreign young lady' of marriageable age, Brooke's daughter Gertie. Such was life in the new frontier settlement of Yokohama.

Expatriates strove to make Yokohama as livable as possible. Before the foreigners arrived, Yokohama had been a swamp. Much of that was drained to make way for the new arrivals. The Blacks did not live near the swamp. They lived in the hills where they had the advantage of the fresher sea breezes. Occasionally a foreign circus troupe visited the community, or local Japanese acrobats enlivened the scene, but, for the most part, foreign families made their own entertainment in their homes, although in later years they used the nearby Gaiety Theatre.

Beyond the confines of the expatriate settlement lived the Japanese, the poorest of whom settled near the swamp with its fetid smells coming off the abattoir in summer and its unhealthy damp in winter. Their way of life did not necessarily equate to expatriate notions of being civilised. For most expatriates in Japan in those early years, the Japanese were the uncivilised ones.

---

1 For detail about Brooke and his daughter Gertie, see Williams 1958:162–163. Williams' book is an excellent source of information about expatriate life in Meiji-era Japan.

Restless spirits

Henry Black's parents were British. His father, John Reddie Black, was born in Scotland.[2] John was educated in London at Christ's Hospital and later joined the Royal Navy. John's wife, Elizabeth Charlotte, was English.[3] In July 1854, John and Elizabeth Black left London for Australia on the barque *Irene*, arriving off Adelaide on 29 October that year.[4] Despite Henry Black's subsequent claims that he was born in Brighton (Nishūbashi 1905:293) or London, England (Nyorai 1896), his birth certificate shows he was born in North Adelaide, South Australia, on 22 December 1858.[5] Little is known of the Blacks' activities in Australia, other than that John Black was also at the gold diggings at Ballarat in the adjoining colony of Victoria in 1862 (Black, JR 1883:I,348). There is no evidence that he succeeded as a gold miner, but he did establish a reputation there as an amateur singer (Brooke 1880).

There is no firsthand account of the timing and reason for John Black's departure from Australia after an eight- or nine-year stay. Nor is there any record of his arrival in Japan, although a *Japan Herald* obituary marking his death in 1880 cited 'business with him taking an unprosperous turn' as the reason for departure from Australia. It stated that he reached Japan 'after traveling through the Australian colonies, India, and China' (Brooke 1880). John Black himself offered no evidence of a burgeoning interest in Japan prior to his arrival there.[6] In the posthumously published compilation of recollections he penned in 1880, *Young Japan*, John Black recalled that

---

2 An extract, dated 28 August 1975, from an entry in 'an Old Parochial Register' in the Parish of Dysart in the County of Fife, Scotland, held by the Registrar Of Births and Baptisms at the General Register Office, New Register House, Edinburgh, records John Reddie Black's birth on the 8 January 1826 to John Reddie Black and Sophia KI Hurdies. He was baptised in the Episcopal Chapel, Kirkcaldy. Sir Walt John Tierney Bart and G Spence Esq recorded as sponsors. The extract was in the possession of Henry Black's niece, the late Mrs Joy Currie.

3 Letter from Mrs Joy Currie to the author, 28 October 1993. According to Mrs Currie, Elizabeth's maiden name was Bonwell.

4 *The Adelaide Times* of 30 October 1854 lists the Blacks in the ship's passenger list. *Irene* carrried wool and gold as well as passengers. In a memorandum dated 28 October and published several days later in *The Adelaide Times*, the Blacks and 15 other passengers expressed their appreciation and gratitude to the ship's captain, D Bruce, for conveying them safely to Australia.

5 My thanks to Mr David Sissons for a copy of Henry Black's birth certificate, sourced from South Australia's registry of births and deaths.

6 In Ballarat in 1862, the year before his probable arrival in Japan, he met 'a gentleman' who related his experiences in Japan to him, but recalled that 'nothing my new friend told me imparted to me any special desire to go there; for at the time my thoughts were turned in a totally different direction' (Black, JR 1883:I,248).

he 'arrived on a visit, without an idea of becoming a permanent resident' (Black, JR 1883:I,248). Nevertheless, his subsequent transfer of wife and son to Japan suggests he was among a small but growing number of inquisitive Europeans who ventured to Japan in those years. In *Young Japan*, John Black admitted that his 'own personal sympathies [were] so strongly with Japan and the Japanese' (Black, JR 1883:I,vii) and that visitors such as himself 'found everything strange, and every human being he met, full of interests and attraction' (Black, JR 1883:I,2).

After an initial stay in Nagasaki, the offer of a job as editor-in-chief of the English-language *Japan Herald* in Yokohama enticed John Black to move. Yokohama was a rapidly growing port, offering more promise than Nagasaki as it was closer to the political and administrative capital of Edo. The offer came from Albert W Hansard, head of an auction and commission business. Hansard had launched the *Japan Herald* on 23 November 1861. Grace Fox's preface to the 1968 reprint of *Young Japan* describes the *Japan Herald* as 'the official organ for the publications of the legations of the treaty powers in Japan' offering 'kindly criticism of the Shogun's government' (Black, JR 1883:I,viii). It was published every Saturday evening. From December 1863, John Black also edited the *Daily Japan Herald*.[7]

Henry Black was almost seven years old when he arrived in Japan in 1865, three years before the *shōgun* relinquished power in what was to become known as the Meiji Restoration. The family was to live in Yokohama for seven years until moving to Tokyo in 1872. A younger brother, John Reddie Black II, was born on 6 April 1867, when Henry was nine years old. Their sister, Pauline, was born on 25 July 1869.[8] This meant that Henry was about a decade older than his two Japan-born siblings.

For John and Elizabeth Black, Japan was the geographic end-point of a lengthy journey. It had taken them first from London in 1854 to the British colony of South Australia and the goldfields of Victoria and beyond to the new frontier of Yokohama. But for Henry Black, Japan was to become his home. Japan was the beginning of everything.

---

7 John Black is listed for the first time in 'Merchants, Professions, Trades etc.' (1866:235) as a resident of Yokohama and is shown as working at AW Hansard and Co., auctioneers, *Japan Herald* office. The listing was published in January of each year. Grace Fox gives additional detail about John Black's relationship with Hansard and the *Japan Herald* in her preface to *Young Japan*.

8 Henry Black rarely referred to his childhood in interviews. Although his father wrote of the period in *Young Japan*, he did not give family details. According to Henry Black's niece, Mrs Joy Currie, documents that might have shed light on this period in the family's history were lost in Japanese raids on Singapore in the Second World War.

Japan at the crossroads

The years immediately after the arrival of the Black family in Japan coincided with a weakening of the *bakufu*, the government of the Tokugawa shogunate. The catalyst for this development had been the arrival in July 1853 of Commodore Matthew Perry, envoy of the United States President. Perry had dropped anchor at Uraga in Edo Bay and handed over documents urging the Japanese to open diplomatic and trade relations with the United States. He returned the following year for an answer. Following several weeks of negotiations he secured the Kanagawa Treaty under which the Japanese guaranteed good treatment for shipwrecked American sailors, permitted access to the towns of Shimoda on the Izu Peninsula and Hakodate in Hokkaido as supply stations, and gave the United States most-favoured nation status. The United States also gained consular representation in Shimoda. The treaty set a precedent for others to follow. It became the model for similar treaties between Japan and several other Western nations, including Britain.

But the debate within the shogunate, which Perry's intrusion set off, was not harmonious. Reflecting ancient allegiances, differences emerged within the *shōgun*'s palace over the extent to which Japan should co-operate with Western powers. The advent of the steamship had accelerated encroachments into the East Asian region by Western powers at a time when the centuries-long hold over Japan by the *bakufu* was beginning to weaken. *Shōguns* had always ruled in the name of the emperor (*mikado*), but the incursions by the obviously powerful and technologically more adept Western powers posed a challenge to the legitimacy of their rule. To shore up their hold on the country, some of the *shōgun*'s advisers favoured total exclusion of foreigners. Others saw contact with the Western powers as a means to monetary gain from trade or as a way of expanding their influence at the expense of the *shōgun* through access to Western know-how.

These differences took more than a decade to play themselves out as the various domains or fiefdoms, each under the control of its *daimyō* or lord, flexed their muscles. While this continued, the power of the *shōgun* gradually waned. In 1863 the southwestern domain of Chōshū, acting independently of the central government, shelled foreign ships in Shimonoseki Straits between the southwestern tip of Japan's main island of Honshu and nearby northern Kyushu. In response, British ships shelled the town of Kagoshima, also in the southwest. The following year, English, French, American and Dutch ships shelled Chōshū batteries at Shimonoseki (Jansen 1989:22–23). The skirmishes were symptomatic of a loosening of control by the shogunate. *Samurai* who resented the presence of foreigners instigated the skirmishes, but foreign retaliation easily emphasised to all parties, including the *shōgun* and various *daimyō*[9], the strength of the Western powers.

More perceptive *samurai* in these southwestern domains were alerted to the need to end old domainal divisions and to develop a more centralised government that would be better able to withstand foreign threats and adapt Western technology. In 1865, the year of Henry Black's arrival in Yokohama, the Satsuma domain in Kyushu broke with a central government rule against contact with the West to send 15 students to England. Far-sighted people in the domain knew that knowledge lay in the West.

The Satsuma domain had a long history of resisting the shogunate. Tokugawa *shōguns* had from 1603 consolidated Japan under their rule following a series of battles in which Satsuma was defeated. Satsuma *daimyō* subsequently had to swear allegiance to the central government, but the memory of defeat remained a simmering source of resentment. The region's geographic proximity to the Asian mainland had also long afforded its rulers insights into developments in other parts of the world ahead of any central government in distant Edo. The southwest included Nagasaki where Portuguese and later Dutch traders had maintained a trading post, giving *daimyō* in the vicinity knowledge of Western military, medical and scientific prowess superior to that of the central government of the *shōgun*. Disaffected, but perceptive, *samurai* in these southwestern domains had ample and early knowledge of the Western powers' abilities.

It was to be some years before *samurai* reformists could achieve their aim of uniting the country (Jansen 1989:23). Eventually, in 1868, a coalition of mainly low- to medium-ranked *samurai* from domains in the southwest of Japan succeeded in wresting power from the *bakufu*. Their solution, on taking power, was to give the boy emperor, Mutsuhito, nominal power while they held the daily reins of government. Having overthrown the *bakufu*, these far-sighted *samurai* then embarked on a program of rapid modernisation and consolidation of the country in emulation of the Western powers with which the shogunate had signed its treaties. Their task was now to oversee the creation of a country that could withstand any predations from Western powers and reverse many of the disadvantageous terms written into the treaties. To achieve this, they systematically dismantled the

9 *Daimyō* were military lords who were, in theory, subservient to the *shōgun*. By this stage, the sense of allegiance to the central government was beginning to weaken among many *daimyō*, particularly those in the southwest of Japan.

domainal structure and concentrated power in a centralised, but civilian-led administrative capital. In the process, they symbolically transferred the malleable Mutsuhito from the imperial palace in Kyoto to the *shōgun*'s palace in Edo. To emphasise the significance of this move as a complete break with the past, they declared 1868 as the first year of a new era, the Meiji (enlightened rule) era. Mutsuhito became known posthumously, therefore, as Emperor Meiji, and the symbolic reinstatement of the emperor to prominence became known as the Meiji Restoration. To emphasise their desire for change, the new rulers renamed Edo (river entrance), the old seat of the *shōgun*, as Tokyo (eastern capital), declaring it the new administrative centre of Japan run by a civilian bureaucracy. Years later, Henry Black's younger brother John recalled in an interview how he and Henry witnessed Emperor Meiji journeying to Tokyo from Kyoto (Hanazono 1926:78). While John claimed he remembered seeing the procession in the Spring of 1869, this is unlikely as he would only have been two at the time. It is more likely the two brothers witnessed the emperor moving in state on one of the many official journeys encouraged by the civilian rulers as a way of impressing on the populace the importance and status of their monarch in the years after the Restoration.

The years between 1868, which began with the Meiji Restoration, and 1912, when Mutsuhito died, thus delineate the Meiji era. Since the changes during the period were revolutionary in nature, some historians have suggested that the Restoration is more appropriately described as a revolution.

Knowledge shall be sought

To promote their reform agenda, the new governing elite issued a series of edicts in the name of Emperor Meiji. In 1868, the first year of the Meiji era, the emperor placed his seal on one such document, the Charter Oath. This was a five-clause statement of the aims of the government:

> An assembly shall be widely convoked and all measures shall be decided by open discussion.
>
> High and low shall be of one mind, and the national economy and finances shall be greatly strengthened.
>
> Civil and military officials together, and the common people as well, shall all achieve their aspirations, and thus the people's minds shall not be made weary.

> Evil customs of the past shall be abandoned, and actions shall be based on international usage.
>
> Knowledge shall be sought all over the world, and the foundations of imperial rule shall be strengthened (Japan 1993:177).

For their time, the aims of the oath were revolutionary. They spelled the end of the *samurai* as a caste and held out to all Japanese the possibility of aspiring to become something more than they then were. The reality was, of course, far different, because members of the former *samurai* caste, particularly those in the upper ranks, had a head start in terms of education and connections. These were the people who, at least in the early years after 1868, filled the ranks of the new civilian bureaucracy. But not everyone benefited. Unable to fend for themselves in a new Japan, where an understanding of money, the currency of the once despised caste of traders and merchants was now a guarantee of security and prosperity, just as many former *samurai* fell by the wayside.

The quest for modernity

In the preamble to a story he narrated in 1891, Henry Black spoke of vast changes he witnessed in the years following his arrival. He recalled how foreigners had lived in constant fear of death at the hands of sword-wielding *samurai* resentful of their presence (Eikokujin 1891:2). Their resentment had quickly yielded to admiration of all things foreign. In the same story, Henry Black recalled the aspiration on the part of many Japanese to own a Western-style brick home, 'whether or not the breeze is bad and they are unbearably hot', and the fashion among men to copy a Western-style moustache, 'even though it gets in the soup' (Eikokujin 1891:2). Such amusing and entertaining comments were typical of the many Black interspersed throughout his stories with the aim of informing audiences about Western customs and thought associated with modernity as it was then perceived.

As the Charter Oath implied, the Meiji years were synonymous with rapid and far-reaching change of the sort Henry cited. Henry Black lived through these years and well understood that the path to modernity was neither smooth nor even. He understood that definitions of modernity among Japanese and foreign residents alike varied over time, reflecting continuous reassessment of the modernisation process by all involved (Pyle 1969:4). But of all people, Henry Black was well positioned to participate in the debate over these differences. As the son of a newspaper editor who associated with prominent Japanese intellectuals and political figures and as a capable speaker of Japanese, he had daily access to the opinions of both foreigners and Japanese over the big questions of reform and the nature of modernity.

While the governmental shapers of Meiji modernisation did not have it all their own way, they at least attempted to control the process. Given the example of the partition of neighbouring China at the behest of Western powers, their immediate aim was to achieve, as rapidly as possible, a country whose economic, bureaucratic, political and defence capabilities would insulate it from Western dominance.

One of the most radical of the reforms instituted by the post-Restoration government was the early abolition of the *samurai* class. To symbolise the move, the new government ordered *samurai* to cut off their topknots, surrender their swords and forego their hereditary stipends. This signalled to the entire population that the old order, based on a feudal caste system with the *samurai* at its apex, was now obsolete. While this meant that the son of a farmer could in theory now aspire to become a merchant or prime minister, in practice it was the more adaptable and ambitious of the former *samurai*, who with the advantage of a good education, were able to take positions of power in government and bureaucracy. At the same time, however, many ex-*samurai*, stripped of the income their former high status had given them and unable to manage their financial affairs, became destitute. The old order had been overturned. In the new Japan, there were new winners and losers. There was opportunity and there was resentment.

Much of the resentment was directed against the government over its signing of treaties with Western powers between 1858 and 1869. There were valid reasons for this resentment. Driven originally by the desire for coal to supply modern steamships which could traverse great distances at undreamed of speeds to service the China trade, Western powers, including Britain, had urged Japan to sign treaties guaranteeing foreigners extraterritoriality in several Japanese 'treaty ports'. Extraterritoriality guaranteed foreigners immunity from Japanese law. The treaties also subjected Japan's external trade to tariffs imposed by foreign powers. These terms motivated a decades-long drive on the part of governments and their domestic opponents to end the treaties.[10] It was also a powerful reason

---

10 For summaries of the circumstances surrounding the early development of Yokohama as a treaty port, see Hoare (1994:1–17) and Jansen (1995:283–285).

why many Japanese harboured feelings of ambivalence and even hostility toward foreigners residing in Japan at the time.

The achievement of a degree of modernity commensurate with that of the Western powers inspired a drive to import the trappings of what many understood as civilisation in order to achieve cultural and economic parity with the foreign treaty powers. This meant that many of the notions associated with modernity in the region originated in the West. Many of the changes in Japan following the Restoration were therefore synonymous with Westernisation. Early Meiji debates among intellectuals and government figures over the nature of Westernisation and the meaning of enlightened civilisation were therefore aimed at defining priorities for national development. But divisions caused by disparate dialects and historical allegiances to the old regional domains and cultures stalled any quick and unanimous resolution to the debate (Hall 1983:10). Within the governing elite, factionalism driven by these ancient divisions also contributed to policy confusion. Despite agreement on the need for modernisation, this delayed civil reform by at least five years and the establishment of central government authority by a further five years (Jones 1980). Some historians opt for a longer period, with one describing the first two decades of trial-and-error policy-making as 'a period of dialectical discourse' (Burks 1985:257). Despite the factional disagreements, a process of compromise and 'decision by a kind of bureaucratic collegial consent' resulted in the eventual emergence of an official response to policy imperatives (Jones 1980:26–27).

The formula the Meiji governments eventually chose, after some years of trial and error, as their means to modernise was a combination of Western scientific know-how and Japanese spirit. This formula was adopted on the advice of Japanese returnees from Europe and North America. The returnees included people such as the politician and scholar Sakuma Shōzan who coined the motto 'Japanese spirit, Western knowledge' (*wakon yōsai*) (Japan 1993:1301,1304). Others who influenced thinking at this time were the members of the Iwakura Mission led by senior minister Iwakura Tomomi. The mission visited the United States and Europe between 1871 and 1873 to examine Western society and discuss the revision of the 'unequal treaties'. What impressed mission members were the practical trappings of the modern Western nations they visited – national education systems, large-scale mechanised factories, constitutional government, centralised bureaucracies and conscripted armies. The findings of the Iwakura Mission and subsequent similar missions shaped a program of modernisation whose planks within the first decade of the Meiji period included bureaucratic efficiency, industrialisation, networks of efficient communication and transportation, a stable currency and the strengthening of the country's military and technical prowess. 'Civilisation' and 'enlightenment', two words frequently used by Henry Black in his narrations, became the government mantras as it worked toward the 'paraphernalia of modernity' (Gluck 1985:24). The government's reform agenda was also to include the writing of a Prussian-style constitution, the marshalling of patriotism directed at a reinstated and malleable figurehead emperor and the inculcation through a mass education system of selected cultural and religious beliefs and practices aimed at uniting the country.

Foreigners as agents of change

As a part of the reform process, the government also positively encouraged the importation of foreign employees known as *oyatoi gaikokujin* (literally, hired foreigners), or *oyatoi*. During the Meiji years, the word *oyatoi*, or its less obsequious version *yatoi*, became a Meiji neologism for 'government foreign employee' (Jones 1985:248). The government also encouraged the sending of Japanese *ryūgakusei* (overseas students) to North America and Europe (Burks 1985:187–206,145–160). One estimate puts the number of Japanese students who studied in American institutions of higher learning alone between 1867 and 1902 at about 900 (Burks 1985:153). Both strategies were aimed at speeding up the importation of ideas (Burks 1985:145–160; Ishizuki 1985:161–186). Of the two strategies, the hiring of foreigners received priority in the first decade and a half of the Meiji period (Jones 1980:xv,21–23). The *yatoi* were usually imported on fixed-term contracts as advisers and educators. There were also many foreigners who were not officially invited, among them the missionaries, teachers, traders and newspaper editors such as John Black. Although not officially invited as a *yatoi* when he arrived, John Black was to become one in 1874 when he accepted the government's request to serve as an adviser to the Sa-In, the left chamber of the Dajōkan (Council of State).

The foreigners brought new ideas, but their presence also inspired hostility, curiosity and fear of cultural violation (Irokawa 1985:38). The mixed reaction to their arrival made the foreign presence a litmus test of government reform measures. While attitudes toward foreigners evolved over time, the ambivalence evoked in 1862 by one *bakufu* bureaucrat's description of *yatoi* as 'live machines' (Jones 1980:125) was never shed. Like machines, when they became obsolete, *yatoi* were expendable, a fact that a disappointed John Black encountered when sacked from the bureaucracy in 1875.

The presence of *yatoi* contributed to the creation of a hierarchy within the foreign community and complicated the debate within that community about the Japanese reform agenda. Symptomatic of the hierarchy was the Japanese ban on non-*yatoi* foreigners outside treaty ports, a rule that later hampered the development of Henry Black's career as a storyteller, since it prevented him travelling to the regions to perform.

The large number of foreigners in Meiji-era Japan make this period perhaps unprecedented in the history of cultural borrowing. Figures indicate that at the time of the 1868 Restoration there were only 92 *yatoi*. Six years later, in 1874, the year John Black was employed as a *yatoi* in the Sa-In, the number of *yatoi* peaked at 854. Numbers then fell steadily to below 200 for the first time in 1883, when it was 196, and to 58 by 1900.[11] *Yatoi* came from many countries, including Britain, France, the United States and Germany (Jones 1985:225). The most numerous throughout this period were the British, which explains the acceptance of John and Henry Black as conveyors of British ideas via newspaper and stage. Many Japanese intellectuals of the time looked to Britain for inspiration. John Stuart Mill's *On Liberty* and Samuel Smiles' *Self Help* were standard intellectual fodder at the time (Yokoyama 1987:xxii). Britons helped shape the Meiji years.

Beef and soirees

> Referring to the account of Mr Black's Japanese readings which appeared in our columns yesterday, a correspondent writes that he well remembers him as a small boy in Yokohama. Young Black's companion was one of the Salabelles. The two lads were of a most daring and adventurous disposition and got themselves into numerous boyish scrapes. On one occasion they started from Yokohama for the Bonin Islands in an open boat, and after getting as far as Kannosaki, some twelve miles distant, returned to Yokohama half starved (*Kobe Weekly Chronicle* 1901).

---

11 Many hundreds of foreign entrepreneurs and adventurers were not official invitees. The total number of *yatoi* alone during the Meiji period may have been as high as 4000.

By 1865, when the Black family reunited in Yokohama (Asaoka 1987:11–14), the settlement was transforming from a village on the edge of a swamp to a bustling frontier town surviving on trade and commerce. Yokohama's foreigners came principally from China, Britain and the United States. The new foreign enclave flourished on the margins of a sometimes hostile country. The town's foreign residents were occasionally targeted by sword-wielding ultranationalists who perceived their presence as a threat to Japanese sovereignty and sensibilities. Ghastly reminders that the central government could not control events included the gruesome pre-Restoration death in 1862 of the retired British businessman Charles Richardson in an encounter with a group of sword-wielding *samurai* while out riding on the Tokaido, the main trunk road which connected Tokyo in the east with Osaka in the west (Black, JR 1883:I,125–138). Richardson and his party were fatally punished after they had refused to dismount on encountering the retinue of the father of the *daimyō* of Satsuma. So seriously did the foreign community in Yokohama take these and other attacks that, at a meeting on 24 September 1862, residents had created a volunteer corps to protect themselves. Four weeks later, the savagely mutilated body of a soldier attached to the French legation was found in the village of Hodogaya on the same Tokaido road. John Black, who recorded the incident, said the soldier had sustained 'some twenty wounds…most of which were sufficient to cause death' while 'his bridle arm had been severed from the trunk, with a portion of the reins yet in hand; and this was found ten paces from the body' (Black, JR 1883:I.263).

Even after the Restoration, death could still come suddenly and unpredictably in the form of a drunken ex-*samurai* bent on retribution with a sword. Although he did not specify the year, Henry Black experienced such terror as a boy while cowering in the family's horse-drawn carriage one day as a sword-wielding *samurai* confronted them on their way to a party in the foreign quarter. He mentioned the incident in his 1891 *Eikoku Rondon gekijō miyage* (Story from a London theatre) (Eikokujin 1891). He also elaborated on it in an interview given to a Japanese journalist at the height of his career, recalling how the drunken *samurai* had drawn his sword as he and his mother alighted with American consular staff from a carriage. The *samurai* was pacified by 'an official' (Nishūbashi 1905:294).

Despite the dangers, Yokohama prospered, so that by the late 1870s its foreign population surpassed 3,000. Over half of these were Chinese, many of them coolies working the wharves or servants in the homes of wealthier Europeans. The largest European contingent was the British, including those who, like the Blacks, came via Australia[12] and other British colonies.[13] This strong British presence was a consequence of Japan's entry to the world trade system at a time when Britain's rate of economic growth was at a peak and its Industrial Revolution was powering trade expansion (Jansen 1995). The second largest number of foreign nationals was Americans.

To make themselves more at home in Japan, foreign expatriates strove to maintain lifestyles to which they were accustomed. The Blacks lived 'quite a luxurious life' typified by John Black's fondness for 'a large joint of meat on a dish', which he would carve for the family (Hanazono 1926:78). Beef was a rarity in the early days. During the 1860s cattle were slaughtered at two 'odiferous cow-yards' within the foreign settlement at Yokohama. By 1872, beef was being shipped to Yokohama from Kobe 'on the hoof' at the rate of 'forty or so head of cattle per steamer' (Williams 1963:96–97). Recreation for expatriates included wild geese hunts, although this was officially discouraged because of sensitivities toward the Japanese. British residents also staged foxhunts using mongrel dogs. A foreign circus or acrobat troupe occasionally visited, but members of the foreign community otherwise provided their own entertainment with soirées in their homes (Williams 1963:51–52). John Black was an enthusiastic participant on these occasions. A cartoon in a September 1873 edition of *Japan Punch* (reproduced in Morioka & Sasaki 1983:137), depicting him as a kilted Bonnie Prince Charlie at St Andrew's Day commemorations, attests to his participation in amateur concerts, which may have influenced Henry Black's later aptitude for stage appearances. The Scottish traveller and diarist John Francis Campbell (1822–1886), who visited Japan in 1874, referred to John Black as 'that Scottish Lion of the Press' and mentioned his ability to 'sing old Scotch songs like a born musician, and jingle Japanese ditties on a piano and denounce them' (Campbell 1876:247). The *Kobe Weekly Chronicle* (1901) also alluded to this, quoting an unidentified reader as recollecting that John Reddie Black,

12 The question of the impact on Japan of Britons from nearby colonies, in particular Australia, has been explored by Endō Masako (1985) and Harold S Williams (1958; 1963).

13 Neville Meaney (1999:10) notes that this early trickle of British or mainland European-born foreigners into Japan via Australia was to reflect a growing perception among European migrants to Australia of Japan as 'central to both their understanding of Asia and the definition of themselves. The few Australians who in the latter part of the nineteenth-century experienced Japan were fascinated by this "Oriental" nation which, instead of succumbing to the superior power of the European empires, had preserved its independence by learning Western ways and converting itself into a modern state.'

> the father of the gentleman who is now a storyteller in Japanese theatres, was ...also very in the habit of giving public readings and concerts. He possessed a fine personality and commanding presence on the stage, with a powerful, clear and sonorous voice, and most old residents will remember his famous renderings of favorite Scotch songs. His son, it appears, inherited his father's gift for public readings.

By the 1870s, much of the initial antagonism toward foreigners had dissipated to be replaced with curiosity as people began to equate change and modernity with Westernisation. During this stage of the relationship, the Japanese developed an insatiable appetite for information about the West. The growing number of government-sponsored students, official delegations, intellectuals, writers and the just plain curious, who had travelled to Europe also began to have an impact. Their letters, diaries and newspaper articles contributed to the construction of a composite vision of Europe that gradually filtered through to the rest of the population.

But there was another Europe that was more accessible. Within easy horse-riding distance of Tokyo and by 1872 a short train ride from Tokyo's Shinbashi Station, it was called Yokohama. In these years, the town's foreign population assumed the quality of an easily accessible museum exhibit. Woodblock print artists and their proxies flocked there to sketch the town's foreigners for the mass-produced prints that constituted a new genre known as *Yokohama-e* (Yokohama pictures). These prints, the contemporary equivalent of picture postcards, portrayed foreigners engaged in the balls, picnics and country excursions Henry Black experienced, of which John Black wrote in *Young Japan* (Black, JR 1883:I,380). As portrayals of the Japanese view of foreigners, *Yokohama-e* became 'instruments for satisfying curiosity and conveying information' (Suzuki 1997:684) to a curious population elsewhere in Japan. Outside Yokohama, this curiosity was also catered to in the 1870s through exhibitions (*hakurankai*) at which Japanese could view the products of foreign cultures as tangible representations of modernity (Tomio 1997:724). This same sense of curiosity was to sustain interest in Henry and his stories when he became a storyteller. *Yokohama-e* raised expectations. They represented a lifestyle beyond the average person's reach. The average person could only gaze at them and wonder what the future would bring. All around them, the citizens of Japan witnessed the encroachment of modernity in the form of new train lines and the march of telegraph wires across the country. People in villages, who had only known the sound of frogs in paddy fields, now experienced the whistle and clang of the steam train that could take them to Tokyo. The metropolis was no longer as distant as it had seemed.

Historians continue to dispute the extent of the influence of foreigners during this period. This debate centres on whether the Japanese engaged in imitation, selective borrowing and adaptation, or combinations of these. There is evidence that, prior to the Restoration, Japan already had resources to cope with modernisation by comparison to nearby China. According to this argument, these resources included the pool of well-trained and educated *samurai* who manned the civilian bureaucracy after the Restoration. Japan also had a preexisting urban base and an extensive domestic transport infrastructure (Jansen 1989:xv). Certainly many foreigners, including John Black perceived and appreciated the existence of these resources. Nevertheless, an informed analysis of the role of foreigners as invited or uninvited participants in the modernisation process is integral to an understanding of developments in the Meiji period (Garon 1987:7). The foreign presence served as a catalyst for change. Many foreigners, in the form of educators and advisers, played a role in informing, at the highest levels, those leaders whose policies shaped the reform process.[14] A minority of foreigners felt so at home in Japan that they stayed permanently. And some, like Henry Black, or his contemporary the Irish-born journalist and teacher Lafcadio Hearn, empathised so profoundly with Japan that they even adopted Japanese citizenship.

But while the motto propounded by the progressive *samurai* and intellectual Sakuma Shōzan, 'Japanese spirit, Western knowledge' (Japan 1993), was acceptable to a government whose members wanted to control the reform agenda, many wanted more from the West than utilitarian trains and telegraph lines. For these people, there was one thing missing. Western technology brought prosperity, but not participation in governance.

Ultimately, this struggle for democratic change was to involve the Blacks. It was to become a formative experience for a young Henry Black – an experience which provided him with the will and the means to embark on a career entirely unanticipated by his family.

---

14 For an evaluation of the role of the *yatoi*, see in particular Burks (1985) and Beauchamp and Iriye (1990). Burks' 1985 book resulted from a 1967 conference at Rutgers University, probably the first conference on the subject of hired foreigners in Japan during the Meiji Period. Beauchamp and Iriye's 1990 book is the outcome of a second conference on hired foreigners held in Fukui in 1985. See, for example, analysis in Burks (1985:4).

Chapter 2

Old Japan – New Japan

> All top bureaucrats often toil away honestly, showing compassion and not discriminating against those below them, but when you get down to the lower ranks, they are apt to be oppressed and there are some who are quite unreasonable. I very much doubt that such a disgraceful thing would happen in Japan. Needless to say, all the bureaucrats are the epitome of integrity and absolute incorruptibility (Satirical comment in Ishii 1896:2).

The modernity project

Foreign residents and travellers in Meiji Japan were excellent observers of developments in the country. They wrote diaries in which they mentioned their meetings with the influential as well as their encounters with the seemingly inconsequential. The young American woman Clara Whitney recorded an outing to witness a hot-air balloon as well as her impressions of the extended family of the educator, writer and Westerniser Fukuzawa Yukichi (Whitney 1979). The British traveller Isabella Bird ventured deep into the countryside and wrote of bed bugs and fleas at inns (Bird 1984). Fortunately, Scottish diarist and adventurer, John Francis Campbell wrote of his encounters with John and Henry Black during his journey through Japan (Campbell 1876). And John Black's own book, *Young Japan* (1883), is invaluable to historians. It is noteworthy that the emphasis on youth and the new should have so interested John, given that everyone knew Japan possessed an ancient civilisation and was quite possibly the world's oldest continuous monarchy. But from the outset, the Meiji years were a time of rapid change when government-initiated reform measures caused widespread upheaval and disparity as new sets of winners and losers emerged. There were good reasons for John Black's emphasis on the new.

Perhaps one of the more striking things to emerge from the writings of these observant foreigners is their constant fascination with the co-existence of the old and the new, the exotic and the familiar. It is a theme that continues to preoccupy travellers to Japan even today. One of the more evident disparities in the Meiji era was between rural poor and urban rich, although as industrialisation progressed, urban areas also experienced the advent of slums alongside the wealthier parts of cities. As observers of Japan, including foreign residents, watched these trends, they began to speak wistfully of an Old Japan as compared to a New Japan. Old Japan was associated in the minds of many with an idealised agrarian past represented by images of rice paddies, thatched roofs, the distant night chorus of frogs and a slower pace of life. New Japan was represented by steam trains and telegraph lines traversing the country, as well as factories and the trappings of a Western lifestyle, such as brick buildings and bowler hats.

Many foreigners shared the sense of nostalgia for a disappearing past, but combined this with a desire to educate the Japanese to Western ways. Having arrived before the Restoration and having witnessed the changes, Henry Black was in a unique position. At the height of his popularity in the 1890s, Henry liked to appeal to his audiences' sense of humour by depicting characters confused and victimised by the rapid pace of reform. The country's bureaucrats, who were responsible for carrying out the reforms mandated by the government in its haste to modernise, were the butt of such jokes. So if you couldn't criticise the government, it was still possible to criticise the bureaucracy. This meant that Henry Black was able to tap a rich vein of public resentment over incompetent and venal ex-*samurai* members of the bureaucracy.

At the time of the Restoration, there existed a large perception gap between ordinary people and elite former *samurai* who had assumed government positions. For ordinary people, the Restoration had little immediate impact, although it served to raise expectations. The replacement after the Restoration of one group of *samurai* rulers with a new civilian bureaucracy largely drawn from the same *samurai* class merely inspired distrust and the suspicion that nothing much had changed (Waswo 1996:24). The perception gap was reinforced by the wording of the 1868 Charter Oath and other edicts.

While the Charter Oath stated that 'knowledge shall be sought all over the world, and the foundations of imperial rule shall be strengthened', in practice it was former *samurai* who possessed the wherewithal to travel or to bolster their own positions of control (Gluck 1985:25). Furthermore, although the same document mandated 'open discussion' of 'all measures' and was predicated on an assumption that 'high and low shall be of one mind', participation of the non-*samurai* classes was not immediately facilitated. This was why, for citizens of non-*samurai* background, a trip to the theatre to hear a storyteller satirising the new ruling class was a cathartic experience. Storytellers like Henry Black could provide them with uncensored social commentary well leavened with humour.

To achieve their reform aims, the new rulers, who in the main were former *samurai*, issued an unprecedented number of edicts in the name of the emperor directed at the general population. Bureaucrats, who were also in the main former *samurai*, were largely responsible for ensuring that the edicts were carried out. The impact of this social engineering has been described as a 'partial samuraization of Japan' (Waswo 1996:22). The implications for the general populace were enormous over time. By mid-Meiji, any indifference on the part of the general populace had changed as policies propounded by a coterie of former *samurai* began to involve the entire population in a selective makeover of Japan in the image of a modern Western nation-state.

One result on a practical level was that 'the patriarchal family became the model for all families, displacing in law, if not always in reality, the looser, more flexible practices of marriage and inheritance that had long prevailed among commoners especially in the countryside' (Waswo 1996:22). References Henry Black made to Western marriage customs and inheritance laws in his narrations were within this context. The government's new mass-education policy also helped promote participation on the part of the people with its 'subversive doctrine' that the entire population should share in the same education ideals once restricted to the *samurai* class (Burks 1985:255). Changes to *samurai* ranking systems and the elimination of many *samurai* privileges also helped reduce inequities based on social status (Yazaki 1968:299). Topographical changes accompanied social change. Formerly quiet rural villages were transformed by the train or linked by the telegraph wire. Such changes also provided new opportunities for movement and human contact.

Like Henry Black, other foreigners were also caught up in the debate these changes inspired. But among them, opinion on the merits of modernisation varied. Some, like Basil Hall Chamberlain, the English Navy School teacher and later instructor in Japanese language and linguistics at Tokyo University who lived in Japan between 1873 and 1911, displayed mixed feelings over the passing of what many described as 'Old Japan'. By 1904, Chamberlain declared that 'Old Japan' was 'dead and gone', citing a long list of symbols of modernity, including 'the steam-whistle, the newspaper, the voting paper, the pillar post at every street corner and even in remote villages, the clerk in shop or bank or public office hastily summoned from our side to answer the ring of the telephone bell, the railway replacing the palanquin' (Chamberlain 1984:7).

Those who lamented the passing of 'Old Japan', under the impact of the foreign influence, feared that modernity would destroy the Japanese identity. This probably derived from a sense of responsibility for the changes, since British institutions frequently served as prototypes for Meiji government reformers. Diaries and accounts of visits to Japan published in Britain fed this fear by idealising aspects of 'Old Japan' as a 'paradise' rapidly fading (Yokoyama 1987:150). For example, Scotsman John Francis Campbell, who met the Blacks in 1874, found the Japanese exotic and wrote that he was 'so vastly amused by this strange, wild country' which was so utterly unlike anything I ever saw or dreamed of. The people are the most polite. The landlord goes down on all fours and knocks his noddle on the ground, and grins and gives a parting gift to each guest…Truly the manners and customs of these amiable seals are wonderful. I have some sketches, but really I have little time to do anything but rush about, and gape open-mouthed at everything and everybody like a fresh-caught greenhorn (Campbell 1876:183–184).

In a style of writing which has ever since characterised the 'discovery' of Japan as an exotic mix of East and West by many from the West, Campbell found it odd that old and new co-existed. Writing of the fad for 'toy-books' illustrating life in Tokyo, he commented that it was a 'strange thing' to see in them depictions of such symbols of modernity as 'photographic cameras, carriages, horses, and European clothes jumbled up with the manners and customs and costumes of old Japan. It is all true to nature. Polo is on one page; a native naked in a bath on another. That is the modern taste' (Campbell 1876:51–52).

Concern about the loss of Old Japan also reflected 'growing anxiety about Britain's "Mission of Civilization" in the Far East' as ordinary Britons became increasingly aware of their country's involvement in the detrimental effects of the China opium trade (Yokoyama 1987:163). Misgivings over the direction in which the Meiji Restoration would take Japan also may have reflected British concerns over the revolutionary nature of the 1871 Paris Commune (Yokoyama 1987:139).

For his part, John Black was a sympathetic participant in the making of the New Japan, taking the debate over reform directly to the pages of the newspapers he edited. John Black's opinions were in part determined by his identity as a Freemason. If you walk through the section of the Yokohama Foreigners' Cemetery where John Black and his contemporaries are buried, you will notice that a large proportion of the gravestones of the men there bear the insignia of the Freemasons with its compass and carpenter's square.[15] This attests to one of the less well-documented aspects of foreign influence on Japan in the Meiji era – that Freemasonry inspired the zeal with which many British and American expatriates approached the task of bringing Western civilisation to Japan.[16] Records show that John Black served as organist and director of ceremonies at the Yokohama Masonic Lodge in 1870 and 1871 and as 'senior warden' and 'worshipful master' of the Otentosama Lodge from 1872.[17]

The Blacks were from a generation of Britons who believed in the positive influence of manufacture, free trade, individualism and self-help. They were the mid-19th-century intellectual and religious inheritors of what American historian of Victorian literature Walter Houghton characterised as an 'age of transition'. What Houghton had in mind was not so much a transition from the preceding 18th century or the then still relatively recent 'Romantic period'. Rather, he meant a transition from the Middle Ages with their mediaeval tradition of 'Christian orthodoxy under the rule of the church and civil government under the rule of king and nobility; the social structure of fixed classes, each with its recognised rights and duties; and the economic organisation of village agriculture and town guilds' (Houghton 1957:2). The Blacks, who lived in the age of Queen Victoria, belonged to a country whose citizens were in the midst of an industrial revolution with its trappings of prosperity and empire. Much that they associated with pre-Industrial Revolution Britain must have seemed positively antiquated and obsolete. The irrevocable nature of the transition the Victorians experienced was ensured by the development of individualism, which facilitated the erosion of belief in absolute truths (Houghton 1957:16). But despite the erosion of belief, any skepticism in the minds of people like John Black was not yet

---

15 John Black refers to the early presence of Freemasonry in Yokohama in *Young Japan* (Black, JR 1883:II,15–16.

16 See Bond (1947:13–14). In an address printed in *The Ashlar*, attributed to 'Brother Apgar' and delivered at a meeting of Tokyo Bay Masonic Club in Yokohama on 22 November 1945, Brother Apgar claimed that the first Freemason Lodge in Japan was known as Sphinx Lodge. He claimed that Sphinx Lodge operated 'under the Grand Lodge of Ireland in the years 1862 to 1865 a few years after the opening of the [treaty] ports of Japan by Commodore Perry'. He stated that Yokohama Lodge secured its charter from the Grand Lodge of England on 26 June 1866 and that Otentosama Lodge received its charter on 28 July 1894, under the Grand Lodge of England. Brother Apgar warned, however, that the dates given 'may be somewhat inaccurate' because records had been confiscated by the Japanese authorities at the outbreak of the Pacific War.

17 In editions of *Chronicle and Directory for China, Japan, and the Philippines*, JR Black is listed as: organist at the Yokohama Masonic Lodge in 1870; organist and director of ceremonies in 1871; senior warden of the 'O'Tentosama' Lodge in 1873; 'worshipful master' of the Otentosama Lodge in 1874; member of the Otentosama Lodge in 1875.

completely undermined by the subsequent relativism and rationalism of early 20th-century sociology, anthropology and psychology (Houghton 1957:13).

This great schism with the past, this leap forward, underpinned John Black's faith in Japan's apparent determination to move from old to new. People like John Black possessed the confidence to think they were the inheritors of a set of beliefs that could inspire Japan. The 19th-century egalitarian and liberalist legacy thus equipped them for the social and intellectual changes they encountered in Japan. Freemasonry gave John Black the added zeal to deal with the challenges.

By the 1850s, a number of other forces set in train by the Industrial Revolution also reinforced the notion of a civilising mission on the part of many expatriates and *yatoi*. The Blacks belonged to a newly literate middle class whose numbers increased rapidly during the 19th century and who increasingly exhibited concern for the poor. Such concern derived from a belief that the wellbeing of the poorer classes could be improved if they followed a middle-class example of 'sobriety, thrift, hard work, piety and respectability' (Hibbert 1988:601). For the 19th-century British middle class, godliness was also a prerequisite for respectability (Hibbert 1988:602). Henry Black's mother Elizabeth and his sister Pauline exemplified this. Both took an interest in Christian missionary activities while in Japan. Pauline at one stage contemplated becoming a missionary in the Ogasawara Islands about a thousand kilometres to the south of the Japanese mainland.[18]

The increased concern among the middle class over the plight of the poor resulted in pressure for more state responsibility for social welfare and an acceptance of a greater state role in social regulation. As a young man, Henry Black gave expression to many of these notions in speeches at gatherings of supporters of the Freedom and Peoples' Rights Movement. It later influenced his choice of material for adaptation from European authors in the 1890s when he became a professional narrator.

John Black's own comments, frequently repeated in *Young Japan*, attest to his sense of mission to civilise the Japanese. His book's title echoes sentiments expressed on its pages that the Japanese had responded well to tutelage from the West and were by 1880 finally 'born into the family of nations' on the occasion of the signing of 'the Treaties of Mr. Harris and Lord Elgin' (Black, JR 1883:I,v).[19] Japan had on that occasion experienced 'a new birth'.

---

18 Personal communication between the author and Morioka Heinz and Sasaki Miyoko, 25 June 1985.

19 Townsend Harris, the first American Consul-General in Japan, and Lord Elgin, who negotiated diplomatic links between Britain and the pre-Restoration *bakufu*.

> She now attains her majority! Then, boasting herself as one of the most ancient Empires in the world, with an Imperial Dynasty extending over two thousand five hundred years, she was for the first time born into the family of nations. In the most literal sense may she have been said previously to speak and think and act as a child; but now she is of age she has put away childish things (Black, JR 1883:I,2).

Despite this, John Black was also convinced that many in the *samurai* caste lacked the qualities that would enable the country to modernise as quickly as he would have liked. While he praised the *samurai* for a number of traits, including their administrative abilities, which he considered prerequisites for the attainment of modernity, he was also scathing of their ignorance of the outside world and their domination of the rest of the population.

> They knew, with a few honorable exceptions, nothing whatever of the outside world; and were puffed up with the conceit that Japan was – if not the world, at all events the greatest country in it…The very existence of the *samurai* was a frequent curse to the respectable citizens and commoners; and if the exclusion from foreign intercourse was productive of ignorance, that ignorance was – anything but innocence, and certainly not – bliss (Black, JR 1883:I,150–151).

It was this sort of ignorance, found in bureaucrats drawn from the former *samurai* caste, which could annoy anyone who knew better. On the whole, however, he found the *samurai* determined and dedicated, and it was this that sustained his involvement in the push to modernise the nation. His enthusiasm for the modernity project motivated his determination ultimately to stay on with his family in Japan, unlike many of his countrymen who might have been tempted to eventually return to Britain.

Committing to Japan

When Hansard sold the *Japan Herald* and *Daily Japan Herald*, a determined John Black saw an opportunity to add his voice to the debate over modernity via a newspaper of his own. John Black quit the *Japan Herald* and set up the first of his own newspapers, Yokohama's first evening newspaper, the *Japan Gazette*, publishing its first issue on 12 October 1867. He also published a fortnightly summary, the *Japan Gazette Fortnightly*, and an annual *Hong List and Directory*.

In investing in a newspaper of his own, Black committed to a lengthy stay in Japan. His interest in and passion for Japan had brought the family to its final home. He, Elizabeth and all of their offspring were to live out their lives in Japan. All died there and are buried in foreigners' cemeteries in Yokohama and Kobe. Black published the first issue of *Japan Gazette* just a few months before the events now associated with the 1868 Meiji Restoration. The turbulent years that followed ensured a constant supply of news about their adopted country. These events were to bring John and his eldest son Henry into conflict with the government, which brought ultimate disappointment and rejection for John, but inspired Henry to an even closer engagement with Japan.

Chapter 3

The move to Tokyo

> My father came to Japan about three years prior to the Boshin Civil War. At first, he devoted himself to newspapers in Japan, with the *Herald* in Yokohama. At the outset, it was a partnership, but later they couldn't get on with each other so he left it to the other person and devoted himself separately to the *Gazette*. Then in Meiji 5 (1872), he published the *Nisshin shinji shi* in Tokyo…It was the first time a newspaper was produced in Tokyo. Some while later there was the *Yomiuri shinbun* and the *Tokyo nichinichi shinbun*. Around that time in the government, there were the three In, the Sa-In, Sei-In, and the Genrō-In. My father was made an official of the Sa-In and ceased (work with) the newspaper, but maybe in Meiji 9 (1876), when the Sa-In was abolished, he briefly returned to his country (Henry Black, aged 36, speaking about his father and quoted by Nyorai An [1896]).

By the 1870s, the government, sensitive to foreign criticism and wanting desperately to prove that the country was civilised and enlightened, had begun treating Yokohama's newspapers as valued sources of information about overseas events and customs. It monitored and even subsidised a number of foreign-language papers in Yokohama (Hoare 1994:141). The presence of a lively foreign-language press in the treaty port of Yokohama ensured that the town was an important element in the government's attempts to project an image of a civilised nation. This continued the policy of the pre-Restoration shogunate which had ordered Japanese-language translations of foreign-language newspapers for distribution to domainal officials around Japan.[20] Here was a government that wanted its stakeholders to know what was going on in the rest of the world and what the rest of the world thought of Japan. It also wanted foreigners informed of developments within Japan,

20 For information on the Japanese-language translations of foreign newspapers, see Neilan (1993)

since the foreign population could influence the decision-makers in their home countries when it came to revision of the unequal treaties.

This was also precisely what John Black wanted to do. While he was officially editor of the *Japan Gazette* until 1874,[21] in all practicality he relinquished its editorship in 1870 to devote himself to the publication of an illustrated literary journal called *The Far East*. His stated motive for initiating each of these publications was the encouragement of interest in Japan among foreigners resident there and overseas. The first issue of *The Far East* came out on 30 May 1870. Initially a fortnightly publication, it went monthly in 1873 (Black, JR 1883:I,ix). The last issue is dated 31 August 1875.

But these ventures were not enough to sustain his interest. As an experienced editor with access to persons of influence and status, John Black also sought to influence affairs within Japan. In 1872, inspired by the idea of establishing a British-style newspaper aimed exclusively at Japanese readers, he moved the entire family to Tokyo. The Blacks left behind the foreign enclave of Yokohama with its brick and stone edifices and its neat gardens and houses filled with clergymen and merchants who paraded in their Sunday best on the Bund. By this time, Japan's governing elite aspired to turn Tokyo into the capital of a great nation-state modeled on Paris and London. But it was still very much a wooden city, parts of which regularly burned to the ground in great fires. It was an old city of temples and shrines, with jugglers, wrestling matches and toy-sellers clustered around their entrances. The Blacks were given accommodation in the temple complex of Zōjōji. Outside, the muddy streets played host to blind masseurs calling their trade, filthy rag pickers, night-soil collectors and splendidly costumed *geisha*. The city was also full of vaudeville theatres where storytellers narrated their tales and *kabuki* theatres where all-male troupes of actors played roles in great sagas that took all day to perform.

Henry was 13 years old when the family moved to Tokyo. Relocation to the capital placed the Blacks at the heart of domestic Japanese politics. To achieve his aim, John Black put into practice his conviction that the best of the former *samurai* were natural allies in the mission to civilise by employing some in the new project, the publication of the Japanese-language newspaper, the *Nisshin shinji shi*. The first edition came off the press on 17 March 1872.

---

[21] Editions of the *Chronicle and Directory for China, Japan, and The Philippines* from 1869–1875 list John Black as the editor of the *Japan Gazette*.

In a comment indicative of his sense of mission to instruct and edify readers and publishers of Japanese-language newspapers, John Black disparaged two earlier attempts at creating Japanese-language newspapers, the *Mainichi shinbun* published in Yokohama and the *Nichi nichi shinbun* in Tokyo. He explained that he intended to show Japanese readers what a true Western newspaper was in style and content.

> Neither [the *Mainichi shinbun* nor the *Nichi nichi shinbun*] dared to write leading articles nor to comment seriously on the occurrences of the day; and their columns were always defaced with such filthy paragraphs as to render them worse than contemptible in the eyes of foreigners; though they appeared to be enjoyed by the Japanese, who, for the most part, had no conception what a newspaper was, nor what were its uses (Black, JR 1980–81:I,364).

Crucial to the venture was a Macao-born Portuguese resident and former editor of the *Japan Commercial News*, Mr F da Roza, then a 'commercial Merchant' residing in the foreign concession of Tsukiji in Tokyo.[22] Da Roza arranged for the *kanji* characters used for typesetting to be fashioned from hard boxwood. This was not without its problems. When the type-carver failed to meet a production deadline, with resultant delays in the publication of the newspaper, John Black had to resort to seeking an indictment against the carver (Hayashiya, Ishii & Aoyama 1998:32). Da Roza also introduced Black to the authorities in the Monbu-Kyō (Secretary of State of the Education Department) where he gained the necessary licence for publishing his newspaper (Black, JR 1883:I,367–372). The newspaper received strong government support. The government supplied a Japanese editor and, over the objections of the municipality of Tokyo (Campbell 1876:243), a residence and printing premises in the Genkōin Temple within the Zōjōji temple complex.[23] At one time, Zōjōji had 66 hectares of land with over 100 buildings and 3,000 novices training for the priesthood (Waley 1984:361–364). While the Blacks were there, some of these buildings were rented out to foreigners. By comparison to its earlier grandeur, Zōjōji is now a fraction of its original area, making it difficult to

22 In 1872 the *Japan Gazette*'s 'Hong List and Directory' lists F da Roza as a 'commercial Merchant' residing in the foreign concession of Tsukiji in Tokyo. In 1875 and 1877 editions he is listed as a resident of Moto Bizen Yashiki, Ozakimura, in Tokyo, and the 1878 edition lists him as resident at Kiu-Bizen (*sic*) Yashiki, Shinagawa.

23 In its 1875 edition the *Chronicle and Directory for China, Japan, and The Philippines* lists John Reddie Black as residing at Genkoin, Shiba, Sannai in Tokyo.

imagine what it looked like when the Blacks were there. The huge, modern bulk of nearby Tokyo Tower and the Tokyo Prince Hotel now dominate the scene.

According to John Black, the new newspaper was read 'with avidity by officials; but it took some time to find a firm footing for it among the common people'. To remedy this, he and da Roza resorted to cold-calling potential customers to persuade them of the benefits of a subscription. During one such visit to a business in an industrial district, the proprietor indicated he already had a copy, even producing it and praising them for the interesting news it contained. But when da Roza suggested the proprietor take out an annual subscription, the man declined, explaining that he already had a copy and did not need any more. After much laughter from other staff, it was left to a young clerk to explain that each day's issue contained different news. According to John Black, the proprietor exclaimed: 'What? As much as this changed and fresh every morning? I cannot believe it possible!' The man flatly refused to take out a subscription, arguing that if he wanted a fresh copy he would find it at a bookseller (Black, JR 1883:II,371).

In July 1872, four months after the first edition came off the press, the government increased its support for the venture by buying copies for distribution to all prefectural headquarters. Then on October 20, the left chamber of the Dajōkan (Council of State), known as the Sa-In,[24] contracted the newspaper for three years to publish announcements and articles about its proceedings, a development which ensured that the paper became 'a paragon of government–press symbiosis' (Huffman 1997:53). The record of Sa-In proceedings shows that the chamber decided to use the *Nisshin shinji shi* in this way for the purpose of 'ensuring prosperity and strength by leading the people to enlightenment' (Satō 1989:14–16). This permission may also have owed more to the government's agreement with John Black to help with publication of the paper since Black was 'pressed for finances' (Huffman 1997:53).

The Sa-In was at the time investigating the possibility of establishing a bicameral legislative assembly and its members saw John Black's newspaper as a way to publicise their motives for the new parliamentary structure. Several other newspapers were available for the Sa-In to use

---

24 The Sa-In 'nominally an appointed legislature', together with the U-In (Right Chamber) advised the Sei-In (Central Chamber), which advised the Emperor; see Beasley (1989:64).

in this manner, but John Black's access to overseas news, his ability to publish daily in Tokyo, his speedy use of moveable type, rather than a single carved woodblock per page, and use of editorial comment, rendered *Nisshin shinji shi* the newspaper of choice for the Sa-In (Satō 1989:19). In an interview, Henry Black described his father's status at this time as *yatoi* (Nishūbashi 1905:294). John Black had become one of the government's 'live machines'.

Such direct government support for and patronage of newspapers was not unusual at the time. From 1872, the government had begun supporting a number of newspapers financially through Finance Ministry (Ōkurashō) purchases of copies of the *Shinbun zasshi*, the *Tōkyō nichi nichi shinbun* and the *Yokohama mainichi shinbun* for distribution to every prefectural headquarters. From 1873, the ministry even guaranteed free mailed delivery of journalists' articles for inclusion in newspapers (Satō 1989:15). The government also promoted the use of newspapers in schools as educational aids. Ōkuma Shigenobu, who was Finance Ministry head from 1873, used *The Japan Mail* to print government spending and income details for the perusal of foreign nations.

Given this kind of support, John Black's new enterprise thrived. In a diary entry covering several days prior to and including 4 December 1874, Campbell gave a vivid description of the scene at the Zōjōji Temple offices of the *Nisshin shinji shi*:

> The compositors were on the floor, and they were all gentlemen of the soldier class in their national dress. They were *Samurai*, well-educated men of good family, employed about literature. The Japanese characters in use amount to thousands, and their number grows continually (Campbell 1876:242).

Henry Black, then almost 16, conducted Campbell to the temple on the visit he described. We can thank Campbell for creating the earliest extant English-language record of Henry ('Mr Harry Black') knowing 'a professional story-teller'.

> One of these mornings Mr. Harry Black conducted me to the office of the Japanese newspaper, of which his father is editor. We walked to the Buddhist temple, in which the Jupiter of Tokio lodges, and walked thence through the main streets. My guide carried a magnificent hunting hawk on his wrist. It had no hood and gazed about composedly at the sun and the crowds of people. The falconer followed. He was a

> Japanese gentleman and looked like it. We were seeking a professional story-teller. He was off his beat, so we went on, hawk and all, to the editor's room, and the equivalent of the Queen's Printers (Campbell 1876:242).

Although the storyteller is not identified, Campbell's memoir tells us that Henry was at this time already familiar with a member of the profession. The presence of the hawk and the falconer, with which *samurai* hunted, indicate further an interest in Japanese culture.

In describing his work as a journalist some years later, John Black recalled how, in the *Nisshin shinji shi* in particular, he had created a forum for topical political discussion with a strong editorial flavour. He recalled, for example, that if he approved of the behaviour of the police, he praised them, taking pains to explain to those police who later came to thank him that in the future he might even have cause to censure them. The issue of *Nisshin shinji shi* for 12 May 1875 was no exception to his policy of impartiality. It criticised the Japanese government for spending vast sums of money over four years on what amounted to a very short length of railway track and claimed that the shoddy construction of telegraph lines was giving the government a poor reputation (Okitsu 1997:5–7).

John Black was also critical of behaviour he considered uncivilised by British standards. When in 1872 he accompanied da Roza to apply for the licence to publish the *Nisshin shinji shi*, the two entered a tiny wayside entertainment booth where they paid to witness what turned out to be a boy devouring a raw rabbit. The boy's dogteeth 'were extraordinarily long and dog-like', prompting John Black to conclude that 'this may have given his parents the idea of training him accordingly, with a view to exhibition'. John Black's sensibilities were offended. He subsequently investigated the state of 'street exhibitions', concluding that many were 'indecent and objectionable'. He later printed 'a very strong paragraph on the subject' with the result that 'within three or four days, every one of them was swept away; and never since has any such obscenity been permitted in any part of Tokio' (Black, JR 1883:II,369–370). The response demonstrated the government's sensitivity to foreign criticism of 'uncivilised' behaviour.

Black's approach gave the *Nisshin shinji shi* a reputation as 'a model of the first "modern" newspaper, with Japan's first editorial columns and a broader range of articles than could be found in other newspapers' (Huffman 1997: 53). Years later, in 1926, a writer for the *Mainichi shinbun*, summing up John Black's contribution to Japanese journalism, wrote that he had been a 'realist' who had 'understood the useful function that a newspaper can discharge'.

> While the *Chūgai shinbun*, the *Moshihogusa*, and the *Kōko shinbun* dealt principally in very unsophisticated political discussion and strange jottings reminiscent of the preceding era, Black told his readers of the vicissitudes of farming, of prices, of new inventions, of exports and imports, of transactions as far apart as the sale of upland pastures and the purchase of battleships. No doubt the readers could tell from this that it was a real newspaper and could see the scrupulous care with which he treated everything. His was the first newspaper to list exports and imports at Yokohama and the time-table and fares of the railway… It is apparent that its strength was that it caused people to realize that newspapers are useful (Ōdawara,1930:222).

In his mid-teens, Henry Black worked closely with his father in the venture, frequently commuting on horseback between Tokyo and Yokohama on errands for the newspaper. On one such occasion, travelling to Yokohama to arrange for the supply of newsprint, he was followed by a mysterious man on horseback. Afraid of the stranger, he spurred on his horse only to find that the stranger did the same until he arrived safely at his destination. He later learned that the stranger had followed him because he was worried for his safety as a foreign boy alone. The incident attests to the dangers which still attended foreigners in Japan in the 1870s and the risks taken in gathering news (Nishūbashi 1905:294). It also indicates that Henry Black was acquainted with newsgathering from an early age. His ability to gather together the strands of a story was to serve him well in later years.

Friends in high places

The work at the *Nisshin shinji shi* facilitated contact between the Blacks and a number of prominent post-Restoration figures. As Henry himself recalled:

> Around that time, my father was on familiar terms with Saigō Takamori, Count Itagaki, Count Gotō, Count Kawamura, and other well-known Chōya figures. Etō Shinpei and others used to come quite often to our place, and he even came for dinner the night before he returned to Saga (Nishūbashi 1905:294).

All these men were leading political strategists and critics of the Meiji government. Henry's association with them during his formative years helps explain his enduring interest in Japan's development and his subsequent affiliation with activists in the pro-democracy Freedom and People's Rights Movement.

Saigō Takamori (1827–1877), for example, led the movement for the overthrow of the *bakufu*. He served as head of a caretaker government while members of the Iwakura Mission were overseas, but resigned after mission members refused to support his proposal for a military expedition to Korea. Saigō then returned to his domainal home of Kagoshima from where he led an army of disaffected former *samurai* against the central government. The army was defeated and Saigō committed suicide on 24 September 1877 (Japan 1993:1293).

Itagaki Taisuke (1837–1919) was a former *samurai* who supported Saigō Takamori in attempts to get rid of the *bakufu* prior to the Restoration. Itagaki joined the post-Restoration government, but like Saigō, resigned over the government's refusal to become embroiled in Korea. Itagaki was a founding member of the Aikoku Kōtō (Public Party of Patriots) (Japan 1993:6350) and a leader of the pro-democracy Freedom and People's Rights Movement.

Gotō Shōjirō (1857–1929) was a former *samurai* from the Tosa domain who also urged the *bakufu* to hand power to the emperor. He was appointed to a government position after the Restoration, but resigned over the government's refusal to sanction the proposed military expedition to Korea. Gotō joined Itagaki in forming the Aikoku Kōtō (Public Party of Patriots) and again joined him in 1881 to form the Jiyūtō (Liberal Party) (Japan 1993:470).

Count Kawamura Sumiyoshi (1836–1904) was an admiral from the Satsuma domain. After the Restoration, he rose to become senior vice minister of the navy at a time when other cabinet ministers saw the appointment as a compromise requiring a balance between the Satsuma and Chōshū domains. Much later, in his seventies, he was to be entrusted with the welfare of the son of the crown prince (Keene 2002:272,277,359,573).

Etō Shinpei (1834–1874) was a former *samurai* from Saga Prefecture. Following his appointment as Minister of Justice in 1872, Etō accomplished a number of legal reforms, including the drafting of the penal code (Japan 1993:351). Henry's acquaintance with Etō is important because in the 1890s Henry displayed an interest in the debate about law reform by including references to British and French legal codes in several of his narrations. Etō also resigned from government service in 1873 out of dissatisfaction over the government's refusal to mount a military expedition to Korea. Etō then returned to Saga where he led an unsuccessful uprising against the government in 1874.

Another of the prominent figures John Black met was Kido Takayoshi (1833–1877), who negotiated the alliance between the Chōshū and Satsuma domains, which overthrew the Tokugawa shogunate and ushered in the Meiji Restoration. Kido later worked against the Freedom and People's Rights Movement, but played a pivotal role in abolishing the feudal system and replacing it with a centralised bureaucracy. In 1869, Kido directed the surrender of domain registers (*hanseki hōkan*) (Japan 1993: 776) as part of a strategy to convert the domains into prefectures within a centralised government. In a diary entry for 11 April 1869, written while Kido and John Black were aboard the *Costa Rica* on a sea journey from Yokohama to Kobe, Kido recorded that 'inasmuch as the Briton Black is fluent in Japanese, I talked about world affairs with him' (Kido 1986:I,457).

Although John Black did not mention meeting Kido in *Young Japan*, he devoted several paragraphs to documenting Kido's journey to Yamaguchi, the Chōshū domainal capital, in 1869 to persuade key domainal figures to agree to dismantle the feudal system. Kido recalled in a diary entry on 26 February 1871 that his purpose in instigating the return of the registers was 'to put the nation on a course of building a still stronger foundation that we may be able to stand side by side with the rest of the nations of the world' (Kido 1986:I,457). In his assessment of Kido's actions, John Black wrote of the 'absolute necessity for centralization…for feudalism and constitutionalism could not exist together' (Black, JR 1883:II,252).

Overstepping the mark

Such contacts gave John Black inside information, but did not guarantee immunity from crossfire in domestic Japanese politics. In 1874, his outspoken style and preparedness, as an editor, to criticise the government led to his sudden loss of a job.

The catalytic incident had its origins in the proposal put to the government by Saigō, Itagaki, Gotō and dinner guest Etō, in the autumn of 1873 for a punitive military expedition to Korea. Iwakura Tomomi, who led the mission to Europe and the United States in 1871–73, and Ōkubo Toshimichi, by now both prominent government figures, opposed the proposal. This prompted Saigō, Itagaki, Gotō and Etō to leave the government. On 17 January 1874, eight disgruntled former government members, including Gotō and Etō, presented an appeal to the Sa-In for an elected assembly. They leaked the details of their appeal to John Black who knew a scoop when he saw one (Sissons 1978:7–8). His printing of the appeal in the following day's edition prompted other newspapers to take up the issue of an elected assembly (Asaoka 1989:50–63). Debate over an elected assembly was now out in the open. The impact of his action was alluded to by the scholar Sakatani Shiroshi in the June 1874 issue of *Meiroku zasshi*, the journal of the Meirokusha, a society of intellectuals and Westernisers, in which Sakatani mentions the key role of *Nisshin shinji shi* in the debate (*Meiroku zasshi* 1976:149).

John Black's decision to publish the appeal in his Japanese-language newspaper was a defining moment in the history of politics and journalism in Japan. It contributed to a shift in attitude within the government toward a greater perception of the role of the press as a potential voice for the opposition. Although the Meiji government promulgated its first regulations pertaining to print media in 1869, these had dealt only with the publication of books. Book and press regulations pertaining to newspapers between 1871 and 1873 were initially aimed at encouraging the growth of the newspaper industry. But after mid-1873, they grew progressively draconian and restrictive (Asaoka 1989:55; Mitchell 1983:13–100). Indicative of this were regulations issued in October 1873, which specified that newspapers must have 'no evil tendency'. The legislation listed permissible topics, including translations of foreign writings and official notifications, but stipulated that no newspaper could be established without official permission. The rules also prohibited attacks on the Constitution, the discussion of laws, or the casting of 'obstacles in the way of the working of the national institutions by the persistent advocacy of foreign ideas'.[25]

Under the circumstances, John Black's decision to publish the opposition's appeal for a legislative assembly did not endear him to a government which had regarded *Nisshin shinji shi* as its mouthpiece. The incident galvanised the government into developing even harsher penalties against its critics.

Betrayal

Retribution was swift. The government reacted by enticing John Black out of editorship of the *Nisshin shinji shi* with an offer of work as foreign adviser to the Administrative Section of the Sa-In. He at first refused to resign the editorship, but was later convinced that the Sa-In would shortly be abolished and replaced with an elected legislature which would continue to patronise the paper. In January 1875, John Black resigned as

[25] 'The Newspaper Press Law, Notification No. 352, Oct. 19, 1873' (McLaren 1979:534).

Nisshin shinji shi editor to take the new post (Asaoka 1989:56). Then in June 1875, the government promulgated its Defamation Law and Press Regulations prohibiting criticism of government policy and specifying that 'no other persons than Japanese subjects can be proprietors or directors, editor or chief editor'.[26] A week later, John Black was transferred from the Administrative Section of the Sa-In to languish in the Translation Bureau. Then in July 1875, the government dismissed him from that bureau. It had effectively silenced him (Morioka & Sasaki 1983:134–136). One of the great ironies of the entire episode is that Black's Japanese editor colleagues did not complain about his 'martyrdom' since 'they had long resented his special privileges and had promoted the rule against foreign ownership of vernacular papers' (Huffman 1997:81). John Black was no more than a disposable 'live machine'. He had passed his use-by date. In January 1876, he tried to establish another Japanese-language newspaper, the *Bankoku shinbun*, but the government invoked its press regulations, penalising the printer and terminating publication. He appealed through the British consul, Harry Parkes, for compensation from the government (Asaoka 1989:57), but Parkes was unsympathetic and the appeal went nowhere. In April 1876, with little prospect of employment in Japan, a bitterly disappointed John Black left for Shanghai where he edited the *Shanghai Mercury* until his return to Japan for health reasons in June 1879 (Hanazono 1926:77).[27]

When John Black had left Zōjōji Temple for a larger office in the Ginza, he presented the priests with a chandelier as an expression of his gratitude for housing the family and the newspaper printing works. We know of this from *Osaka mainichi* journalist Kanesada Hanazono (1926:77):

> As I was told by Ishii Black that his father presented a chandelier to the Zōjōji Temple, when he was removing his office from the Genkoin, one of the temples in the old compound of the Zōjōji to the Ginza, I went to the Zōjōji and the Genkoin. In the Zōjōji, I was ushered into a gallery, and was shown the chandelier in a rather damaged condition, but beautifully shining as if to tell of its origin. Black made a present of the chandelier just after it was received from Holland.

There is surely no more incongruous setting for an ornate European chandelier than a Buddhist temple. Could the gift have been John Black's

26 'The Newspaper Press Law, Notification No. 101, June 28, 1875' (McLaren 1979:593).

27 Black notes his return to Japan in June 1979 in his preface to *Young Japan* (Black, JR 1883:I,v).

attempt to blend gratitude with some tangible example of European civilisation and enlightenment? There is a degree of consistency here. While John Black constantly gave what he could to Japan in a manner consistent with his Freemason ideals, his actions offended many in authority. Like a chandelier in a Buddhist temple, he was not always appreciated.

A lasting legacy

While John Black suffered from the government ban on his participation in the news media, his chief legacy was to turn newspapers into lively participants in a dialogue with the government over its reform agenda. The closure of the *Nisshin shinji shi* and his sacking from the Sa-In highlighted two things: government determination to gain control of the reform agenda by taming the press, and; increasing resentment of involvement by non-Japanese in the reform debate.

Several other factors combined in the mid-1870s to make restrictive government reaction against the press inevitable. Although the Finance Ministry had promoted the use of newspapers as an aid to enlightenment following the Restoration, responsibility for the use of newspapers was transferred in November 1873 to the powerful new Home Ministry, which was formed in the government's attempt to restructure local government. This sequence of events lends weight to the suggestion that the process of devising more oppressive regulations stemmed more from bureaucratic wrangling than from agreement within the government (Huffman 1997: 55).

John Black's campaigning style had one further legacy. With the *Nisshin shinji shi* as an example of how the press could work for a cause, many of the government's critics, including powerful but disgruntled bureaucrats who wished to make their views on the meaning of civilisation and enlightenment known, set about establishing their own newspapers. Japan experienced the rise of a partisan press with newspapers as vehicles for the projection of power and influence (Freeman 2000:35). Diversity among newspapers also increased, which serendipitously worked to Henry Black's later advantage. This diversity led to the creation of two different types of newspapers – the *ōshinbun* (major newspapers), which catered to elites by focusing on political issues, and the more apolitical *koshinbun* (minor newspapers), which catered to the masses by focusing on entertainment and sensation (Freeman 2000:35). The *ōshinbun* became vehicles for debate over the proposal for a popularly elected legislature (Satō 1989:14). Although powerful bureaucrats had originally backed selected newspapers by favouring them with leaks and privileged information, they found that editors were beyond their control. Editorial staff at the *ōshinbun* ceased to be willing and uncritical acolytes of the government. They became active participants in the national debate, shaping their editorial stance to reflect the debate and to influence it. At the same time, the *koshinbun* specialised in sensationalist reporting of crime and gossip as entertainment. By the 1880s, the *koshinbun* were including serialised versions of stories narrated by professional storytellers, including those of Henry Black.

With the departure of John Black to Shanghai, the government had eliminated foreign influence from the vernacular press. Nevertheless, John Black had helped revitalise journalism as a medium for carrying on the debate over reform. Until the mid-1870s, the Meiji government had only had to contend with local opposition movements; from the mid-1870s, its opponents, backed by the popular press, began to demand alternative institutions.

Like his father, Henry Black was to retain a disputative and critical disposition which, many years later, he at times brought to bear on his colleagues within the storyteller fraternity with unfortunate results. But the ban on his father's participation in the media sent him an early warning that the government would not brook interference from foreigners. A later hardening of the policy eventually terminated Henry Black's direct involvement with the pro-democracy movement, but, ironically, influenced his decision to become a *rakugoka*. The foundations for that career were laid while his father was absent in Shanghai.

Chapter 4

A novice on the stage

> He [Hori] said to me; 'you're used to Japanese. Why don't you make a speech?' I was young and foolish at the time, so devoid of political thoughts or opinions as I was, I said I would, and took on the task. So I made a speech before the public and that was at the Yūraku Theatre, which no longer exists, in Kōjimachi. (Henry Black on one of the earliest occasions he spoke on stage, urged by orator Hori Ryūta [Nishūbashi 1905:295])

As a storyteller, Henry Black was fond of embroidering the truth about his formative years. In an interview with Nishūbashi Sei (1905:295), for example, he claimed to have spent some of his early years with his mother in Seattle. According to this version, relatives in Seattle urged him to become a businessman (*jistugyōka*) or to go into banking, but Henry felt the apprenticeship for these fields was too long compared to working with his father in Japan. So he decided, he said, to return to Japan to work with his father. Henry Black's surviving relatives on his mother's side are unaware of any family members having settled in the Seattle area. In another interview in the *Yomiuri shinbun* (Nyorai 1896), Henry claimed to have spent the years during his father's absence in Shanghai with his mother in London. None of this appears to have been true because Japanese newspapers recorded him appearing on stage in Japan while his father was absent in Shanghai.

If he never stayed in the United States and remained in Japan throughout his father's absence, why then did he claim otherwise? The answer lies in his need to embroider the truth. In the 1880s and 1890s, in interviews granted when he was at the height of his career, Henry Black invented a past spent in the West to bolster his credentials as a foreign-born entertainer with a talent for adapting material from foreign sources. In the years when he was supposed to have been in Seattle or London, he was in Japan laying the foundations for a future career on the stage.

Just three months after his father left for Shanghai, in July 1876, 17-year-old Henry Black made his first documented stage appearance. This was a performance of magic at the Yoshikawa Theatre in Tokyo's entertainment district, Asakusa. That month the *Yūbin hōchi* newspaper also recorded that 'the English magician Black' would perform 'strange magic' with the entertainer Yanagikawa Ichōsai 'this coming 16th at the Kanbagawa Theater in Nishi Torigoe'. Henry also performed at the Seizōin Hall in October in 1876, but this reportedly did not meet with the acclaim of the previous performances.[28] Henry does not appear to have considered these performances integral to the development of his storyteller career. He did not refer to them when interviewed on how he came to his storyteller career, even though they were an essential part of his path to becoming a stage performer. Rather, according to the version he related to chronicler and journalist Nishūbashi Sei (quoted above), he was encouraged to appear on stage by his father's acquaintance, retired naval officer and public orator Hori Ryūta. The date of the performance in the Yūraku Theatre in Kōjimachi is unclear, but it appears to have been while his father was absent in China.

His experience in the Yūraku Theatre led to contact with Shōrin Hakuen (1831–1905), a prominent exponent of the didactic *kōdan* style of storytelling, who coached him in the art. *Kōdan* drew from a long narrative tradition that included stories of the lives of Buddhist saints, 'tales of heroic protectors of the common people' and tales of military prowess (Morioka & Sasaki 1990:5). Hakuen's influence was as an innovator. Although born in the Edo period, he seized opportunities for renewal in his art provided by the flowering of new ideas in the Meiji period. Hakuen specialised in *sewamono* (stories portraying duty and obligation), but had a talent for innovation in creating new stories or entirely novel variations on old ones. He considered himself an artist first and secondly an educator. In 1871, for example, Hakuen popularised a version of the story of Columbus. He also made famous a narrated version of a journey around the world entitled *Sekai isshū ochiriya sōshi*, eight years before the translation of *Around the World in Eighty Days* was published, which indicates his ready eye for a good story.

---

28 For reports of the July performance in *Yūbin hōchi shinbun*, 13 July 1876, and *Yomiuri shinbun*, 8 July 1876, see Kurata (1981–87:I,157). Morioka and Sasaki (1983:136) mention the Seizōin Hall performance, citing *Tokyo hanauta*, 25 October 1876, in Kurata (1980:85).

Hakuen's story about a robber (*nezumi kozō*) won him the nickname 'Robber Hakuen', which backfired when he was hauled in by the police for interrogation after a real robber claimed to have been influenced by Hakuen's story. Hakuen charmed his interrogators by telling them the full-length version of the story. Doubtless, the police enjoyed this and when word of the incident spread, his fame grew. Audiences flocked to his performances and newspapers took an interest. Contacts with the newspapers led to serialisation of some of his stories, further boosting his popularity among the literate, educated and informed classes. His popularity explains why Henry credited Hakuen as one of the more influential persons in his career.

Hakuen is reported to have seen the intellectual, Fukuzawa Yukichi, making a speech using a table and chair on the stage in 1875. He later incorporated this practice into his performances and even became the first *kōdan* narrator to appear during performances wearing Western-style clothes. Several illustrations of Henry in later years show that he also used a table and Western clothes, although it appears he did not do so all the time.

After Hakuen's coaching, Henry Black's next reported stage appearance was in December 1878 at the Tomitake Theatre in Bashamichi, Yokohama's main entertainment and theatre precinct. As the Tomitake opened in December 1878, Henry's appearance was probably part of its inaugural program. On that occasion, he spoke about Joan of Arc and the exiled pretender to the Scottish throne, Charles Edward Stuart. The owner of the Tomitake Hall was Takeuchi Takejirō, operator of three other vaudeville entertainment theatres (*yose*) on Bashamichi in Yokohama (*Yokohama shi shikō* 1973:252–254). *Yose* were typically the venues for a wide variety of cheap, mass entertainment, including jugglers, musicians, magicians, contortionists and storytellers. By this stage, Henry was almost 20 years old.

The lives of the two mythologised and tragic nationalist heroes, France's Joan of Arc and Scotland's Bonnie Prince Charlie, fitted well with the *kōdan* presentation style which in the early Meiji years was still more popular than *rakugo*. Given Henry Black's Scottish ancestry and the timing of the performance, it is not surprising that he should have chosen their stories.

The mythologisation of Charles Stuart and Joan of Arc as prototypes for 19th-century nationalist heroes was not necessarily lost on Japanese audiences whose quest for a national identity was already integral to the quest for modernity. The tragedies of these two European nationalist heroes were similar to that of Black family confidant, Saigō Takamori. They served as warnings about the threat of colonisation by the British, whose military prowess had largely English philosophical underpinnings. These links suggest that Henry Black was already sensitive to nationalism as one of the attributes of the 19th-century European nation-state to which the Japanese aspired.

Other factors were also at work in determining his relationship with audiences. From the beginning Henry Black was aware of his status as a foreigner on the Japanese stage. In the Nishūbashi interview, referring to his narration of the lives of Bonnie Prince Charlie and Joan of Arc at the Tomitake Theatre, he attributed the 'full house' to the novel (*mezurashii*) nature of the topic and the speaker (Nishūbashi 1905:296).[29] But in his interview with Nyorai An, he explained that he still had some way to go before polishing his ability as a storyteller. Foreignness alone was not yet enough to guarantee an entertaining and professional performance. Elaborating on this, Henry explained that, when the Yūraku Theatre performance led to his sharing the bill at speech meetings with Shōrin Hakuen, his initial reception owed much to the presence of Hakuen. As Henry recalled 'when Hakuen didn't appear, we only got a few customers, so I appeared all the time with Hakuen' (Nyorai 1896).

Henry Black soon improved. By the spring of 1879, when he visited Hakuen at the Tomitake Theatre in Yokohama, the scene of his performances in December the previous year, Hakuen suddenly asked him to give an impromptu performance. As Henry described it,

> He said to me: 'Ah, Black, you've come at a good time. Fortunately, I'm just about to take a break, so would you give a talk?' I had no idea what to do, but I said I would do it, so I gave a humorous talk (*kokkei banashi*). There was tremendous applause and it was a great success. That's how I began appearing in *yose*. From that time, I gave speeches in various *yose*, performing Western history stories and I was quite popular (Nyorai 1896:1).

By this stage, Henry Black was acquiring many of the attributes he would utilise throughout his career in storytelling – fluency and confidence in the Japanese language before audiences, knowledge of domestic and international affairs and of Western and Japanese cultures, and a talent for gathering story material that would appeal to Japanese audiences. The novelty of his sourcing of material from the West was without doubt a

---

29 Black tells the interviewer: 'Chārusu issei no hanashi to ka, mata wa furansu no jon [*sic*] dāku no den nado wo yarimasu to, mezurashii no de koi ga sono hijyō no ōiri.' (When I did the story of Charles I or the life of Joan of Arc from France, it was novel so we got a full house.)

major reason for his initial success with audiences. There was also the unique distinction of being a narrator with European ancestry. When he recalled this period (Nyorai 1896), he explained that his performances of *seiyō no rekishi banashi* (Western history stories) led to his becoming *jūbun ninki ga yoku nariyashita* (quite popular).

But there were obstacles in his way. Although Hakuen and other storytellers encouraged his storytelling talent as an opportunity to modernise their art, Henry's immediate family and some of his associates considered it demeaning and inappropriate. Occasional appearances on stage might have been acceptable, but they did not regard storytelling as suitable for a full-time career.

Chapter 5

The activist years, 1878–1886

> In my country of Britain, gambling and women are in just the same position...On the surface it is forbidden to openly engage in business by putting out a sign saying 'We have rooms so come and buy a woman'. And of course according to one argument, if businesses are permitted to trade openly they will cause considerable harm to society, so it shouldn't be tolerated. But there are many people who secretly operate gambling dens or brothels in London. If any of them are reported, the police enter the premises and it is immediately closed down ... Take the case of Tokyo and you'll see what I mean. Yoshiwara and Susaki are famous places. The streets are wide and the buildings are fine and beautifully decorated. When someone from the country comes to see the sights of Tokyo, if he doesn't go there to take a look, he can't claim to have seen Tokyo. He'll be stuck for something to talk about when he gets back to his hometown and will get laughed at. (Henry Black's condemnation of the Yoshiwara licensed prostitute quarter in Tokyo in his 1891 narration (Eikokujin 1891:133), an adaptation of Mary Braddon's 'Her Last Appearance' [Braddon 1877]).

By June of 1879, six months after Henry Black's performances at the Tomitake Theatre in Yokohama, his father John Black returned to Japan from China to recuperate from an illness. The family were together again in Yokohama, which was no longer the frontier shantytown they had known immediately after their arrival in Japan. Superstitious Japanese no longer threw buckets of water at passing trains on the Tokyo–Yokohama line because they belched smoke from their engines. Mary Kidder's school for girls had been joined by many others and a generation of foreign children were growing up never having known the country of their parents. Gas lit the streets. The Grand Hotel had opened for business on the Bund. The British and French garrisons had been closed permanently in 1875. In Tokyo in May 1877, a young American girl called Clara Whitney had written in her diary of her enjoyment on viewing the ascent of a balloon over the Naval Ministry while sharing genteel tea and cakes on the balcony. Selections from Clara's diary (Whitney 1979) would be published a century later as a record of events in an exotic country.

During John Black's absence in Shanghai, the discourse about modernisation had further evolved. Many of the early leaders of the Freedom and Peoples' Rights Movement, including Itagaki Taisuke and Gotō Shōjirō who were known to John and Henry Black, were at least as much interested in gaining or regaining political power from the ruling oligarchy as in enlightening the masses about their democratic rights (Jansen 1995:243–244). Despite their mixed motives, their calls for a representative assembly had by 1878 attracted increasing numbers of adherents from outside the *samurai* class. The movement had developed a momentum of its own and was seeking new ways of reaching a wider audience through the press and oratory.

But in the rush to carry out its reforms, the Meiji government did not want troublesome opponents. To forestall opposition, it legislated, or used the police to intimidate and imprison opponents. However, by the time John Black returned from Shanghai in the late 1870s, those excluded from running the reform agenda were becoming better organised and more vocal. They now agitated for a greater say in the nation's affairs. The Blacks, with their belief in the freedom of speech and press, were natural allies of the pro-democratic elements in a struggle which was to pit John Black against the government and Henry against the police.

The 1870s in Japan were 'one of the most stimulating and optimistic eras in modern Japanese history' (*Meiroku zasshi* 1976:xviii). A spirit of participation, debate and enthusiasm for new, mainly Western ideas culminated in the formation by intellectuals late in the decade of societies to propagate Western ideals of progress and equality. These societies contributed to the national discourse about the nature of modernisation and reform by publishing journals containing the writings of their members.

The Blacks counted several members of these societies among their acquaintances and friends. Prominent among them was the intellectual, Fukuzawa Yukichi, who was responsible for the establishment of Japan's first private university. Henry's sister, Pauline even taught English to Fukuzawa's offspring in her later years (Morioka & Sasaki 1986a:65). In the late 20th century, yellowing copies of Fukuzawa's works were found preserved in farm storehouses, attesting to his widespread popularity among rural adherents of the pro-democracy movement. Fukuzawa taught a rationalist, pragmatic approach to modernisation and encouraged the questioning of authority, but ultimately favoured compromise with the government and even opposed early establishment of a national assembly, one of the planks of the pro-democracy movement (Irokawa 1985:67).

Fukuzawa belonged to one of the more prominent of the societies for promotion of Western ideas, the Meirokusha, whose members campaigned against 'everything that smacked of bigotry and superstition in Old Japan'.[30] Members used their journal *Meiroku zasshi* to define the then popular slogans of 'civilisation and enlightenment' (*bunmei kaika*) and 'prosperous country and strong army' (*fukoku kyōhei*). Their writings and lectures covered a variety of themes, including the separation of church and state, the status of women, economic policy, the uses and benefits of chemistry and language reform (*Meiroku zasshi* 1976:xix). In an essay in the journal's ninth issue, for example, Mitsukuri Rinshō examined the use of the word 'liberty' from its early Latin origins to British philosopher John Stuart Mill's *On Liberty*. Tsuda Mamichi, in the 24th issue, argued that an easing of the government's restriction on foreigners travelling throughout the country would help bring enlightenment to more people (*Meiroku zasshi* 1976:298–301).

Fukuzawa is important to the story of Henry Black because he pioneered using the public speech meeting as a way to spread ideas to large gatherings in halls and other venues in Tokyo and throughout the countryside. Fukuzawa's idea quickly took hold and between 1878 and 1886 societies dedicated to promoting debate over democratic ideals sprang up around Japan. Many of them sponsored gatherings with invited speakers; many also began to establish newspapers to transmit their ideas. These societies constitute the core of what we now know as the Freedom and People's Rights Movement. The movement was both a struggle for power and a struggle for control over definitions of modernity.

As the movement grew in strength and influence, the government reacted by progressively restricting right of assembly and freedom of the press. The government did, however, partially meet some of the movement's demands. Its decision to accede to the demand for the establishment of an elected assembly and a constitution eventually split the movement.

---

30 Meirokusha was established in 1874 by Mori Arinori, Japan's first diplomatic representative to Washington, and like-minded scholars of Western society (see *Meiroku zasshi* 1976:xix).

Orators, newspapers and people's rights

By the time John Black had returned to Japan from Shanghai in June 1879, the press had undergone a number of changes in reaction to the imposition of government regulations. In the early Meiji years, editors and journalists, including John Black, had displayed a relatively uncritical propensity to support the government. They did so through a shared desire to inculcate ideas of progress and enlightenment in readers. From around 1874, however, in reaction to government restrictions imposed partly because of John Black's actions, the press spent the following several years cultivating a more independent stand on issues (Huffman 1997:68–71). This situation was to be resolved between 1881 and 1886 when there was a further shift in the role of the press denoted by the growth of partisanship, whereby a significant number of influential newspapers began to serve the newly formed political parties.

The government's increasingly draconian restrictions on the press drove editors to identify less with the government's interests and more with alternative elements, including activists in the Freedom and People's Rights Movement. Even John Black, who described the government's actions as at times amounting to 'persecution', noted that the measures 'seemed to strengthen the growth and importance of the Press' (Black, JR 1883:II,448). It should be remembered, however, that this shift in emphasis remained in essence a struggle over the reform agenda involving members of an educated, but numerically small, elite.

The new preparedness of newspaper editors to criticise the government, in spite of legal restrictions, matched the rapid increase in the number of popular rights societies around the country, which were more highly politicised than the Meirokusha. Their growth, which began around 1878 and culminated in the formation of the Jiyūtō (Liberal Party) in October 1881, was indicative of a period of promotion and organisation by participants in the Freedom and People's Rights Movement (Bowen 1980:109). Japanese scholars find it hard to quantify the number of popular rights societies, but Irokawa Daikichi cites evidence that there were 'more than 150 "well-known political societies"' between 1878 and 1881 (Irokawa 1976:176). The figure is approximately the same as Gotō Yasushi's findings that 149 political societies affiliated with the Jiyūtō when it was formed in October 1881 and that by November 1880, these 149 societies managed to mobilise over 135,000 people for a petition advocating establishment of a national assembly (Bowen 1980:113). In 1879, Tokyo had 12 societies, second only to Kōchi which had 17 (Bowen 1980:114).

Many of the societies and political parties were started by ex-*samurai*, ostensibly to achieve a representative assembly as a way of eliminating what they regarded as unrepresentative rule by an oligarchy dominated by former *samurai* from domains in the southwest (Bowen 1980:114). But the leaders of this movement were hardly radical revolutionaries. The early democracy movement was very much a power struggle with its adherents mostly favouring a constitutional monarchy and endorsing the patronising view of Fukuzawa Yukuchi that 'liberal ideas such as freedom and independence had to be instilled in the people' (Hane 1983:92). It was very much a revolution delivered from above by an educated elite of ex-*samurai*.

The societies used the rhetoric of natural rights to garner support for campaigns for self-government, local autonomy and class equality (Hane 1983:109). The doctrine of natural rights, articulated by John Locke in his *Second Treatise*, and subsequently by Rousseau and Jefferson, had inspired moves throughout the 17th and 18th centuries to eliminate feudal society. But in Europe, the governments that emerged to ensure the efficient working of a liberal market society based on this theory were invariably dominated by the propertied class. The lack of trust in ordinary people by the propertied class who dominated government explains why the leaders of the Freedom and People's Rights Movement in Japan could appear both democratic and illiberal.

But the story of Meiji democracy is more than the history of the political parties and prominent leaders of the Freedom and People's Rights Movement. At grassroots level, large numbers of people were inspired by the introduction of new ideas, including those of Fukuzawa, to imagine that they could aspire to a new constitution that guaranteed them individual freedoms (Irokawa 1985). The dialogue the leaders of the movement had initiated in the late 1870s was soon joined irrevocably by increasing numbers of disaffected persons, including journalists, ex-*samurai* and intellectuals. These people took the message of natural rights and their demand for a new constitution to meetings across the country.

A number of political societies actively supported their demands. The larger, more renowned political societies were the early liberal Ōmeisha and Aikokusha. There was also the Seikyōsha, whose members studied political science, economics, history and even natural sciences and held regular weekly lecture meetings at which they discussed classics of Western political thought, such as *On Liberty*, *The Spirit of Laws*, *The History of English Civilization* and *The Social Contract* (Jansen 1995:243). Gatherings such as these were increasingly common from the mid-1870s (*Meiroku zasshi* 1976:xxii).

Between June 1879 and January 1880, Henry Black addressed a number of meetings organised by the political societies. He had already proved his ability to perform in Japanese at the request of Hori Ryūta and as a protégé of Shōrin Hakuen and both men shared the stage with Henry Black at some of these speech meetings.

The first of these was a meeting of the Kun'yūsha at Yūrakuchō on 1 June 1879,[31] when Henry spoke in Japanese on 'a theory of people's rights' (*minkenron*).[32] Hori Ryūta also spoke at the meeting (Nishūbashi 1905:295). Advertisements in the *Chōya shinbun* in June attest to Henry addressing other meetings of the Kun'yūsha at two venues, including Fukagawa, on the topics of 'revision of the treaties' (*jōyaku kaisei*) and the 'pros and cons of a prison system'. He addressed a meeting of the Kun'yūsha on 6 July 1879 regarding 'defamation' (*zanbō no setsu*) and a meeting on 11 July regarding 'a theory of Napoleon' (*Naporeon no ron*). Advertisements promoting his speeches described him as 'the Briton Black' (*eijin Burakku*). Over eight months between June 1879 and January 1880, both John and Henry Black maintained a hectic schedule addressing gatherings on topics including 'abolition of the Yoshiwara', 'the demerits of opening up Japan', 'extraterritoriality', 'criminal procedures', 'cholera prevention', 'the case for using juries', 'the abolition of jails', 'trial by testimony', and 'the rice price hike' (Oizuru 1986:10–11). In addition to the Kun'yūsha, other societies, including Hokushinsha and Kōyō Gakusha, sponsored the gatherings.

At a meeting on 5 November 1879, John Black spoke on the topic of 'Sino-Japanese Relations'. Three days later, at a meeting of the Sanrakusha, which succeeded the Kun'yūsha, he spoke on 'a theory of people's rights' and Henry spoke on 'the source of a country's prosperity'. John Black also attended a meeting with Doi Kōka in Urawa just north of Tokyo on 9 November. At Sanrakusha meetings on 23 and 24 November, Henry spoke on 'The relationship between the people and government' (*jinmin to seifu no kankei*), while his father spoke on 'the rights of a nation' (*kokken ron*). The advertisement for the Sanrakusha meeting printed John Black's surname in large-font *kanji* and described him as 'a Shanghai newspaper editor'. The professional storyteller Shōrin Hakuen also addressed the meeting, again attesting to the involvement of storytellers in the pro-democracy movement.

The topics show a preoccupation with the practicalities of social and legal reform aimed at achieving what the movement's adherents understood as

31 Advertised in *Chōya shinbun*, 30 May 1879 (see Oizuru 1986:10–11).

32 Henry Black was listed as *Hāre Burakku*, reflecting that his immediate family called him Harry, not Henry. For details on the advertisements, see Oizuru 1986:10–11.

modernity. They include legal code reform, health and hygiene, governance and public administration, the opening up of Japan, and women's rights. Many of the topics recurred as themes in the narrations that Henry Black delivered in later years as a professional storyteller.

The topics need to be understood within their historical context. Interest in Louis Napoleon Bonaparte, for example, stemmed from Japanese curiosity over European experiments in styles of governance and legal codes and from the Japanese government's eagerness to superimpose Parisian-style grand boulevards and imposing edifices on central Tokyo. After Louis Napoleon Bonaparte became President of France in 1851, canals were dug and rivers widened to improve the French transportation network and Baron Georges Haussmann was hired to remodel Paris. Paris became a transportation hub and hosted two world's fairs, and new lending institutions stimulated agrarian and industrial development (Lehan 1998:60–61). Napoleonic law was used as a model for the framing of many laws in post-Restoration Japan when the new government employed French jurist Gustave Boissonade in 1876 as a *yatoi* to supervise the compilation of a new penal code (Pflugfelder 1999:170).

Other topics such as 'defamation', 'criminal procedures', 'juries', and 'the abolition of jails' reflect the contemporary interest in law reform. One motive supporting the inclusion of these topics in the reform agenda was the experience of imprisonment of some Freedom and People's Rights Movement adherents when they were *samurai* in the 1840s and 1850s. The former *samurai* campaigned to revise early Meiji penal codes which still reflected the *bakumatsu* practice of prescribing methods of torture and punishment according to a criminal's social status (Umemori 1997:735). As a result of pressure for prison reform, the first Western-style penal code was introduced into Japan in 1880 (Umemori 1997:735). The code reflected a new epistemology of the jail system, to which Henry Black contributed at the speech meetings in the preceding year. Behind the reforms was a new psychology of prisoners as reformable humans, which arose from new definitions of self that were derived from the European natural rights philosophers. Further revisions of the penal code in 1890 eliminated discriminatory punishments based on social rank, affirmed that a crime and its penalty should be mandated under law and enshrined the notion of the protection of private property (Umemori 1997:747).

The themes of these reforms were all ones that Henry Black used later in his narrated stories. A prime example is his 1891 *Shachū no dokubari* (The poisoned pin in the coach) (Kairakutei 1891b) in which, in spite of high social status, retired and respectable opera-going businessman Mr Yamada is jailed as an accomplice in the death of his niece. Just as in the Paris of *Shachū no dokubari*, under the new legal code framed with the help of Boissonade, all were equal before the same law that a judge could refer to in determining appropriate sentences. At the heart of *Shachū no dokubari* is the appropriate disposal of an inheritance.

Henry Black's use of themes such as these in his speeches and narrations attests to the extent of government and audience participation in the contemporary discourse about these new definitions of self. His references to legal reform in his 1879 speeches and, 12 years later, in his 1891 narration illustrate the manner and timing of the transfer of the new concepts beyond an educated elite both to a broader audience in the theatres and to those at home reading printed versions of the story.

The issue of abolition of Tokyo's brothel quarter, Yoshiwara, was the subject of newspaper editorials at the time. It was not unusual for poor families to sell daughters into prostitution, many serving out contracts in licensed quarters like Yoshiwara. The practice of setting aside land for licensed brothels originated in pre-Meiji times in a number of feudal domains and spread nationwide under the centralised government after the Meiji Restoration. Most brothel inmates in Tokyo, which was then home to the largest single number of licensed prostitutes in Japan (Tsurumi 1990:181–182), had parents in dire economic straits. Prostitutes in such quarters worked long hours and lack of sleep left them subject to illnesses. Contracts were difficult to fulfil because of high overheads imposed by employers. Women wanting to flee prostitution found it physically difficult because their quarters were fenced and guarded (Tsurumi 1990:181–187).

The issue of abolition of licensed brothel quarters like Yoshiwara stimulated sentiments such as those expresssed by Tsuda Mamichi in *Meiroku zasshi* issue 42. Tsuda denounced the licensing of brothels as inappropriate for a nation desirous of enlightenment. In his article, published in October 1875, Tsuda acknowledged the high level of indifference or hostility toward his proposal, concluding that 'the public generally may only laugh scornfully and that even men of intellect may reject my views as empty theories easy to set forth but impossible to carry out' (*Meiroku zasshi* 1976:518). The article also presaged anti-prostitution campaigns orchestrated by Christian groups in the late 1890s and the independent press in the early 1900s.

Henry Black referred to the debate about regulating prostitution in his narration *Eikoku Rondon gekijō miyage* (Story from a London theatre) (Eikokujin 1891). The story deals with a young Englishwoman Gātsurudo (probably Gertrude) whose spendthrift husband provides Henry with the opportunity to note the harm caused to families and society by men who squander their money at the Yoshiwara licensed quarters. He also mentions the tricks pimps and others use there to fleece customers and informs listeners that the British parliament, that paragon of civilisation and enlightenment, had passed a law banning gambling dens and brothels.

The extraterritoriality of foreign residents, revision of the treaties with the Western powers and the demerits of opening up Japan were interrelated issues for all Japanese. Naturally enough, they were preoccupations shared by members of the Meirokusha. The fifth issue of *Meiroku zasshi* contained an essay by Tsuda Mamichi (1874) deploring the large outflows of capital as a result of the high level of imports and the protective tariff regime established by the unequal treaties with Western powers (*Meiroku zasshi* 1976:56–59). Pro-democracy movement adherents constantly railed against the injustices of the treaties and were active in the nationwide push to abolish them. Extraterritoriality rankled with many Japanese because it meant that foreigners remained beyond the reach of Japanese law and were subject only to the laws of their respective countries in spite of crimes they might commit in Japan.

Taxation and rice prices were topics of concern to hard-pressed farmers, since the government had promulgated a new law restructuring the old feudal land-tax system in 1873. The new system rationalised tax assessment, basing it on the value of farmland rather than on estimated rice production, on which the old Tokugawa land tax had been based (Jansen 1995:210). The drastic overhaul of the taxation system led to protests by farmers who disputed the valuations accorded their land by bureaucrats. Dissatisfaction over rice prices prompted many *gōnō* (wealthy farmers) to join the pro-democracy movement around this time, making it a 'predominantly rural and increasingly mass-based movement' (Bowen 1980:108).

The final report of speech-making by John and Henry Black appeared in the *Tōkyō e-iri shinbun* (Tokyo illustrated newspaper) of 4 January 1880. Further corroboration of the Blacks' participation in speech meetings comes from the journalist Miyatake Gaikotsu (1867–1955), who wrote in his memoirs that 'John Black delivered some speeches in public' in 1879 (Miyatake 1928, quoted in Morioka & Sasaki 1983:138 fn19). Although Miyatake would have been around 12 years old at the time, he came to know Henry Black intimately seven years later.

The societies associated with these meetings, their organisers and the proprietors of the newspapers that advertised them were linked through a network of friendships and alliances across Japan. The web of connections is a measure of the extent of the respect in which Henry Black and his editor father were held at the time by members of the pro-democracy movement. The Hokushinsha, for example, was a Fukushima-based society which was 'in correspondence' with the Sanshinsha in Miharu (Bowen 1980:219). The founding president of the Sanshinsha was Kōno Hironaka, an ex-*samurai* from the Miharu domain, who helped organise the Sanshisha in the town in 1878. Two years earlier in 1876, Kōno organised and served as founding president of the Seikyōsha (Open Society) in Ishikawa district while serving there as *kuchō* (ward chief). The rules of the Seikyōsha and Sanshinsha show their inspiration owed much to the English doctrine of natural rights. Since as president Kōno was responsible for correspondence with other societies, it can be assumed that Hokushinsha also drew from similar philosophical origins (Bowen 1980:216–220). The Sanshinsha founder, Kōno, went on to become a founding member of the Jiyūtō (Liberal Party) in October 1881.

The *Chōya shinbun*, which announced many of the meetings in its pages, was known as *Kōbun tsūshi* at its inception in January 1872. It had earned praise from John Black for seeking to appeal to a less-educated audience by using the phonetic script *furigana* to gloss the pronunciation of difficult *kanji* words. But in keeping with the move toward political partisanship in the nation's press, when it was renamed *Chōya shinbun* in September 1874 upon Narushima Ryūhoku assuming the chairmanship, the paper revamped its pages and campaigned on behalf of the Freedom and People's Rights Movement. Narushima eliminated *furigana*, in line with the *ōshinbun* nature of the paper, but introduced an editorial section before other vernacular papers did and placed official announcements and general news on the front page (Oizuru 1986:10–11). Little wonder that the newspaper reformist John Black gave it his approval.

In his interview with Nishūbashi Sei, Henry Black confirmed that, during this period, he associated with several orators who later founded political parties or established newspapers. They included Numa Morikazu, Takanashi Tetsujirō, Arakawa Takatoshi and Doi Kōka (Nishūbashi 1905:296), all of whom possessed determination and clear leadership qualities.

As a young man, Numa Morikazu (1844–1890) studied Western military science. Although he sided with the shogunate in the Boshin Civil War and was briefly imprisoned, he joined the new government following the 1868 Meiji Restoration. He later disagreed with the government over its policies on freedom of speech, resigned from the Genrōin (Chamber of Elders) and devoted himself to the Freedom and People's Rights Movement. He purchased the *Yokohama mainichi shinbun* in 1879, moved it to Tokyo and renamed it the *Tokyo Yokohama mainichi shinbun*. The paper became an organ of the intellectual organisation Ōmeisha (Huffman 1997:103), which railed against the fact that nearly two-thirds of government higher officials came from the four domains that had led the Restoration (Huffman 1997:75). In 1881, Numa became a founding member of the Jiyūtō (Liberal Party), but later left it to join Ōkuma Shigenobu's Kikken Kaishintō (Constitutional Reform Party) (Japan 1993:1118). Numa was 'one of the period's half dozen most influential journalists' who fervently believed in the power of journalism to cultivate debate and bring enlightenment. He was typical of many *ōshinbun* owners at the time who used their papers and organised study groups to promote their version of freedom and people's rights (Huffman 1997:103).

Another of the protagonists mentioned by Henry Black, Takanashi Tetsujirō, possessed a voice capable of projecting his words a considerable distance – a distinct asset in the days before electricity and loudspeakers. In December 1890, the *Jiyū shinbun*, commenting on one of his speeches in the Diet, noted that he employed 'extremely powerful means, including a voice of far-reaching stentorian quality'.[33]

Another of Henry Black's associates, Doi Kōka (1847–1918), was born on Awaji island in the eastern Inland Sea. Doi taught at the Tokushima clan school and subsequently become a public speaker, serving as head of the Hokushinsha and then president of the Gakunan Jiyūtō party. He became editor-in-chief of the newspaper *Tōkai gyōshō shinpō*, wrote a number of books and produced a translation of Henry Thomas Buckle's *Introduction to the History of Civilization in England* (Matsuō 1990:96; *Meiji ishin* 1981:648; *Dai jinmei* 1953–56:393). Works by European natural rights proponents such as this were considered dangerous by the oligarchy, which in 1881 banned from schools the Japanese translation of Mill's *On Liberty* (Lehmann 1982:246).

Victim of suppression

As people like Numa, Takanashi, Arakawa, Doi and the Blacks became more organised and more outspoken, the governing oligarchy's unease deep-

---

33 The article praised Takanashi's enthusiasm, but cautioned him not to get too carried away by scaling the lectern when he got angry. Details, including *Jiyū shinbun* extract, collated from *Meiji bungaku* 1965–1967:13,391 and 36,311.

ened. The government, which had already introduced a number of restrictive measures covering the press, introduced increasingly draconian regulations pertaining to political gatherings, including the type of meetings Henry Black addressed. The first of these measures, the Ordinance on Public Meetings (*shūkai jōrei*), was promulgated on 5 April 1880. It gave police sweeping powers to investigate and regulate political parties and to ban public meetings.

The English-language *Japan Weekly Mail* took a conservative stand on the issue. In an editorial on 10 April, it claimed that 'the Government was right in restricting the number, and exercising some control over the nature, of written discussions and treatises on the difficult subject of popular representation'. Commenting on a proposed gathering in Shimane to urge the establishment of a national parliament, the paper declared that the gathering was 'undesirable' and that the authorities were justified 'in the very interests of the people themselves, to prevent them from being disquieted in their minds, and interrupted in their peaceful avocations, by the declamatory nonsense which is pretty certain to form the substance of communications proposed to be addressed to them' (*Japan Weekly Mail* 1880).

In an article on 12 April, a more critical *Mainichi shinbun* claimed that the government's clear purpose was to stifle opposition. 'It appears evident', the paper said, 'that they are to be applied to political meetings.' The newspaper also criticised the regulations for their vagueness and for the manner in which they authorised the police to pass judgment over the content of the meetings and their potential to infringe 'public welfare'. The paper complained that the meeting regulations are quite inconsistent with the principles of law, for the character of a political discussion or lecture is to be judged by the police authorities, and police officers will have to know all that may, in a future time, happen to enter the minds of the members of a political society (*Mainichi shinbun* 1880).

Among the reasons that police officers could cite for forbidding the holding of a meeting, the paper listed content of debate 'pernicious to the public welfare or conducive to the committal of offences against the established laws; or if persons who are not allowed to attend the meeting are present and refuse to leave when ordered to do so' (*Mainichi shinbun* 1880).

Within days of the promulgation of the new regulations, Henry Black became one of their first victims. With his father engaged since January 1880 on the compilation of his book *Young Japan*, Henry embarked in early April on a speaking tour of parts of Kanagawa Prefecture. His route included Odawara, about 70 kilometres southwest of Tokyo where the Tōkaidō, the main trunk route between Tokyo and the Kansai region, passes through the foothills of Mount Fuji near Sagami Bay. Henry was quite at home in the area. With an Australian-born friend, George T Marsh, he made occasional trips on horseback on the Tōkaidō where Marsh collected curios, which he later sold in a shop in San Francisco.[34] The intent of the journey in April 1880 was political and police intervened to prevent a meeting he was to have addressed. In its account of the incident, *The Japan Daily Herald*, quoting from the vernacular *Kinji hyōron* on 28 April, suggested that Henry Black had made history by becoming the first foreigner to run foul of the regulations.

> It has not unfrequently happened that Japanese have been prohibited from delivering lectures, but we hear, for the first time, of the suspension of a lecture delivered by a foreigner, and an Englishman, Mr. Black, is the first who has been restricted by our police authorities from the liberty of speech…At any rate we believe that our police authorities would not without reason, have suspended the lecture of Mr. Black; and we are unable to state when and on what grounds the said Mr. Black intends to sue the chief of the police station at Odawara, on his return to the capital…Mr. Black had delivered lectures in several places, and at one time he proceeded to Odawara, where he lectured upon the effects of a national convention, and upon the subjects respecting the laws of conscription. On the third day of his lecture, he was officially ordered by the police authorities to abstain from lecturing, but in opposition to this order, he again announced his work. This time again, on the third day, a similar order was given him. Utterly disgusted at the proceedings of the officials, he immediately set out for Hakone, and after having taken the baths there for a few days, he quitted that place on the 19th instant. It is said that soon after his arrival in the metropolis, he will bring an action against the chief of police at Odawara for having suspended his lecture (*Kinji hyōron* 1880).

It was perhaps no coincidence that the party planned their trip with Hakone as their destination. Accounts by others written on other occasions attest to Henry's fondness for soaking in mineral springs and public baths, making Hakone's hot springs a conveniently placed diversion for him.

---

34 Details are from a 1959 letter to Australian businessman Harold S Williams from an American acquaintance Gordon Bell, who knew Marsh. The letter is in Harold S Willliams Collection, National Library of Australia MS6681/1/1.

The cleanliness of the Japanese was cause for comment among foreigners. British scholar Basil Hall Chamberlain wrote that there were over 1,100 public baths in Tokyo and that 'every respectable private house' had its own bath. 'The charm of the Japanese system of hot bathing is proved by the fact that almost all the foreigners resident in the country adopt it', Chamberlain (1984: 60–61) wrote. Henry's father also commented on the custom, writing in *Young Japan*, 'Every country house has its bath tub in which the body can be purified and reinvigorated after the toils of the day by being parboiled.' (Black, JR 1883:I,116).

These days there is a train from Odawara to Hakone that zig-zags into the foothills, from where tourists can walk to the inn of their choice. In Henry Black's day, horses would have transported his group there. Many of Hakone's baths are outdoors. Henry was there in April when the views would have been of green leaves dappled with the faint pink of wild cherry blossom and azalea.

The interruption to Henry's speaking plans on that day in April 1880 was not an isolated incident. Police records indicate that 131 political meetings were disbanded in 1881 and 282 in 1882. Many other meetings simply did not take place because police denied permits to the organisers (Vlastos 1995:248).

Seeking other outlets

Two months after the incident in Odawara, personal tragedy struck. On 10 June 1880, at the age of 53, John Black suffered a cerebral haemorrhage. He died the following day, the incomplete manuscript for his book *Young Japan* still on his desk. His funeral was held several days later, the cortege moving in procession from the family home at Yokohama 116-ban to the nearby church and then on to the foreigners' cemetery up on the Bluff.

JH Brooke, editor of the *Japan Herald*, which John Black had once edited, penned a dismissive obituary to mark his passing:

> Mr Black was a native of Scotland; he emigrated to South Australia, and resided in that colony for some years. Business with him taking an unprosperous turn, he was induced to turn his fine vocal powers to account, and after traveling through the Australian colonies, India and China, he at length reached Japan, where with the exception of a short stay in China, he has ever since resided. The deceased's career was a checkered one. Of a hopeful and cheerful disposition, his views were always sanguine. His industry was great, but his business enterprises

> were seldom crowned by success. Year after year, he struggled manfully with his difficulties, but the Fates were unpropitious. At one time, he held the editorship and sustained the management of this journal (Brooke 1880).

Brooke's opinionated obituary made cursory mention of John Black's book, *Young Japan*. Brooke was not to know that it was to become a respected source of information on the period, still frequently quoted by historians.[35] Such was the smallness of the world in which the expatriate community lived in those days. Little wonder Henry Black sought wider horizons in another culture.

When Elizabeth came home from the funeral, she closed the front door on the outside world and climbed the stairs to the study. Then her hands began sorting through a pile of papers until she found what she was looking for – a copy of the already published first volume of *Young Japan*. Elizabeth opened it and read the dedication.

> To one who, all her life long, has devoted her energies to the welfare of others, disregarding herself; and who, for more than thirty years has made my well-being and happiness her first care. To my dear wife: my companion: my comfort: and my crown: This narrative of a period, the greater part of which we have spent together in this land of promise, is dedicated with the deepest affection and respect (Black, JR 1883:I,[iii]).

Henry Black was 21 at the time of his father's death. The event obliged him to think more seriously about his own future. In the normal course of events, he might have been expected to find work by relying on his father's support and contacts within the hongs and insurance agencies which supported the foreign trading companies in the treaty ports. Alternatively, he might have sailed to Britain, America, or Australia, to find work. But Henry chose to throw in his lot with Japan. Cast between two worlds, some choose to live solely in one world. But for others it is possible to remain fully at home in both or to be more at home in one while reaching

---

35 According to Williams (1958:163), Brooke used the *Japan Herald* to criticise the Japanese government severely, prompting the government to subsidise the *Japan Mail* under the editorship of Captain F Brinkley. Thus began an enduring rivalry between Brooke and Brinkley. When *The Japan Herald* went out of business, Brinkley had the last say, describing the *Japan Herald* thus: 'It has been a disgrace to foreign journalism. Its methods have been the methods of the thug. The *Japan Herald* has been as effective and annoying as the viperist shrillings of some sideway slut.'

some accommodation with the other. Sometimes this becomes an act of individual will, perhaps because of external pressures in the form of glances from others or unspoken expectations of parents or friends. Sometimes our choices are made for us. And sometimes we just grow into our lives. In an interview with the journalist Hanazono Kanesada, Henry Black once recalled that he 'did not know what to do', after his father died, but became a storyteller 'on the advice and persuasion' of his father's colleague, Numa Morikazu (Hanazono 1926:75). This was the same Numa known to Henry through his participation in speech meetings for adherents of the people's rights movement. By this stage, Numa was owner of the Ōmeisha organ, *Tokyo Yokohama mainichi shinbun*. His influence on Henry at the time rated mention years later in an obituary for Henry in the *Japan Weekly Chronicle* in 1923. The writer also recalled that Henry's political addresses included 'a wealth of anecdote and the interest they aroused raised the suggestion that he should appear as a professional story teller' (*Japan Weekly Chronicle* 1923). We can safely assume that Numa was among those who appraised his storytelling potential highly, even at that early stage.

Henry's career choice at this moment enabled him to circumvent the ordinance on public meetings by joining a *gundan* (military stories) group under Hōgyūsha Tōrin (Kurata 1981–87:II,96). The move allowed Henry to reach an audience through another form. The didactic *gundan* genre originated in the early Edo period when masterless *samurai* read war tales to audiences in towns. Their inspiration was the *Taiheiki* (The chronicle of great peace) a 14th-century war chronicle. (Morioka & Sasaki 1990:5). Hōgyūsha Tōrin took his performances very seriously. He was not averse to chastising the audience if they did not pay attention. According to one anecdote, when the audience failed to receive one of his performances as well as they had the famous San'yūtei Enchō, he contemplated suicide. He was a strict but benevolent disciplinarian. His straight-laced demeanour backstage earned him a reputation among colleagues as *ingin burei* (overpolite, or arrogantly modest). Tōrin was also a man of refined taste, being proficient in *waka* poetry and *haiku* and practising tea ceremony. He had 33 disciples in his lifetime, including Henry Black. It is worth keeping Tōrin in mind when looking at Black's subsequent career, as there are a number of parallels. For example, Black also practised tea ceremony and was fond of poetry, and there is strong evidence that he too attempted suicide.

An indication that Henry had embarked on a career as a storyteller is found in the *Asahi shinbun* of 7 September 1883, which refers to him as again giving *gundan* performances with Shōrin Hakuen in Osaka (Morioka

& Sasaki 1983:139). It was Hakuen who had coached Henry before his stage appearances narrating the lives of Bonnie Prince Charlie and Joan of Arc in December 1878 at Yokohama's Tomitake Theatre. Five years later, the 1883 performances with Hakuen outside Tokyo imply considerable early commitment to a career in storytelling. This was no mere part-time job. Henry Black is mentioned in the 7 March 1884 edition of *Jiji shinpō* as appearing in a number of theatres. It also mentioned that he was to be seen in the *Tōkyō keizai saibansho* (Tokyo Court of Petty Sessions) 'taking detailed notes with a view to producing one or two narrations' (Kurata 1981–87:III,81). Sourcing stories from the courts was entirely consistent with a fad for newspapers and storytellers to turn real-life drama into serialised accounts for mass audiences.

Henry Black's participation in the *gundan* genre was symptomatic of the growing links between proponents of democratic reform and those who used vernacular Japanese as a medium for reaching ordinary people. The nationwide oppression of political orators resulted in similar crossovers between oratory and storytelling elsewhere around this time. A typical example was the political novelist and civil rights activist Sakasaki Shiran (1853–1912), who embodied a crossover between oratory, storytelling and, later, written Japanese. Prevented from making political speeches in Kōchi in 1881, Sakasaki reacted by organising his own group of storytellers, who presented 'accounts of European liberals and the French Revolution' (Twine 1991:127). Sakasaki applied the narrator's conversational style to spread the pro-democracy message when he later joined the newspaper *Jiyū no tomoshibi* (antecedent of *Tōkyō asahi shinbun*) and became an editorial writer (Twine 1991:127).

The Black family remained in Japan after John Black's death. John's wife Elizabeth, their offspring Henry, Pauline and the younger John, had all put down roots in Japan. Elizabeth lived on until 1922, looked after to the end by her spinster daughter, Pauline. An ageing Pauline even lived through the Second World War in a house in Tokyo. The younger John later married in England, but returned soon afterwards to work in an insurance company in Kobe. Two years after Henry's father died, in a diary entry dated 2 June 1882, adventurer and traveller Arthur H Crow, recorded a visit to Elizabeth's house in Tokyo with English diplomat, linguist and scholar Ernest Satow (1843–1929). Crow wrote that Elizabeth lived in 'a purely Japanese house, but with, of course, European furniture' which was 'some miles away' from Kaizenji Temple. The temple is in present-day Tokyo's Taito Ward. There is no mention of Henry Black or his siblings in Crow's diary entry, but in an indication that the government respected John Black's contribution to journalism, Crow noted that Mrs Black was allowed to live outside the foreign concession of Tsukiji 'by special favour of the Government' (Crow 1883:26–27).[36]

A newspaper report indicates that by 1885 Henry Black resided apart from his family and may have been experiencing financial difficulties following the loss of family support after his father's death. It stated that he was living at No. 2 Shinsakae Chō in Tsukiji, where he was engaged in an illegal *sake* brewing enterprise (*Japan Weekly Mail* 1885). Although the venture may have been designed to earn money, given indications that Henry was a heavy drinker, it may simply have been intended to provide a cheap source of alcoholic refreshment. In a letter to the British Consul on 23 July 1885, Henry apologised for the *sake* brewing and promised 'that in future I will have nothing to do with any such business'. The letter was transcribed into the Consulate's records by the Assistant Vice Consul JC Hale and in an annotation on the opposite page it is noted that the case was a result of a 'complaint by the Japanese government'.[37] The embarrassment caused by newspaper coverage of the event, followed by the formal apology to a representative of the British crown, drove a wedge between Henry and his family. Henry Black was showing all the signs of going native as a storyteller and family and friends in the expatriate community did not approve.

---

36 The house was probably at the Yamato-chō, Kanda address cited in the 1883 and 1884 editions of the *Japan Directory*.

37 A copy of Black's letter was supplied to the author by Asaoka Kunio. It misspells his place of residence as 'Shinsakei-cho'.

Chapter 6

From English teacher to *rakugoka*

> What cigarettes do you usually smoke?
>
> Those manufactured by Iwaya Matsuhei.
>
> Does he manufacture good cigarettes?
>
> Yes, I think they are the best made in Japan.
>
> What tobacco are they made of?
>
> The best Kagoshima grown tobacco.
>
> Yes, the best tobacco in Japan is grown there.
>
> Do Europeans smoke much?
>
> Yes, but not so much as the Japanese.
>
> Is it true that English women do not smoke?
>
> Yes, it is considered rude to smoke in their presence
>
> (Extract from *Yōi dokushū: Eiwa kaiwa hen* Lesson 8 (Burakku 1886:58).

In January 1886, front-page advertisements in *Chōya shinbun* announced that Henry Black would teach English at the Tokyo Gakkan. He began work at the institution in February and had to give up work as a storyteller under the *gundan* banner. He did so in response to the entreaties of friends and family who insisted that a career in storytelling was 'disreputable' (Nishūbashi 1905:297) and would bring shame on his deceased father. In his account of the reasons for abandoning work as a narrator, Henry explained that friends questioned whether being a *yose* performer (*yose geinin*) was an appropriate occupation. He does not explain whether the friends were Japanese or foreign, but this was perhaps immaterial. The reasons he gave reflected opinion among many Japanese and foreigners alike that, although *yose* were popular venues of entertainment, the entertainers themselves were 'low class' (Morioka & Sasaki 1990:3).[38] Henry Black was an extremely busy English teacher. At the height of his teaching career, he worked at another school in addition to the Tokyo Gakkan, and claimed in an interview that he worked from 9 am to 10 pm on some days to meet demand.

Work at Tokyo Gakkan facilitated an association with yet another famous Meiji-era figure, journalist and cultural historian Miyatake Gaikotsu (Japan 1993:989). Miyatake Nanbai, an elder brother of Gaikotsu, ran Tokyo Gakkan. By this stage, Henry Black was 29 and Gaikotsu 19. The two would have encountered each other at the school where Gaikotsu helped his brother after coming to Tokyo from the country. In November 1886, Gaikotsu inaugurated his *E-iri kōkoku shinbun* (illustrated advertiser newspaper), the first of his many satirical publications. Given Gaikotsu's flair for humour and political satire, he and Henry Black would have found much in common in spite of their ten-year age difference.

The first edition of Gaikotsu's newspaper stated that it had the official endorsement of several *rakugo* luminaries, including Henry Black and the prominent *rakugoka* San'yūtei Enchō, who was the head of the San'yū guild of professional storytellers. This is the first known occasion that the names of Henry Black and Enchō, who was to become Henry's mentor, shared the same page. In later years, Enchō sponsored Henry's affiliation with the San'yūha and the two engaged in friendly rivalry over their adaptations of Western stories into Japanese. The appearance of their two names in Gaikotsu's newspaper indicates when Henry's association with members of the San'yūha began. It also proves that he maintained his association with storytellers, in spite of his English teaching and the disapproval of friends.

Henry Black continued his interest in Gaikotsu, including when Gaikotsu was jailed in 1889 for three years after running foul of the government on a charge of *lèse-majesté*. The charge related to a parody in the witty magazine Gaikotsu founded in 1887, *Tonchi kyōkai zasshi*, on the promulgation of the Meiji Constitution. Henry Black was among friends and relatives waiting at the jail exit to welcome Gaikotsu on his release (Asaoka 1986:2–3).[39] Henry's association with a prominent critic of the government such as Gaikotsu

---

38 The authors note that 'a *yose* performer is proud of being called a *geinin*, artiste of the common people, although the expression *geinin* – because of its association with "low class" – has been included in the list [compiled by media associations since 1973] of "discriminatory vocabulary" which should be avoided in public.' The extremely erudite polymath and *rakugoka* San'yūtei Enraku once lamented this fact to me.

39 Asaoka also cites Gaikotsu writing in *Meiji bunka kenkyū* 4 (January 1928) that Black was among those who welcomed him on his release from jail.

indicates that his sympathies remained with pro-democracy opponents of the government and with notions of freedom of the press and artistic licence to criticise government actions.

One outcome of Henry Black's English teaching was his editorship in 1886 of a 100-page English grammar book (Burakku 1886). The book is divided into two sections, one dealing with vocabulary and the other with conversations. The first section includes some 700 items of vocabulary in 14 thematically collated lists or 'lessons' devoted to topics including 'Relationships', 'Parts of the Body' and 'The Weather'. The second section contains 25 conversation 'lessons'. Japan's National Diet Library holds the first and second editions of the book. To browse through them is to experience something of what it was like to live in Japan at the time. They offer a time capsule with snapshots of Meiji life in their references to trams on Ginza streets, firemen in Asakusa and the buzz of excitement at the Yokohama races or the *kabuki* theatre. Occupations such as the now rare 'stonemason' are mentioned. By today's standards, the conversation lessons in Henry's book seem antiquated and based on questionable linguistic and pedagogical theory. While the conversations are grammatically correct, they reflect 19th-century upper-class English morality and gender roles, suggesting that the author saw himself as a purveyor not only of the English language but also of a culture, in keeping with the sense of mission shared by many fellow expatriates. They also shed light on a bygone way of life in Meiji-era Tokyo, offering insights into annual events such as the viewing of plum blossoms at Kameido, the cherry blossoms at Koganei and shopping at Ginza – or the danger of fires in Kanda and Asakusa.

> I cannot understand why people set houses on fire.
>
> They do it so that they can enter the houses near the fire and steal. (Burakku 1886:Section 2, Lesson 19).

Or the merits or otherwise of horse-drawn trams.

> Shall we go in a tram?
>
> No, the trams are always too crowded.
>
> Then shall we take a *jinriksha*?
>
> No, let us walk. (Burakku 1886:Section 2, Lesson 2).

The conversations section contains possible insights into Henry's interests and lifestyle. A reference in Lesson 8 to Ikaho's hot springs confirms

Henry's fondness for such places, something already attested to in his decision to take to the hot spring waters of Hakone in 1880 after the police put a stop to his speech-making in Odawara and further evidenced from others who knew him later on. In Lesson 15, several sentences devoted to *kabuki* actors and the differences in style between English and Japanese drama take on added interest, given that Henry later went on to perform *kabuki* roles. After a query about the difference between English and Japanese drama, for example, the text alludes to the greater verisimilitude of sets and dialogue in English drama where 'everything is more real than in Japanese plays'. And after a question about who might be the 'best actor' in Tokyo, the text notes that the great *kabuki* actor Danjūrō is certainly the 'cleverest'. Danjūrō was to tutor Henry in acting some years later. Another sentence, which notes that 'actors are very much despised in Japan', bluntly encapsulates the reasons why Henry delayed for so long his ultimate transformation to stage performer, settling, at least temporarily, for the more socially acceptable status of English teacher. Reading through the text and encountering this sentence, the reader is struck by how out of place it seems. It is as if hidden within the respectable English teacher there lay a performer longing to escape the confines of other people's expectations. It is a gem that perhaps reveals his true feelings. And was Henry Black interested in gambling too? How else do we explain the devotion of three conversation lessons to horse racing?

The first edition of the book was published in September 1886 and the second edition in June 1887. The second edition has a white cover with a blue design incorporating cherry blossoms and a crown of the style worn by European royalty. As a marketing gimmick, the back cover has a table that readers could use to calculate how many Sundays there were in any month of any year between Meiji 20 and Meiji 36. The front inside page of the second edition contains an apology noting that errors in the first edition had been corrected; nevertheless, there are almost as many spelling errors in the second edition as in the first.

By late 1886, work as an English teacher became more difficult because, according to Henry, of widespread resentment of foreigners following the postponement of the revision of treaties concluded with Western powers in the 1850s and 1860s. Public opinion turned further against foreigners that year, following the sinking of the British steamship *Normanton* off the coast of Wakayama Prefecture in October. The British captain of the *Normanton*, John Drake, rescued only the British crew and did not assist the Japanese passengers and Indian crew, all of whom drowned (Lehmann 1982:293). A hearing at the British Consulate in Kobe exonerated the crew, but, after a public outcry, a second hearing was held at the Consulate in Yokohama. Feeling over the incident ran high, as it was thought that the terms of the unequal treaties had led to an injustice. The lenient three-month sentence given to the captain and the crew's freedom from any sentence, at the Yokohama hearing further strengthened the resolve of many Japanese to revise the treaties with Western powers and eliminate extraterritoriality under which foreigners could not be subjected to Japanese laws (Japan 1993:1114).

Another factor was in play in the general revulsion toward all things foreign. The Rokumeikan was an ostentatious Western-style building opened in central Tokyo in 1883, so that members of the Cabinet and the foreign and diplomatic community could attend functions intended to impress the foreign community with the 'sophistication' of the Japanese. If the Cabinet could dance the waltz in a venue such as the Rokumeikan, then surely the Japanese people were enlightened enough to have the unequal treaties revised. In November 1884, Count Inoue hosted a ball there on the Emperor's birthday at which the visiting United States Governor Lowe's wife wore her blue diamonds. Her diamonds dazzled Miss Boissonade, daughter of Gustave Boissonade, the professor at the Faculty of Law in Paris who was helping to draft Japan's new penal and criminal procedure codes. 'Very *distingué*', the impressed Miss Boissonade whispered to Clara Whitney, who recorded the comment in her diary (Whitney 1979:335).

The Rokumeikan was designed by a British architect and built by the Japanese government. It contained a large dining room supervised by a French chef, salons, parlours, games-rooms, ballrooms and 'a corridor for promenading' (Barr 1988:12). But such extravagances failed to impress the locals. In 1887, the last of several outrageously expensive fancy dress balls was held there. Ordinary Japanese were shocked to learn that the prime minister had attended dressed as a Venetian nobleman. Newspapers lampooned the event. It was all too much. Too divorced from the realities of life. Too preposterous to contemplate. In serving as a venue for the rich and fortunate to fraternise with similarly rich and fortunate foreigners, the folly that was Rokumeikan merely reinforced the impression that the ruling elite were out of touch. In 1893, an earthquake severely damaged the building. Repairs were found to be too expensive and the Rokumeikan was left to decay. Ordinary Japanese did not lament its passing.

So the *Normanton* sank and the Rokumeikan offended sensibilities. People stopped learning English and when English language schools went bankrupt, Henry found himself looking for an alternative source of income.

Reversion to storytelling

For Henry there was always the theatre and storytelling. So instead of choosing an option of the sort favoured by family members and seeking work with a foreign trading firm in Yokohama, Henry listened to his inner voices and toyed with the idea of a career as a storyteller. As a first step, in 1886, he collaborated in the production of an adaptation of then popular British author Mary Elizabeth Braddon's (1837–1915) novel *Flower and Weed*. As a native speaker of English, Henry had access to a vast trove of fictional material emanating from America, Britain and its English-speaking colonies. He would have sourced stories from books and journals, through lending libraries, subscriptions, or from friends. Henry appears to have freely translated *Flower and Weed* verbally to a stenographer who captured what he said in shorthand. The translation was published with the title *Kusaba no tsuyu* (Dew by the graveside) (Buradon 1886). A note at the front of the book attributes the story to Braddon and credits Henry Black with 'dictation' (*kōjutsu*).

Braddon was not entirely unknown in Japan. In 1882, the regional newspaper *Doyō shinbun*, in the city of Kōchi, in southern Shikoku, had begun a serialised translation of Braddon's celebrated work *Lady Audley's Secret* as *Eikoku kidan – dokufu Ōdoroku koden* (A Strange Tale from England – The Wicked Woman Ōdoroku) (Yanagida 1966:33). The newspaper had begun life as an organ of the pro-democracy Risshisha in Meiji 10 (1877) and the choice of Braddon's story about a strong-willed female character was consistent with the movement's early aim of promoting women's rights, with which the newspaper's sympathies lay for some years afterwards.[40] Publication of the paper was temporarily suspended before all episodes of the story were published, but the novel was eventually serialised in its entirety in *Kokkai shinbun* in 1883 (Yanagida 1966:33–34). Braddon was one of the top-selling British authors at the time, although George Bernard Shaw, who, early in his career, reluctantly reviewed one of her books for the *Pall Mall*

40 In Meiji 17 (1884), after the pro-democracy activist Ueki Emori (1857–1892) returned to Kōchi, the *Doyō shinbun* ran stories every day taking up issues related to the household, women and education having a big influence on women in Kōchi.

Gazette, complained facetiously to his sub-editor that her work was hardly the kind of material befitting his intellect:

> Why condemn me to read things that I can't review – that no artistic conscience could long survive the reviewing of! Why don't you begin notices of boots, hats, dogcarts and so on? They would be fifty times as useful and interesting as reviews of the last novel by Miss Braddon, who is a princess among novel manufacturers (quoted in Holroyd 1988:214).

Shaw detested Braddon's formulaic works. He complained that the novels of Braddon and other writers of women's sensation fiction perpetuated false romantic conventions. Sensation novels, not least those of Braddon, relied on a panoply of stereotypical devices, including avalanches, fatal and deliberately arranged falls from horses, large and threatening dogs, daggers, snake venom, mistaken identity and bigamy. But Braddon had thousands, perhaps millions, of readers in the English-speaking world. In Japan, intellectuals and proponents of 'pure' forms of literature also turned their noses up at detective novels, but enough people bought and read them to ensure a thriving market. Writers and translators gladly adopted the genre to cater to this demand. Henry Black was one of its early proponents and astutely recognised Braddon's work as the sort of material his own audiences would appreciate.

In the preface of the printed version of *Kusaba no tsuyu*, stenographer Shitō Kenkichi described 'the Briton Black', as 'having lived a long time in Japan, and being fluent in Japanese and familiar with the customs of Japan, has for many years now wanted to venture into the field of novels, but till now has not had the chance to do so' (Buradon 1886:preface). Unlike later versions of Black's stories, which usually accord space at the beginning or end of the book for a stenographer's name, *Kusaba no tsuyu* cites Shitō Kenkichi for 'note-taking' (*hikki*) and not stenography. *Kusaba no tsuyu* was produced by Black relating his own Japanese-language version and Shitō transcribing this onto paper with his own elaborations of Black's Japanese. In the preface, Shitō explained that the adaptation contained bracketed commentary from Black, 'for explanation or where the writer, fearing that it might be difficult to comprehend the differences in customs and emotion (*ninjō*) between Japan and England, which are thousands of miles apart from each other, has each time queried Mr. Black and had him clarify the situation in his own country' (Buradon 1886:preface).

Kusaba no tsuyu faithfully adheres to Mary Braddon's rags-to-riches tale about a female protagonist who escapes the slums of London and displays a natural talent for acquiring the ways of the upper class. Henry Black's 1886 publication of the story in Japan came only two years after the advent of stenography in Japan and four years after the Braddon original was published in London in the 1882 edition of the annual Christmas magazine *Mistletoe Bough*, which Braddon had founded in 1878.[41] Unlike most of his subsequent adaptations, whose characters bear Japanese names, Henry retained the original names of the Braddon characters, with only minor variations resulting from transliteration into Japanese.

Braddon's *Flower and Weed* harked back to the manor novels of late 18th-century Britain and the onset of the Industrial Revolution. Henry Black's adaptation of it as *Kusaba no tsuyu* can be read as a metaphor for the dangers posed to a feudal status quo by a British-style Industrial Revolution, then occurring in Japan. With its reference to the intrusion of the city into the country and its calls for legislated measures to aid the poor, *Flower and Weed* contains elements of nostalgia for a feudal past tempered with an early warning that unchecked industrialisation can lead to disruption. The nostalgia for the countryside portrayed in Black's version had parallels in the expressions of regret by foreign visitors and diary writers in the 1860s and 1870s about the passing of Old Japan under the impact of European-style industrialisation.

Like *Flower and Weed*, Black's *Kusaba no tsuyu* is set mainly at Ingleshaw Castle in Kent, home of Lord Ingleshaw and his young daughter, Lady Lucille. It tells of Bess, a destitute young woman who, while attempting to escape the London slums, is found ill and starving in the castle grounds. Lucille takes Bess in and has her taught the social graces. Although Lucille and her cousin Bruno are to marry, Bess sets up a love triangle by developing a liking for Bruno. Bess's dilemma is resolved fatally when her estranged husband thrusts a knife into her during an attack on Bruno in the castle.

The 1886 *Kusaba no tsuyu* set the pattern for much of Henry Black's future repertoire. In it, we can see his earliest attempts to experiment with adaptation and language in the search for a successful formula which, by the 1890s, would satisfy the dual purposes of enlightenment and entertainment in his repertoire. Apart from several explanatory digressions, *Kusaba no tsuyu*

---

41 *Flower and Weed* was subsequently reprinted in a book of short stories titled *Flower and Weed and Other Tales* (Braddon 1884).

faithfully replicated the original Braddon storyline, although it was considerably shorter than the original. One feature that sets *Kusaba no tsuyu* apart from later adaptations is its relative lack of vernacular language. The 'flowery style of early Meiji literature' (Morioka & Sasaki 1983:155)[42] found in *Kusaba no tsuyu* had much in common with the experimental *wa-kan-yō-setchū* (mixed Japanese, Chinese and Western style) and *gabun* (decorous elegant style) styles (Miyoshi 1974:38),[43] and even evoked the melodramatic delivery associated with *kabuki*. Henry Black's subsequent works show a transition toward a more colloquial style both in the speech of the characters portrayed and in Henry's own narrative. Its success demonstrated that as an adaptor of European works Henry had come to *rakugo* at an opportune moment in its history. Henry Black and Meiji *rakugo* were products of their times.

Ironically, the same anti-foreign sentiment that had ended Henry's teaching career now become the catalyst for his return to storytelling, a field where being foreign-born and able to adapt English-language works into Japanese worked to his advantage.

The move into storytelling re-established Henry Black as a protagonist in the debate over modernity. This time the venues were not public halls for speech meetings of the pro-democracy movement. They were vaudeville theatres. The anti-foreign feeling that ended his English-teaching career was also the catalyst for a shift in the debate over reform. The shift is attributable to the coming of age of a new generation of Japanese, born after the Meiji Restoration. The new generation was a product of a new education system put in place after the Restoration. For this new generation, the notion of modernisation was beyond question. Its members now sought to take stock of the achievements of the revolutionaries who had engineered the Meiji Restoration and overseen the transition from centralised feudalism to centralised nation-statehood. This new generation were agreed on the need for modernisation, but, by the 1880s, faced a dilemma about the direction of that modernisation. They were, as one historian has noted, 'caught in a confrontation of circumstances that intensified awareness of their heritage

42 Morioka and Sasaki suggest that in *Kusaba no tsuyu* 'whether intentional or not, the vocabulary is at times archaic, thus evoking the world of the Edo period and thereby imparting a quaint, old-fashioned aura'.

43 According to Miyoshi, although *Maihime* (The dancing girl), written by Mori Ōgai and published in 1890, earned a reputation at the time as a book in the *wa-kan-yō-setchū* style because of its use of Germanic words and names, it is more accurately described as *gabun* style. This latter style was noted for its heavy use of ideograms, but contained a more native vocabulary and syntax that was looser than the old *kanbun*.

and at the same time stigmatised it' (Pyle 1969:20). The process of taking stock lasted a decade or more, commencing around 1886, when Henry Black decisively embarked on his storytelling career. The debate was waged in print and on the stage and shared many characteristics with advocates of modernisation in other spheres, including politics and literature, ranging from those favouring thorough and unfettered westernisation to others favouring 'a Japanese path to modernity that did not necessarily preclude Western values' (Waswo 1996:93).

The oral and the written – *rakugo*'s role in the modernity debate

The new generation's reassessment was intrinsically linked to the way that Japanese perceived themselves and their place in the world. It was also bound up with the very language they used to debate and express their ideas. People could not engage in the discourse about modernity unless the language itself was modern. And intriguingly, it was *rakugo* and its storytellers who began to play a role in shaping the language of the discourse. Out of necessity, oral expression was beginning to influence the written.

When the leaders of the San'yūha invited Henry Black to affiliate with their guild, *rakugo* had begun to attract the attention of people experimenting with the written language. Many writers, intrigued by the mass appeal of *rakugo*, attended *yose* to gain inspiration from an art form where the narrator's use of the vernacular afforded instant intimacy with audiences. With tantalising titles such as 'The time-noodle con game', 'Laughing mushrooms', 'How to praise a cow', 'The badger in the gay quarters' and 'The lord who is hell-bent on making buckwheat noodles',[44] the *rakugo* menu was – and still is – replete with humour, satire, intrigue and, of course, plenty of natural, unadorned dialogue.

When a storyteller tells his audience in *Toki soba* (Time noodle con game) about the clever customer who saved a few yen by cheating the noodle seller, those in the audience are not merely savouring a classic tale they have heard before, they are also enjoying the dialogue. *Toki soba* is a well-known tale about a man who enters a noodle shop and orders and eats his bowl of noodles. He finishes the meal and while paying his 10 *sen* asks the noodle-shop proprietor for the time, just as he has counted out six one-*sen* coins. When the proprietor tells him it is eight o'clock, the man thanks him and resumes counting at eight *sen*, saving himself one *sen* in the process. The proprietor does not realise he has been tricked and has lost money in the

---

44 These are just some of the many titles listed by Morioka and Sasaki (1981:339–402).

transaction. Another customer who notices the ruse decides to return the next night and try it out. But the second customer is dimwitted and, after handing over six *sen*, is told it is four o'clock, so resumes counting off the one-*sen* coins from four, thus losing in the transaction. Little wonder Tokyo audiences loved *rakugo*.

People listening to this story in Black's day could easily identify with dialogue associated with the denizens of the city in which they lived and with situations taken directly from their surroundings. *Rakugo* attracted all sorts, including educator Fukuzawa Yukichi and young novelists Natsume Sōseki and Tsubouchi Shōyō. It was Tsubouchi Shōyō who was soon to point out that *rakugo*'s naturalistic dialogue could show the way forward for writers seeking to express new, modern forms of human relationships, as well as internalised thoughts and plots with appeal. Tsubouchi Shōyō's turning to *rakugo* for his inspiration was tantamount to admitting that the vernacular language of the oral storytellers was conducive to conveying and influencing the discourse of modernity and reform.

These developments were not divorced from the social and political environment within which they occurred. But none of this happened overnight. Tsubouchi Shōyō's thoughts on *rakugo* had their genesis as far back as the splintering of the Freedom and People's Rights Movement, soon after Black joined the *gundan* group under Hyōgyūsha Tōrin. The impetus for the pro-democracy movement's demise had been the government's decision in October 1881 to concede to one of the movement's principal aims by announcing its intention to produce a Constitution and convene a national assembly within the decade. In the immediate aftermath of this announcement, Itagaki Taisuke, a former associate of Henry Black's editor father, formed the Jiyūtō (Liberal Party) as a means to further the movement's aims. And in March 1882, former finance minister Ōkuma Shigenobu announced the formation of the Rikken Kaishintō (Constitutional Reform Party). Within days of that announcement, Fukuchi Gen'ichirō had also announced the formation of the Rikken Teishintō (Constitutional Imperial Party). The formation of these parties began a period of intense political jostling, which ended with the dissolution of the Jiyūtō in the face of increased government suppression of its activities in late October 1884 (Bowen 1980:228–280) .

The government's action splintered the Freedom and People's Rights Movement, robbing the movement of much of its impetus (Jansen 1995:249). Through a prolonged process of trial and error, the government fashioned a double-edged policy of buying off members of the opposition with promises of reform on the one hand and repressing its opponents on the other hand. It had begun to set the rules of debate. This drove more radical adherents of the movement to desperate measures, but the movement's more moderate adherents and sympathisers began experimenting with alternative ways of reaching audiences. Banned from organising political gatherings and robbed of support after the land-owning farming class abandoned their cause, they found ways of spreading the word that, ironically, resulted in dispersing the discourse of modernity to a wider and by now better-educated audience.

Some, for example, opted to experiment with the writing of political novels. Typical of the experimentation was Suehiro Tetchō's 1886 novel *Setchūbai* (Plum blossoms in snow), which used the romantic triangle in an innovative way to make its political and ideological message more appealing (Kurita 1997:231).[45] But even writers of this genre struggled to devise new colloquial forms of Japanese capable of making their message accessible to readers. Literary Japanese had been too full of obscure and obtuse Chinese-influenced expressions, which were out of the reach of most ordinary Japanese.

Another front in the battle for hearts and minds was newspapers. Many pro-democracy moderates established their own newspapers through which they continued to expound their views. With the nation's political debate already centred in their editorial columns by the mid-1870s and a rising literacy rate reflecting steadily increasing school enrolments throughout the 1870s (Rubinger 1986), newspapers were beginning to attract increasing numbers of readers.

As mentioned earlier, by the mid-1880s, two types of newspapers – *koshinbun* (minor newspapers) and *ōshinbun* (major newspapers) – were being published in Japan. The *koshinbun* published racy entertainment-oriented stories of scandal and gossip for the newly transformed city populations. Their rise had an important role in taking Henry Black's stories to a mass audience. From their beginnings as media for recording and discussing events of public interest, they quickly expanded their range to include scandal and gossip. Because they used *furigana*, they were easier to read than the *ōshinbun*, whose turgid prose served to maintain the divisions between classes. By 1877, the archetypal early *koshinbun*, *Kanayomi shinbun*, had moved from pure reportage to the serialisation of

45 In this case the message concerned a woman who was a financial patron of the Freedom and People's Rights Movement.

its gossip-oriented news stories with direct quotations inserted to enliven them. Articles had to sustain reader interest over several days (Okitsu 1997:79). Although *koshinbun* proprietors were universally interested in edifying the masses, they learned to sweeten their message with sensational accounts of court proceedings and real-life events. The *koshinbun* rarely contained serious political discussion, but their 'disengagement with the highly refined literary forms of the past' (Twine 1991:130–131) was a new phenomenon that gave ordinary readers access to the modernisation process in their own vernacular. Nevertheless, despite a marked rise in literacy after the 1868 Restoration and the fact that the press was the largest, single medium for the transmission of ideas, it is estimated that daily newspapers had a readership of only 50,000 in Japan by 1890 (Huffman 1997:170). Direct participation in political debate remained an activity for a limited number of charismatic individuals talking to an informed elite (Lehmann 1982:247).

In 1884, in a development that radically altered the course of book and newspaper publishing in Japan, *rakugo* effectively rescued the debate about reform and modernity from domination by the government and an educated elite. Within a few years, it was to reshape the language of the mediums of public debate. The catalyst was the introduction of stenography (*sokki*) to the recording of debates in the new parliament, using a Japanese version of Graham shorthand. Entrepreneurs quickly realised that stenography could be applied to the verbatim transcription of stories told by professional narrators. By placing a stenographer in the wings to transcribe the stories of popular narrators and then printing them for a mass audience, publishers demonstrated that they could make big profits. The first of these stenographic books, known as *sokkibon*, was San'yūtei Enchō's ghost story *Botan dōrō* (The peony lantern) (*Meiji bungaku* 1965).[46]

The tale tells of the student Saburo who is smitten with a beautiful woman called Otsuyu. But when Saburo falls ill, the two are unable to meet. After he recovers, Saburo learns that Otsuyu has died. But one night during the *obon* festival he is surprised to see Ostuyu and her maid carrying a peony lantern passing his house. The two women pass by the house each night. Saburo learns that his aunt had lied to him about Otsuyu's death because she did not want them to marry. He invites Otsuyu in and, from then on, she

46 Enchō's stenographers were Wakabayashi Kanzō and Sakai Shōzō; the book was printed by Haishi Shuppansha.

spends each night with him. One night a servant spies on them and notices that Saburo is in the company of a skeleton. A Buddhist priest recommends Saburo place talismans around the house to prevent the ghost from entering. When Saburo's pining for the woman reduces him to poor health, the servant relents. The ghost again enters the house, but the next morning the dead Saburo is found entwined with the skeleton, but with a look of bliss on his face.

The story became one of Enchō's most famous *kaidan banashi* (ghost stories). It was told in 12 consecutive episodes. The book version was so successful that five more *sokkibon* of Enchō's stories were published the following year (Miller 1997:582–583).

Sokkibon sold well and, although not considered high literature, they were the envy of many novelists and publishers. They were printed on cheap paper, bought by lending libraries and circulated relatively widely. Few *sokkibon* have survived intact because of their poor paper and the low regard in which they were held at the time. But the low cost and the prevalence of lending libraries meant that they reached a wide audience. (Zwicker 2006:66–67,90–92). Their appeal lay in the storytellers' use of vernacular Japanese. In effect, *sokkibon* served as 'reading primers for the minimally literate masses, thereby aiding state efforts at mass literacy' (Miller 1997:583). The popularity of *sokkibon* offered a further channel for the ideas of narrators such as Henry Black and Enchō to reach a mass audience. Publishers of the easy-to-read *sokkibon* capitalised on the relatively high rate of basic literacy even prior to the Meiji Restoration that was partly attributable to the widespread presence of temple schools (Dore 1965).

The *sokkibon* encouraged ordinary people to take a book in their hands and read. Their rise has been described as marking the point 'when an oral narrative tradition suddenly enters the written domain' (Dore 1965:584). Enchō's *Botan dōrō* has been cited as 'the point of departure for modern Japanese literature' (Sakai 1992:91). Not everyone greeted the new genre with enthusiasm. Critics were appalled at the thought that the language of the *rakugoka* should find its way into the novel (Li 1996), but they were backing a lost cause. *Botan dōrō*, a simple *sokkibon* from a professional narrator, sparked in a mass audience an interest in reading and galvanised the movement for introduction of the vernacular in the print media.

The repercussions of the chain of events extending from *rakugo* through to the language of mainstream literature were far-reaching and permanent. To understand how momentous the impact was, one needs to appreciate that written Japanese was at the time almost incomprehensible to all but the most erudite and highly educated. Until the advent of *sokkibon*, literature was written in a form of Japanese heavily influenced by classical Chinese. It was akin to reading the language of Chaucer or Shakespeare today. Among writers searching for a new vernacular style was the young author Tsubouchi Shōyō. In a preface to the second edition of *Botan dōrō*, Tsubouchi extolled the virtues of the colloquial (Twine 1991:136), attributing the book's success to its use of language in exploring 'the essence of *ninjō*' (human nature) (Kornicki 1982:28), a theme at the heart of *rakugo*. Tsubouchi used his treatise *Shōsetsu shinzui* (The essence of the novel), the first chapter of which was published in 1885, to set out the case for raising the status of novel writing.

Tsubouchi and other writers in the late 1870s and early 1880s faced considerable opposition in convincing intellectuals and the public that the novel was not useless. Critics of the movement for reform of the written language engaged in a strong and vociferous rearguard action, even arguing that reform would render the written word too colloquial and 'oral'. They were exemplified by persons such as Nakamura Masanao (1832–1891), translator of Samuel Smiles's *Self Help*, who in 1876 published two denunciations of the novel as morally and educationally damaging (Kornicki 1982:12). A typical proponent of the other side of the argument was the political novelist and journalist Sakurada Momoe (1857?–1883) who noted in the preface of his novel *Jiyū no nishiki* (Brocade of freedom), written in 1881 and published posthumously in 1883, that the novel was a useful device for promoting social reform (Kornicki 1982:13). By the late 1880s and early 1890s, the hard evidence for literature as an agent of social change was available in the *sokkibon*, including those of San'yūtei Enchō and Henry Black.

Futabatei Shimei put Tsubouchi's ideas into practice in his novel *Ukigumo* (Drifting clouds), published in instalments between 1887 and 1889. With its psychological realism and simple language, in what became known as the *genbun itchi* (unification of the spoken and written language) style stripped of old-fashioned classical elegance, many critics consider it Japan's first modern novel (Kamei 2002:9–15). It is worth noting, however, that in his analysis of the origins of the language in *Ukigumo*, Kamei Hideo favours Terada Tōru's 1958 observation that

> the rhythms and ornamental language he uses could in no way have been the *gen*, or spoken language, often associated with the *genbun itchi*

> style. They may have been words used in the storytelling halls or on the *kyōgen* stage, but they are not words that were used in the streets or in the common people's homes (quoted in Kamei 2002:9,fn10).

There was obviously still a long way to go until the colloquial entered the novel as we know it today.

Having been urged by Futabatei to use the language in Enchō's stories as a model for his writing, Yamada Bimyō explained in his preface to *Fūkin shirabe no hitofushi* (Notes from an organ melody) that the story's style was 'a slightly more ornamental version of that of the raconteur's love stories' (Twine 1991:145). Other novelists who benefited from the loosening of constraints on the use of the vernacular in literature include Higuchi Ichiyō and Ozaki Kōyō (Miller 1997:581). Natsume Sōseki's childhood and student interest in *rakugo* shows in his novels too, especially in *Wagahai wa neko de aru* (I am a cat), which contains many themes derived from narrations attributable to San'yūtei Enyū (Okitsu 1979:101–116). Scholarly debate continues over the degree to which the language of Futabatei Shimei and others reflected the vernacular (Kamei 2002:9), but there is no denying that *rakugo* was one source of inspiration and was often alluded to as a benchmark for writers, an indication that the language of the storytellers was a catalyst for change.

The endorsement these writers gave to *rakugo* also helped raise its profile among the masses. The *genbun itchi* movement's adherents sought to modernise the language of Meiji literature and thus engage readers more effectively in the social and political transformation of their country. The ultimate success of the movement can be attributed in part to the recognition by people like Tsubouchi, Futabatei and Sōseki of *rakugo* as having facilitated this engagement. What *sokkibon* storytellers such as Black pioneered, the novelists who were heirs to the *genbun itchi* debate then finessed into a more sophisticated product. The *sokkibon* were the inkwell into which the writers of the *genbun itchi* movement dipped their pens for inspiration (Tomasi 1999:333–355). While the initial inroads made by the vernacular into education, the press and the political novel had been compromised by repressive government measures against Freedom and People's Rights Movement adherents from 1877 (Twine 1991:74), *Botan dōrō* and the interest it sparked in reading among a mass audience helped renew interest in stylistic reform in the print media.

It was some years before mainstream Japanese literature emerged in its final form from the debate about style and content that raged as a result of the impact of Western literary forms. Nevertheless, the appearance of *sokkibon*, which captured *rakugo* stories on paper for the first time, greatly hastened the debate. The flexibility and consequent popularity of *rakugo* as a vehicle for ideas attracted the interest of proponents of the reform of fiction not just because the debate centred on the technicalities of fiction writing but also because it was concerned with morality and the transmission of ideas. The new generation of writers wanted desperately to express the ideas of their fictional characters in language comprehensible to their readers and the reception accorded *sokkibon* proved this was possible.[47] *Rakugoka* had, of course, already been doing this for decades.

As the debate raged, entrepreneurial newspaper proprietors also began to show an interest in serialising the stenographically recorded stories of *rakugoka*. The *Yamato shinbun* pioneered the practice with its inaugural edition on 7 October 1886, when it published the first episode of Enchō's *Matsu no misao bijin no ikiume* (A beauty buried alive) (Yoshizawa 1981:315). By capitalising on its links to key persons in the Sanyū guild, the *Yamato shinbun* became one of the more consistent in publishing stories by the guild's members. Henry Black benefited from this practice. His ability to adapt a good story from foreign sources gave him a head start in the race to adapt foreign material. Combined with the connections with newspaper proprietors he had developed during his years with the pro-democracy movement, this ability served him well. Between 1887 and 1896 *Yamato shinbun* printed at least four of Henry's tales: *Eikoku kidan nagare no akatsuki* (Dawn at the river);[48] *Setsunaru tsumi* (Pitiful sin); *Tsurugi no hawatari* (The sword's blade); and *Natsu no mushi*[49] (Summer insects).

By serialising well-known canonic stories by narrators, commissioning them to create original works and including serialised Western novels in translation or as adaptations, Japanese newspapers were following the example of their contemporary European counterparts. These were lucrative ways of boosting circulation, particularly for the tabloid newspapers. One of the more innovative newspapers in publishing serialisations was *Yorozu chōhō*, owned by novelist and editor Kuroiwa Ruikō (1862–1920). Kuroiwa adapted Victor Hugo's *Les Misérables* in 1902–1903 and Alexandre Dumas'

---

47 For statistics on *sokkibon* trends over two decades, see Miller (1997:586–589).

48 According to Morioka and Sasaki (1983:142), *Nagare no akatsuki* was published in *Yamato shinbun* in 45 episodes from January 1891.

49 The first episode of *Natsu no mushi* was published on 3 August 1894.

Le Compte de Monte-Cristo in 1901–1902 (Japan 1993:847). He also adapted the Mary Braddon mystery novel *Diavola; or, the Woman's Battle* (Wolff 1979:122–126),[50] as *Sute obune* (abandoned small boat)[51] by serialising it in 156 episodes between October 1894 and July 1895, a decade after Henry Black first introduced Braddon's *Flower and Weed* (Ogasawara 1992:26–33). *Sute obune* was so popular with readers that it was adapted for the *kabuki* stage by Kawatake Shinshichi III in a New Year performance at the Kabukiza Theatre in Tokyo in 1898. The stage adaptation illustrates the tremendous burst of creativity that occurred at this time, involving synergies between numerous genres and mediums. It also demonstrates the role that serialised novels of the kind Henry had introduced played in facilitating the intertextual transmission of 19th-century European notions of modernity to a wide and receptive audience during these years.

It is not clear whether Henry sparked Kuroiwa's interest in Braddon's novels. Nevertheless, Kuroiwa's use of a Braddon work is consistent with the way he combined serialised Western novels and 'sensational reportage on social issues' (Japan 1993: 847) to boost circulation – a formula imitated by other newspapers during the boom years of serialised Western novels.

Since a significant number of serialised stories in newspapers were from *rakugoka*, newspapers were a medium commensurate with *sokkibon* in popularising *rakugo* narrations, thus fostering interest in popular literature and stimulating book publishing. Specialist magazines also arose which offered similar stories to readers. The benchmark *Hyakkaen*, for example, which first appeared in 1889, published Henry Black's *Eikoku no otoshibanashi* (The beer drinking contest) in March 1891 (Kairakutei 1891a). Other magazines included *Kōdan zasshi* and *Kōdan kurabu*, published daily in Tottori City (Yoshizawa 1981:316). Magazines like these continued to flourish into the early years of the Taishō period, even after Henry Black's death in 1923.[52] Book publishers formed links with magazine publishers

50 Braddon biographer Robert Lee Wolff notes that *Diavola* was published from 27 October 1866 to 20 July 1867 in *London Journal* 44 (1133)–46(1171). It was shortly afterwards published in the *New York Sunday Mercury* with the title *Nobody's Daughter; or, the Ballad-Singer of Wapping*, and reissued in 1868 as a three-volume novel, *Run to Earth*. Wolff claims that this sensation novel dates from the years when Braddon wrote for 'penny-dreadfuls' and that its subsequent appearance dressed up as a novel was a violation by Braddon and Maxwell, her publisher and lover, of 'contemporary publishing practices'.

51 Ogasawara Mikio (1992:26–33) notes that the Braddon work is also known in Japan as *Diabora*, or *Ienaki Musume* (The homeless maiden).

52 Yoshizawa (1981:317) notes that by 1924 many ordinary general-purpose magazines also contained *kōdan* stories, giving way by the end of the Taishō period to the genre known as *shōsetsu yomimono*.

and issued compilations of the stories as *kōdan tankōbon* (narrated stories in book form) (Yoshizawa 1981:321).[53]

Henry, therefore, came to storytelling as it entered a golden age of creativity. The growing number of *yose* in Japan at this time (Morioka & Sasaki 1990: 251–252) meant that *rakugoka* who performed in them would have reached even more people than the newspapers. In Tokyo alone, there were 163 *yose* in 1880, 120 in 1884, 199 in 1885 and 230 in 1886, when Henry was forming links with the San'yūha members. The stage was set for a brilliant career.

53 Yoshizawa notes that it was not unusual for newspapers to maintain close relationships with book publishers, so that a story serialised in a newspaper would be released subsequently in book form, sometimes with an altered title. Similarly, stories serialised in magazines were published as books. The publishing house Ōkawaya, from mid-Meiji to early Taishō, obtained publishing rights from many companies and issued a large number of books aimed mainly at the lending libraries.

Chapter 7

In the golden age of the narrators

> In the first place the class is large, and, instead of sweeping it away with other mediaeval relics, the new civilization seems to have given it a new lease of life. The reason of this survival seems to be that which has caused the survival of Japan herself as an independent country; as Japan not only saved herself from extinction but attained a higher pitch of power than she had ever reached before by timely modernization, so the story-teller became in like manner a greater power in the land than ever owing to his judiciously identifying himself with the reform movement (McCullagh 1902:207).

In September 1890, at the age of 31, Henry Black formally affiliated with the San'yūha (Morioka & Sasaki 1983:141), thus cementing his already firm links to the guild and assuring him of regular employment at those *yose* traditionally associated with it. It also guaranteed support from his peers and mentors within the guild. According to Black, the *rakugoka* Gorin Ennosuke made the official approach to him on behalf of the school, because 'a Western *rakugoka* is unusual' (Nishūbashi 1905:298). Guild members considered that the presence of the culturally and ethnically different Black offered potential for innovation in the *rakugo* repertoire. Henry Black also credited his long association with Enchō and San'yūtei Enshō IV as influencing his decision to accept membership of the San'yūha (Nishūbashi 1905:298). Henry's earlier successes with narrations of Bonnie Prince Charlie and Joan of Arc may also have appealed to the guild. Furthermore, the popularity of Enchō's adaptations of Western novels would have persuaded Henry that he could achieve similar popularity (Morioka & Sasaki 1983:140). Describing his return to storytelling, Henry Black credited his friend, *rakugoka* Dokyōtei Ryūba, for introducing him to two San'yūha-affiliated *yose* in Tokyo – Tachibanaya Hall in Ryōgoku and the Kiharatei Hall in Nihonbashi. A good relationship with the owners and operators of venues such as these was vital to any storyteller's continued employment. Henry Black claimed that his narrations at these two *yose* had been well received, in part because of the novelty of their presentation by a foreigner. His affiliation with the guild cemented his commitment to Japan and the culture of *rakugo*. It was also a conscious decision to ignore the disapproval of some of his friends and family.

Henry Black's transformation into a fully-fledged, officially recognised *rakugoka* took place in March 1891. On this occasion he was granted *shin'uchi* (principal performer) status and took the professional name Kairakutei Burakku. *Kairaku* is the Japanese word for pleasure in its fully hedonistic sense and *tei* is the suffix appended to the house names of *rakugoka*; Burakku is simply the Japanese rendering of his surname. Reporting on Henry's assuming a professional name, the *Yamato shinbun* of 24 March 1891 noted that Black 'who is pushing the fact that he is someone with different coloured hair,[54] has an increasing number of disciples and it is becoming inconvenient not to have a professional name under the auspices of a guild' (Kurata 1981–87:V,97). Despite the new professional name, it took several more years for newspapers, particularly those in the countryside, to use it when referring to Henry. Many newspaper reports continued to refer to him as 'Eikokujin Burakku' (Briton Black).

Rakugo critic and commentator Kojima Teijin (1988:2–5) once remarked that the choice of Kairakutei as Black's professional name would have conveyed a quirky originality at the time. Kojima surmised that many of Black's associates, and perhaps Henry himself, would have suggested names that reflected his British ancestry or his ability to impart knowledge of the West through his performances. Kojima suggested that the final choice was probably left to Henry himself and that his reasons for choosing Kairakutei may have lain in Western logic and philosophy as perceived in Japan at the time. Western philosophers had considerable impact on economic and social thought at a time when the ultimate aim in Western society was assumed by many Japanese to be the pursuit of happiness. Perhaps there was an element of this assumption in Black's choice of a name that incorporated the notion of pleasure.

As the figures for the numbers of theatres featuring storytellers show, Henry Black's affiliation with the San'yūha coincided with a golden age for storytellers. The time was ripe for Henry to build on his 1886 experience with *Kusaba no tsuyu* (Dew by the graveside), his adaptation of Mary Braddon's *Flower and Weed*.

---

54 A contemporary euphemism for someone who was not Japanese, usually a Caucasian.

Using Mary Braddon

Inspired by the success of *Kusaba no tsuyu,* Henry Black began to adapt freely a succession of mystery novels from European sources, breaking them into narrated episodes and imbuing them with suspense and humour, leavened with revelations about modern life in Europe. He found inspiration for his narrations mainly in the modern Victorian genres, sensation and detective novels. Preeminent among the writers of such novels was the prolific Mary Braddon and at least two of Henry's narrations were adapted from her works. Braddon had embarked on a stage career, but abandoned it in 1860 to concentrate on writing. In her lifetime she wrote more than 80 novels and nine plays. In the 1880s, Braddon was at the peak of her 55-year career. Her novels were being serialised in newspapers and journals in Britain and other English-speaking countries. Braddon's melodramatic plots featured headstrong women and mistaken identity.

Braddon's biographer, Robert Lee Wolff, notes that Braddon was frequently accused of plagiarising the work of popular French and British authors of the day. She was particularly fond of the works of Émile Zola, Gustave Flaubert and Honoré de Balzac (Wolff 1979:8–9). Even if she did not directly plagiarise their works, she was certainly heavily influenced by them. It would not be surprising, therefore, to find that more of Black's works, particularly those set in Paris, owe their inspiration, if not their origin to Braddon's plagiarised, or adapted, versions of French works.

Henry Black's other known sources included Charles Dickens and Frenchman Fortuné du Boisgobey. He may also have composed his own stories based on ideas culled from novels found in lending libraries or borrowed from friends. As Henry's stories included both good and bad examples of life in the West, many in his audiences came to hear what he had to say about the West, making his stories ingredients in the ongoing debate about how to modernise Japan.

There is a studio photograph of Henry Black of the kind that might have been taken to mark the conferring of the name Kairakutei Burakku on him (see cover photo). His appearance is in the style characteristic of a true *rakugoka*. He is in full *hakama* with a crest bearing the intertwined initials HJB (Henry James Black) near each shoulder. He is squatting on the storyteller's square cushion, known as *zabuton*, with the storyteller's fan in his right hand, which rests on his lap. To his right are a teapot and cup. His hair is receding. The image is far removed from anything he would have experienced in distant Adelaide where he was born, or even in Yokohama, where he could easily have chosen to work in some foreign trading company. Henry stares benignly at the camera, with even a certain air of satisfaction and contentment. He has the expression of someone who appears to have found his vocation (McCullagh 1902:218).

But it was not always a smooth ride for the foreign-born Henry Black. Japan's art of oral storytelling has a long tradition and among his peers were people who questioned the worth of wholesale Westernisation. These people regarded Henry Black as an interloper. Unfortunately, Henry's outspoken nature guaranteed that points of difference developed with other members which festered throughout his career and occasionally caused angry clashes with his peers.

Henry Black was inducted into the San'yūha at a time when the wider debate over modernity had begun to have an impact on *rakugo*. Among *rakugoka*, there were purists who fought to retain the old ways. There were others too, aligned with Henry, who felt that the survival of their art lay in experimentation. There were degrees of difference between these two extremes, but sometimes the representatives of these two sides did not see eye to eye. It did not help that Henry was inclined to overindulge in alcoholic refreshment, a habit that occasionally stoked his argumentative side. The differences of character, temperament and inclination played out within the context of the wider debate about reform and social change.

Rakugo and the quest for modernity

By the time of Henry Black's first major story in 1886 the requirement for success – an audience receptive to a foreigner and involved in the reform debate – was in place. The issues that defined and shaped the debate over modernity among *yose* audiences differed from those that had propelled him into the speech meetings of the Freedom and People's Rights Movement in 1879 and 1880. A new set of political imperatives included a new Constitution, promised by 1889, and the prospect of the first general election in 1890. As the post-Restoration generation began to assume positions of influence from the 1880s, Japan began to experience an 'outburst of nation-mindedness' exemplified by the sudden and frequent use of the words *kokka* (nation) and *kokumin* (the people) in the media and popular discourse (Gluck 1985:23). Henry Black's audiences were developing a more sophisticated appreciation of Japan's place in the world. Many in his audiences aspired to Japan's becoming a 19th-century nation-state similar to the example set by the industrialised Western European monarchies.

Other factors were also at play. In Tokyo and other major cities, distances shrank with the introduction of new forms of communication, such as the telephone and telegraph. New forms of transport, such as the railway and the horse-drawn omnibus facilitated travel, and the incorporation of Western styles in housing began to transform people's way of life. New job opportunities began to alter the way people related to each other. New laws transformed their understanding of their rights to justice, to inheritance, to marriage and even to their place in the family and the modern nation-state. Demographic changes resulted in alterations to the composition of the population of Tokyo and other key towns and cities, which had an impact on urban life and the tastes of *yose* audiences.

The people of Tokyo, where Henry Black lived and performed, were first to absorb the changes associated with modernity. The city had undergone a social, political and architectural metamorphosis accompanying its transformation from the seat of the *shōgun* to the renamed metropolis of Tokyo, the capital city of a modern nation-state. The city's new role became more pronounced as the government built a case for revision of the unequal treaties. In the rush to create a modern metropolis that would make Tokyo 'presentable to foreigners' (Smith 1978:50), the government passed the Municipal Improvement Act in 1888. The act was inspired by Baron Haussmann's renovation of Paris, in which that city's narrow streets were opened up to create the grand boulevards and vistas for which it is now famous (Smith 1978:50). The Meiji rulers wanted a similarly monumental setting in which they could parade their Emperor. Tokyo was to be the place where the government built and displayed its chosen symbols of modernity and carried out its experiments in governance and administration (Smith 1978:53).

Tokyo's prosperity had been briefly undercut following the Restoration as the government abolished the alternate attendance system under which regional *daimyō* had been obliged to spend half their time in the city and the remaining half in their domains. Under the system, *daimyō* had maintained sumptuous residences and numerous retainers in Tokyo. But the abolition of this system freed them to return to their home provinces permanently (Smith 1978:55) and prompted a sudden exodus from Tokyo. It was not until the 1890s, about a decade after Henry Black embarked on his career in *rakugo*, that the city's population resumed its pre-Meiji Restoration level (Smith 1978:53). Nevertheless, when Henry came to the stage, the city's population was rapidly expanding again. Between the mid-1890s and the

1923 Great Kanto Earthquake, Tokyo's population doubled to almost four million.

The task of the post-Restoration reformers was facilitated by a pre-existing infrastructure. Edo, which had surpassed a million inhabitants by 1800 (Rozman 1974:91), was at the centre of a well-developed network of roads and shipping lanes. Its strategic and political importance made it the dominant city in terms of culture and economy. The annual migrations of *daimyō* and their retainers as 'messengers of change' (Rozman 1974:100) to and from Edo under the alternate attendance system had established a pattern of cultural dissemination, keeping the provinces abreast of the latest fashions in the metropolis. Emerging from its previous incarnation as Edo, Tokyo, with its concentration of theatres catering to its huge population, its administrative infrastructure and its links to the provinces, was ideally positioned to rapidly disseminate aspects of modernity within and beyond its boundaries (Rozman 1974:92). The city was an engine of social transformation, comparable to London in the same period.

In Henry Black's Tokyo, the presence of new immigrants from the provinces had an impact on the demographics of the *yose* audience. Not all were commoners. Among Tokyo's growing population after the Restoration were well-educated ex-*samurai* bureaucrats from the Satsuma and Chōshū domains in the southwest. Both were domains whose *samurai* had led the push to eliminate the shogunate, so it was natural that their ex-*samurai* filled the ranks of the new administration. Also among new additions to the population were students and apprentices keen to take advantage of opportunities for education and jobs opened up by the drive for civilisation and enlightenment. In a process akin to colonisation (Yano 1999:147), these newer residents gave Tokyo new meaning and, simultaneously, provoked a cultural clash with the older residents.

To the citizens of Meiji-era Japan, the capital epitomised experimentation, novelty and the future. Its residents experienced a daily co-mingling of Western elements and indigenous Japanese influences, thinking nothing of teaming a bowler hat with a kimono or taking *miso* soup with their beef. Many experienced fatigue at the rapid and confusing pace of change, all of which combined to induce a redefinition of the self among the populace.[55]

Rakugo helped its Tokyo audiences cope with change. From the 1880s, an increase in *yose* numbers in the city attests to the role of *rakugo* in satisfying

55 For a good explanation of the changes, see Irokawa (1985:204).

a demand for entertainment and information. *Yose* numbers grew at a rate commensurate with that of Tokyo's population, which meant that the early Meiji years prior to the burgeoning of more modern sources of entertainment and information, particularly the cinema, were 'a golden age' for storytelling in Japan (Miller 1997:582). *Rakugo* had become one of the most prevalent forms of entertainment available in the capital. The number of *yose*, each of which accommodated between 100 and 300 people, increased further throughout the remainder of the 19th century. They were situated in every district of Tokyo, and each provincial city had at least one or more.[56] By 1902 Scottish traveller Francis McCullagh was able to describe *yose* as 'very numerous and popular':

> The number of *yose* or story-tellers' halls in Tokyo is perhaps greater at present than in any former age, being 243 according to recent statistics; and, as a general rule, the number of *yose* in a Japanese town bears the same proportion as the total number of public houses in an Irish town bears to the total number of houses therein (McCullagh 1902:207).

The Times correspondent, Frank Brinkley, writing in 1902, claimed that there were 180 *yose* in Tokyo, describing them as 'comfortless' places:

> – the building rough and totally undecorated; the floor covered with mats but not divided into compartments; the gallery equally without redeeming feature except a semblance of privacy; the dais for the performers slightly elevated but entirely without ornamentation or scenic background. Such is the *yose*. A visitor, whatever his degree, pays an entrance fee varying from two and one-half to six *sen*, makes a further disbursement of half a *sen* for the hire of a cushion, and, thus equipped, seats himself wherever he can find floor-space (Brinkley 1904:105).

Brinkley noted that the low cost covered up to four hours of entertainment, which could include *jōruri* chanting, jugglers, puppets, dance and music. But the storytellers were the main reason for attendance. There were a number of reasons for the popularity of *rakugo*. Although not activists in the style of the Freedom and People's Rights Movement, Black and his fellow *rakugoka* served as social critics and participants in the

56 For details of the size and location of theatres, see Morioka and Sasaki (1990:2) and Kawamura (1989).

discourse on modernity by appealing to a wide range of the population from intellectuals to those who depended mainly on oral sources of entertainment and information (Miller 1997:582). Most accounts of *rakugo* characterise it as an art of the common people. The classic stories that Black's contemporaries learned as apprentices were socially situated in the lower-class lower city (*shita machi*) districts of Edo, ensuring that *rakugo* bore 'clear marks of a close connection to the life of the common people' (Morioka & Sasaki 1990:1). The *rakugo* repertoire was replete with caricatures of Edo residents, many dwelling in the *nagaya*, the long, narrow wooden tenement row-houses of the old part of the city, or the geisha and licensed prostitution quarters.

A typically humorous example is *Father and son drink sake*, in which a father and his son vow not to drink any more alcohol. Soon after making their vow, the father persuades his wife to serve him sake while their son is absent on a New Year visit to a customer. Over his wife's objections, the father demands more and more sake until he becomes blind drunk. At this point their son returns. The father hides the sake bottle and cup and proceeds to question his son on where he has been. The son explains that he had been visiting the Yamadas to collect an outstanding debt, when Mr Yamada began to insist they have a drink to celebrate the New Year. Questioned by his father, the son proudly explains that he refused the offer of a drink. Under further questioning from his father, the son explains that Mr Yamada expressed his admiration for the son's determination to stick to his vow and suggested they drink to that, whereupon the son had agreed and drunk several bottles of sake, coming home drunk. The thoroughly drunk father, whose sight has obviously been affected by alcohol, then chastises his son. He explains that he can not bequeath the house to his son because the son now has eight heads. At this, the son, who by this stage is also blind drunk, retorts that he isn't interested in getting the house because it is 'wobbling all over the place!' This tale, which is still told today, was the sort of fare which audiences loved and expected.

Records of attendance by intellectuals like Fukuzawa Yukichi and acknowledgement by writers such as Natsume Sōseki (Nobuhiro 1986:20) that *rakugo* influenced their work attest to the widespread popularity of *rakugo* among the general population and intellectuals during these years. Fukuzawa is known to have enjoyed San'yūtei Enchō's stories. He took his students to the performances, possibly so that they could appreciate their modern, colloquial Japanese (Nishiyama 1997:247). Journalist, socialist and labour activist Arahata Kanson (1887–1981) also recorded how his father often took him to a *yose* at Isezaki in Yokohama to hear *rakugoka*, including Henry Black (Arahata 1965:20).

Given its low cost and absence of written instructions and rules for performers (Balkenhol & Sasaki 1979:156), *rakugo* had the flexibility to withstand censorship and cultural ossification. Practitioners could shape it into an ideal Meiji-era medium of instruction, enlightenment and mass entertainment. For Henry Black, these characteristics made it an excellent form of cross-cultural communication. It allowed him to participate in a medium that had always been an integral part of the life of Tokyo. Edo's entertainment quarters, which contained the *kabuki* and *rakugo* theatres, were at the heart of Edo culture, ensuring that the theatre remained central to the culture of Meiji-era Tokyo (Seidensticker 1983:17–18). The low cost of *yose* entry compared to *kabuki* throughout the Meiji period, as well as the overwhelming numerical dominance of *yose* compared to *kabuki* theatres, also ensured that *rakugo* remained accessible to many.

The culture clash between new residents and old had several outcomes. In order to survive, the more innovative *rakugoka* responded to the clash by producing new narrations that reflected the newly evolving culture of Tokyo. This gave the *rakugo* repertoire a fresh stock of modern stories, ensuring that *yose* entertainment continued to provide an accessible catharsis for residents dealing with the stresses of rapid change caused by modernisation. It also ensured that *yose* had a dual function as places for spectators to socialise and to be socialised. *Rakugoka* Katsura Beichō has described how apprentices who came from the country to work in Tokyo or Osaka in these years were often taken to a *yose* by their shop proprietor to learn the ways of the world once they had learned the rudiments of their job. Beichō described how young students flocking to Tokyo from the regions visited *yose* to learn how to relate to Tokyo's citizens. It was through *yose* that the students became familiar with the norms of social etiquette in Tokyo. *Yose*, according to Katsura Beichō were places where Tokyoites could 'learn how to behave toward other people, how to offer greetings, how to use others and be used by others' and even how to use appropriate honorific speech forms.

> Not a few people were taught through *rakugo* the sorts of things one does not learn in the home or at school, like how to mind one's manners at a banquet, or what is standard practice in a red-light district, or even how to hand over a tip. It could be said that *rakugo* is an encyclopedia on life (Katsura 1976:86).

Rakugo in the age of reform

By the Meiji period, *rakugo* monologues of the kind Henry and his colleagues practised had acquired a characteristic structure consisting of a *makura* (preface), a *hanashi* (main story) and a cathartic *ochi* (punchline) (Novograd 1974). *Rakugo* exponents maintain that the *ochi* should make the audience laugh, even if the story has moved them to tears. A number of devices are employed to achieve this. Among them, *ma*, silences defined as 'the space or timing' during a narration and inserted by the narrator for special effect are of paramount importance (Morioka & Sasaki 1990:30).[57] In conventional *rakugo*, the *rakugoka* begins by engaging in a form of intimacy with the audience by discussing a topic of mutual interest such as the weather, a current scandal, or political development. The *rakugoka* uses this to segue into the main story in which he or she assumes the personalities of the persons depicted. This necessitates two simultaneous 'communication events' – 'a metacommunicative event' involving direct communication between narrator and audience, and 'a non-metacommunicative event involving the characters invented by the narrator in the context of the monologue' (Sanches 1975).

In 1899, Jules Adam, a French diplomat who witnessed Black's performances, described *rakugoka* as 'a class of very remarkable and really curious artists', noting that *yose* filled 'a large place in the existence of the Japanese' (Adam 1899:1). Spectators removed their shoes at the entrance and sat on *zabuton* on the floor. A *rakugo* performance involved a single narrator sitting centre stage also on a *zabuton*. Junior ranked storytellers featured earlier in the program and more senior ones performed later. Extremely popular *rakugoka*, including Henry Black, performed at more than one *yose* during the day, relying on rickshaw pullers to take them to the next venue as quickly as possible.

Theatre owners typically formed close associations with the main guilds of *rakugo*, so that performers from those guilds were ensured continued patronage and opportunities to demonstrate their abilities. Theatres advertised programs with banners outside their entrances, displaying the rankings of the performers within the guilds. The content of the narrations was decided by each *rakugoka* who was responsible for ensuring that he did not deliver the same story from the repertoire of well-known classics as a colleague on the same billing. It was not uncommon for *rakugoka* to

---

57 For a full discussion of types of ma, see Balkenhol and Sasaki (1979:156–165) and Morioka and Sasaki (1981:428).

memorise stories from the classics, but each had his own distinctive way of delivering the story. Aficionados savoured these differences, but they did not necessarily appreciate hearing the same story twice in the same day. To prevent duplication, a notebook with the day's program contents to which each performer had earlier contributed was kept backstage for subsequent performers to consult.

By the time McCullagh wrote of the *yose* in 1902, electric lighting was in use at the theatres, but, as with today's *rakugo* performances, traditional stage props had not been abandoned. Props were restricted to a fan and a small cloth known as a *tenugui*. Depending on the story, the fan could double as a pipe, a pair of chopsticks, an oar, or a sword, and the *tenugui* as a sweat cloth, bath towel, or even a wallet.

> [O]n coming to a *risqué* part of his story, or when he simply wants to excite the curiosity of his hearers, or to regain breath, or just get the *mot juste*, the story-teller deliberately pours out for himself a cup of tea and sips it with the slowness and solemnity of a *connoisseur*. The old-fashioned story-teller was also accustomed to snuff the candles, rub his robe with his fan, bring the fan down with a sharp click on a little piece of wood placed before him for the purpose, and do other things at which everybody thought it the proper thing to laugh (McCullagh 1902:212).

Storytellers performed on an otherwise bare stage. This left them completely free to conjure the scene in the minds of the audience. They usually remained kneeling on their *zabuton* for the duration of the story, at times only slightly raising the top half of their bodies from a fully kneeling position to mimic activities such as swimming, parrying with a sword or rowing a boat. Even while kneeling, the knees were rapidly moved up and down to indicate walking or running. These moves are still in use among today's storytellers.

Standard dress for a performer is the kimono with a *hanten* (half-length jacket) over it, both usually bearing the performer's insignia. Henry Black often broke with custom by wearing Western clothing for his performances. Illustrations from this period show him in trousers and jacket, necktie neatly in place, seated on a chair behind a small table with a glass cup and a water decanter, as Fukuzawa Yukichi had first appeared for his lectures in the 1870s. Henry may well have thought that the departure from tradition fitted the prevailing mood for change, enhanced his status as an authority on matters foreign and contributed to his image as an innovator.

The version of *rakugo* that Henry Black knew in the 1880s was one of several genres within the category of *hanashimono* (telling of short stories mostly of a comic nature) traditionally performed in *yose*. Together with *utaimono* (chanted recital with musical accompaniment), *katarimono* (spoken recital with musical accompaniment) and *yomimono* (reading of long stories of mostly tragic nature, including *kōdan*), *hanashimono* made up *wagei*, the oral arts of Japan (Morioka & Sasaki 1990:3–4).

Of the unaccompanied oral arts, *kōdan* was more popular than *rakugo* in the early Meiji years. By the time Henry Black came to it, however, *rakugo* was on the rise. *Rakugo* was associated with humorous stories, while *kōdan* were delivered lecture style from a text. There were also *gundan* (military stories), which Henry had known as an associate of Hyōgyūsha Tōrin shortly after his father died in 1880. Use of the word *kōdan* in newspapers at the time indicates that *kōdan* encompassed more didactic styles, including 'newspaper *kōdan*' (*shinbun kōdan*), 'novel *kōdan*' (*shōsetsu kōdan*), 'popular *kōdan*' (*tsūzoku kōdan*) and even 'enlightenment *kōdan*' (*kaika kōdan*) (Yoshizawa 1981:313).[58]

Many *rakugoka* also performed *kōdan*, and newspapers often made no distinction between the genres. Given the looser definitions of the two forms in the early Meiji years, some *rakugoka*, including Henry Black, were also described as *kōdanshi* (*kōdan* narrator). But since Black was unable to read Japanese, he gravitated to *rakugo*. Its spontaneity, flexibility, and originality meant that it could respond to the debate over modernity and reform. The scope for humour in *rakugo* also made it a popular antidote to the stresses induced by reforms associated with modernisation, which accounted for its growing popularity.

The flexibility of *rakugo* was the product of centuries of the genre's adjustment to suit popular taste, often in the face of government-enforced restrictions on *yose* program content. The *rakugo* repertoire that Henry knew in the 1880s owed its structure and content to links between premodern educator–proselytisers and ordinary people. Scholars of *rakugo* credit chronicler Sekiyama Kazuo with having first identified *rakugo*[59] as 'the offspring and outgrowth of Buddhist exempla tales' (Morioka & Sasaki

58 Yoshizawa's list is extensive and includes 'era *kōdan*' (*jisei kōdan*), 'improvement *kōdan*' (*kairyō kōdan*), and 'new *kōdan*' (*shin kōdan*). Genre appellations could reflect the nature or character of the narrator, particularly when applied to political activists rather than professional storytellers. Examples are 'henchman *kōdan*' (*sōshi kōdan*), and 'student *kōdan*' (*shosei kōdan*), and 'speech *kōdan*' (*enzetsu kōdan*).

59 Morioka and Sasaki (1990:429) note that Sekiyama makes this claim, tracing the genre's lineage to Anrakanu Sakuden, whom Sekiyama described 'as a religious man and great

1990:211) with humorous or fantastic stories to sway congregations. The oldest extant collection of sermon exempla is the *Nihon ryōiki* (or *reiiki*) of 821–822 compiled by the priest Kyōkai (or Keikai) (Nakamura 1973). Its stories each contain a parable or a karma tale and finish with 'an edifying exhortation' (Morioka & Sasaki 1990:212). They contain themes found in *rakugo*, such as the disguised fox and the human skull that returns to life. Two collections of anecdotes and legends, *Konjaku monogatari shū* and *Uji shūi monogatari*, also contain a significant number of features which justify their description as 'the prototype of *rakugo* narration' (Morioka & Sasaki 1990:217). The early 12th-century *Konjaku monogatari shū* contains anecdotes about warriors, tales of supernatural beings, criminals and animals, as well as love stories and tales of ancient times. *Uji shūi monogatari* dates from some 100 years later (Mills 1970). It 'preaches' less than *Konjaku monogatari shū*, while its 'presentation of humorous episodes is more outspoken and pointed'.

In his genealogy of *rakugo*, Teruoka Yasutaka credits the advent of the *Uji shūi monogatari* as 'a clearly defining moment' in the growth of *rakugo*.[60] Teruoka notes that although historians might differ over exactly what collection of tales to credit as the progenitor of *rakugo*, the advent of persons who regularly performed narrations for an audience indicates the emergence of a popular art form. Both collections mentioned above contain word plays, as well as examples of practical jokes, eccentric characters, blustering *samurai*, miraculous happenings, ogres, known as *oni*, and supernatural spirits. They also contain *ninjō banashi* (stories of human feeling), a major genre of *rakugo* characterised as 'dramatic and moving tales of the common people's life'.[61]

In the early Meiji years, *rakugo* was known as *otoshibanashi* (stories with a punchline). But after the introduction of ordinances leading to police surveillance of theatres and story content, police documents using the Sino-Japanese reading of the *kanji* as '*rakugo*', rather than '*otoshibanashi*', led to the word '*rakugo*' entering the vernacular (Morioka & Sasaki 1990:250) .

Rakugo presentation style can be traced to the monk Gyōki (668–749) who preached outdoors in a style known as *tsuji seppō* (crossroad sermons)

---

preacher, as a master of the tea ceremony, as an *otogishū* narrator to the feudal lords, and as an accomplished man of culture'.

60 Teruoka (1978) notes that Minamoto no Takakuni, the chief counsellor of Uji, had been credited with the compilation of the *Uji shūi monogatari*, but that this has now been disproved; Morioka and Sasaki concur with this assessment.

61 *Ninjō banashi* are a fundamental part of today's *rakugo*. Morioka and Sasaki (1990:9) describe them as 'the most frequently performed classical *rakugo*' and devote a chapter of their book to them.

(Morioka & Sasaki 1990:212). The influence of *tsuji seppō* was acknowledged in a paper titled *Kōdan yurai sho* (Document on the origins of *Kōdan*) presented to the Tokyo Metropolitan Police Department in 1882 when police were censoring *rakugo* and *kōdan* (Teruoka 1978:23). A later influence came from the Agui Temple in Kyoto whose preachers provided the model for popular sermons until the Meiji period. They sat on a platform while gesticulating, and sometimes reciting, laughing, or weeping – techniques *rakugoka* still use to dramatise their characters. Once laypersons had taken over the form, it evolved as secular narrative entertainment (Morioka & Sasaki 1990:215).

There was some official patronage of storytellers. During the civil wars of the 16th century, *daimyō* (military lords) employed quasi-professional entertainers known as *otogishū* to inspire them with 'anecdotes about heroic deeds of the past, or to divert them between battles with humorous stories' (Morioka & Sasaki 1990:232). The simultaneous existence of the unfettered offspring of the *tsuji seppō* and the more staid and officially sanctioned *otogishū* is an indication over many centuries of a spectrum of storytelling genres.

Given the propensity for some public speakers from the Freedom and People's Rights Movement, including Henry Black, to seek continued self-expression through the oral arts after the demise of organised forms of the movement, *rakugo* and *kōdan* in particular fell under the purview of the conservative Meiji oligarchy. The surveillance of the oral arts had pre-Restoration precedents. Typical were decrees issued in 1841 by Shōgun Tokugawa Nariaki (1800–1860) which restricted the number of *yose* in Edo to a mere 15 and permitted only lectures on Shintoism and *shingaku* (the practical ethics of Confucianism), the reading of *gunsho* (war tales) and performances of *mukashi banashi* (edifying old tales). The decrees remained in force until 1843, after which the number of legal *yose* increased from 24 in 1842 to over 60 in 1844 and as high as 392 ten years later, giving almost every sub-ward (*chō*) in Tokyo its own *yose* (Morioka & Sasaki 1990:248–249). In spite of restrictions, narrators found ingenious ways to adhere to shogunal law and *samurai* values, while continuing to satirise through techniques including *double entendre*, onomatopoeia, sarcasm and irony. All were the stock-in-trade of *rakugoka* when Henry came to the genre in the Meiji period.

After a brief hiatus during which the press experienced something close to true freedom in the immediate aftermath of the Meiji Restoration, post-Restoration authorities were quick to reintroduce restrictions on most forms of self-expression (Huffman 1997; Freeman 2000). The Meiji government issued its first *yose* control edicts in October, 1869, repeating all restrictions in the 1842 edict, and restricting performances to *gunsho* (readings of tales of great battles), *mukashi banashi* and *jōruri* puppet shows. In the following two decades edicts were issued around the country, variously banning criticism of government officials, obscene stories and even the use of stage costumes in *yose* (Morioka & Sasaki 1990:251). The frequency of these edicts in the first two decades of the Meiji period indicates their ineffectiveness in the face of popular demand. Even the police enjoyed *rakugo*, so were not particularly inclined to enforce the restrictions. One of the ironies of the situation was that the edicts helped 'clarify the definition of *rakugo* as a narrative art and to stabilise its eminent role on the *yose* stage' (Morioka & Sasaki 1990:250).

Henry Black and his peers inherited *rakugo*'s legacy of flexibility when the prevailing mood for reform and consequential rapid influx of new ideas led to a questioning of all aspects of society, including the oral and performance arts.[62] By the 1890s, even the nature and purpose of humour was a subject for debate. Novelist Tsubouchi Shōyō, under the impact of Western genres of drama between the mid-1880s and 1897, raised ethical questions about the worth of certain categories of humour (Wells 1997:81). Fukuzawa Yukichi also turned his attention to humour, although, characteristically, his main concern was with its educative value.[63]

In relation to higher art forms, the debate about humour was carried out among intellectuals in literary journals such as *Waseda bungaku* and *Teikoku bungaku* where the focus was on the impact and influence of Western notions of humour, melodrama and comedy (Wells 1997:59). Proponents of *rakugo*, which was considered by many people a lower art, participated in debate about humour in a number of specialist magazines, including the early benchmark *Kokkei shinbun* and *Hyakkaen* in Tokyo (first issue May 1889), *Hyaku chidori* in Osaka (first issue September 1889), *Hanagatami* and *Azuma nishiki* (Yoshizawa 1981:314). One of the main reform-related issues discussed in these magazines was the question

---

62 Peter Kornicki (1982:17) cites a speech by Akaba (or Akabane) Manjirō (d. 1898) about the reform of fiction, *kōdan*, and drama at a meeting in Saitama in the 1880s as an indication that the oral arts were regarded by Meiji intellectuals as ripe for reform.

63 Wells (1997:57) notes that 'the change in intellectual climate resulting in humour becoming a matter for the positive attention of the great and wise is perhaps most clearly demonstrated by a joke book published in 1892' by Fukuzawa. Fukuzawa's choice of jokes were stories mostly from American newspapers and magazines and 'included jokes about mothers-in-law, pompous politicians, boring preachers, cheeky servants and quack doctors with a smattering of schoolboy howlers'.

of the survival of *rakugo*. *Rakugoka* appeared split into two camps over the issue. Progressives favoured the introduction of novelty, such as that represented by Henry Black. Conservatives preferred a renewed emphasis on the purity of their art. They frowned on experimentation and looked to the classics. Symptomatic of the debate was the second issue of *Kōdan zasshi*, which, in March 1897, declared in an editorial that there was a 'pressing need' (*kyūmu*) for reform in *yose*. After explaining that storytellers (*kōdanshi*) were 'in a vocation in which they are duty bound to offer guidance (*kyōdō*)',[64] the editorial cautioned against debasing the art 'as mere light entertainment'. It urged them not merely to dismiss members of the audience who snored during performances as 'unseemly' (*futeisai*), but to consider such behaviour as, at least in part, a sign of the storyteller's own 'neglect' (*fuchūi*). The editorial went on to warn that, if *yose* were to be made attractive to all, including women and children, the root cause of unseemly behaviour would have to be addressed. It also called on the 'storytelling community in general to appraise highly the popularity of stenography', which was then developing as a means of taking down stories verbatim for use in journals and books. It concluded that if the standard of performances could be raised sufficiently to attract more women and children, audiences and storytellers alike would benefit and a contribution would be made to society (Kōdan 1897:1–2). The *Kōdan zasshi* editorial expressed a persistent concern that narrators not lose touch with the general populace. The editorial indicates that many *rakugoka* saw their art as a medium for all, unlike the high arts of *kabuki* and *noh*, which were associated more with the aristocracy and wealthier upper classes.

Debate about *rakugo* stimulated audience interest and reinvigorated the art form. *Rakugoka* responded in a number of ways, experimenting with story content, presentation style and even the use of props. Differences over these matters, some of which involved Black, sometimes caused rifts within the ranks. The tension between the need to adapt and fears that adaptation would compromise the art form remained unresolved as long as the wider reform debate continued.

One of the earliest experimenters was San'yūtei En'yū. In November 1880, this prominent *rakugoka* broke with metacommunicative convention by performing a comical dance routine at an unexpected moment in the narrative. En'yū suddenly rose from his *zabuton*, tucked the ends of his kimono up under his *obi* sash, exposing his long underwear and pranced around the

---

64 The word *kyōdō* implies *moral* guidance.

stage singing '*suteteko teko teko*' while miming the throwing away of his larger than average sized nose. The onomatopoeic '*suteteko teko teko*' derived from the verb *suteru* (throw away, or discard). The dance provoked outrage from purists, but was an instant hit with Tokyo audiences. On 1 January 1880 the population of Tokyo had rebounded to 957,121, close to its pre-Restoration peak of approximately a million. Many new arrivals in the city did not sympathise with the purists. They wanted novelty. En'yū's popularity rose to the point where he was performing at as many as 30 *yose* a day, and the word *suteteko* entered the lexicon to refer to men's long underwear. It is still in the dictionary today.

The influential head of the San'yūha, San'yūtei Enchō I, responded differently to calls for reform by adapting from foreign sources. By the time Henry Black encountered him, Enchō was considered one of the country's most accomplished *rakugoka*. Enchō's stories were often imbued with a strong moral tone, reputedly stemming from his childhood interest in Zen Buddhism (Morioka & Sasaki 1990:252–254). Although Enchō endeavoured to restrict props to the fan and *tenugui* to ensure *rakugo* remained in essence an oral art, this did not rule out his adapting material from foreign sources from the 1880s onward. Enchō's 1885 *Eikoku kōshi George Smith no den*, about the life of a dutiful child in England, appears to have reached him via an unidentified scholar of Western studies and to have originated in the British author Charles Reade's novel *Hard Cash* (Nakagomi 1998:281 [citing Nobuhiro Shinji]). His *Botan dōrō* is derived from a Chinese ghost story (Ōta 1998:175). Enchō's borrowings came principally from France and included *Matsu no misao bijin no ikiume* (A beauty buried alive) in 1886, *Kōshōbi* (The yellow rose) in 1887, and *Meijin kurabe: Nishiki no maigoromo* (Master artists: the brocade dancing robe), published in 1893 and acknowledged as an adaptation of Victorien Sardou's *La Tosca* (Morioka & Sasaki 1983:152; Nakagomi 1998:281). His last story *Sashimonoshi Meijin Chōji* (Master cabinet maker Chōji), an adaptation of Guy de Maupassant's *Un Parricide*, was published in 1895 as *Meijin Chōji* and was based on a version of *Un Parricide* related to Enchō by the wife of novelist and essayist Arishima Takeo (1878–1923), who had heard the story from one of Arishima's subordinates, a scholar of French literature (Yano 1999:152–153). *Meijin Chōji* was serialised in the *Chūō shinbun* between 28 April and 5 June 1895 and published in book form in October 1895. The story departs from the de Maupassant original in its second half where Enchō goes to considerable length to portray a pre-Restoration style court trial. Relying on a technicality only possible under an obsolete, but still popular, *samurai* code, Enchō showed how a self-confessed murderer could be judged innocent of the charge of patricide.

The timing of narration and publication of *Meijin Chōji* places it in a period when law reform was a topic of intense national debate. A significant number of Henry Black's narrations from these years also contain references to English legal practice, as well as comparisons between European and Japanese legal procedures. The incorporation of these themes into their stories is evidence that these two prominent *rakugoka* participated in the ongoing debate over legal reform in Japan, which involved the wholesale rewriting of the nation's legal codes under the influence of English, French and Prussian models. Whereas Enchō's story exhibits nostalgia for a pre-Restoration neo-Confucian morality, representing a challenge to the reforms, Black's references to the law invariably emphasise Western legal practice as the model for a modern, civilised country. Both exemplify different aspects of the debate over law reform – on the one hand, Enchō's representation of the desire to retain aspects of the indigenous Japanese spirit and, on the other, Henry's argument in favour of bringing the country's laws into line with what were understood as the civilised norms of Western Europe.[65]

A number of Enchō's other narrations probably owe their origins to foreign tales related to him in the same manner as *Un Parricide* without formal translation and without formal acknowledgement from Enchō (Nakagomi 1998). Enchō's initiative was copied by others with varying degrees of success and contributed to the development of a diverse repertoire placing *rakugo* beyond the banal and purely comic. San'yūtei Ensa (1853–1909), a disciple of San'yūtei Enchō, for example, adapted Dickens' *A Christmas Carol* (1843) as the narrated story *Kinoene no matsuri*.[66] The story was published as a *sokkibon* in *Hyakkaen* in March 1900 (Nakagomi 1998:281).

But it was Henry Black who became the preeminent adaptor of foreign material, claiming by 1901 to have 'translated no fewer than 14 English novels into Japanese' for narration (*Kobe Weekly Chronicle* 1901).

Henry Black the rakugoka

Henry Black's induction as a professional storyteller within the San'yūha signalled that the reform debate had reached the top ranks of *rakugoka*. The

65 For a detailed comparison and critique of the theme of legal reform in the narrations of Henry Black and San'yūtei Enchō's *Meijin Chōji*, see McArthur (2008).

66 *Kinoene* is one of the signs or 'stems' on the sexagenary cycle; *matsuri* means 'festival'.

guild's leadership actively solicited him in an attempt to provide something new for theatre patrons. The anti-foreign sentiment, which had caused Black's departure from English teaching, was no impediment to his acceptance by *yose* audiences and his *rakugoka* mentors. As a lower-class *yose geinin*, Henry Black was now no more marginalised than he had been as a shunned teacher of English. From his perspective, the entertainment he provided remained popular, assuring him of a steady income. Newspaper accounts indicate that audiences initially accepted him out of curiosity over his 'Western stories of human emotion' (*seiyō ninjō banashi*), but later appreciated the empathy and enthusiasm for Japan he displayed in his stories and lifestyle. This was a sore point with members of his family who worried that by 'going native' he was becoming uncivilised.

But for his part, Henry Black proved keen to contribute to the art form. His interest in innovation made him an outspoken pacesetter. Like Enchō, Black's response to the problem of the survival of the art form was to introduce adaptations of European novels to the repertoire. These were the major feature of his work in the 1880s and 1890s.

In the eight years between 1886 and 1894, Henry Black produced at least ten full-length, serialised narrations, most of which appear to have had European origins. The stories show an evolution from dogmatic adherence to the original European source to a much freer form of adaptation in which language and content demonstrate a more intimate and conscious engagement with the discourse of reform and modernity. Henry Black had found a formula that was to serve him well. It provided him with means for living, as well as a passage to the core of the spirit of Japan.

Chapter 8

Adapting European sensation fiction

> With the world these days subject to calls for reform (*tōsetsu kairyō*), and with so many things subject to change, everyone is trying their hardest...It would be convenient if there were one eye in the back of our head. Medical scientists are looking into the matter (Henry Black in an aside in his tale *Minashigo* [The orphan] [Kairakutei 1896:53]).

The year 1891 was probably Henry Black's most creative. In this one year alone, he produced seven new tales, including *Shachū no dokubari* (The poisoned pin in the coach), *Nagare no akatsuki* (Dawn at the river) and *Bara musume* (The rose girl), which were tales of murder and intrigue set in Paris. He did this as well as give regular performances of his tales in Tokyo, appear on stage in extracts from at least three *kabuki* plays, publish a self-help book on cosmetics and tour theatres in the Kansai district. Most of his stories from this creative year were from European sources. In terms of publications and adapted stories, the year's output put him well on the way to becoming the pre-eminent *rakugoka* adaptor of foreign material.[67] His stories provided audiences with a window onto life in Western European countries, aspects of whose lifestyles and forms of governance many in Japan now sought to emulate.

In his 1891 narration, *Eikoku Rondon gekijō miyage* (Story from a London theatre) (Eikokujin 1891:90), Henry jokingly proposed that to cope with the problems caused by rapid and confusing social change accompanying modernity, humans might be better off with rear vision. The comment was made in the context of a humorous aside on the need for reform in Japanese drinking habits. With its suggestion that medical science might reconfigure the human head to help cope with the upheavals accompanying reform,

67 Substantiating the English-language *Kobe Weekly* (1901:623) claim that he had 'translated no fewer than 14 English novels into Japanese' for narration.

the joke was in keeping with contemporary confidence in the ability of modern science to help humans overcome their problems. Henry used the same joke five years later in his adaptation of *Oliver Twist* as *Minashigo* (Ishii 1896) when he referred to the theft of a handkerchief from Fukuda Yūkichi's back pocket. In both stories the joke conveyed a hint of empathy with the audience, since it implied that *rakugoka* and audience alike were struggling to come to terms with the social and physical adjustments required to cope with the pace of change in Meiji Japan.

Henry's 1886 story, *Kusaba no tsuyu*, had adhered closely to Braddon's original plot and used highly stylised language similar to that of the *kabuki* theatre. But by 1891, he had evolved a presentation style that relied on vernacular Japanese and capitalised further on Japanese curiosity for all things European by adding liberal doses of information about everything from theatre-going in London to slum life in Paris.

Henry achieved his 1891 creative high point by adapting material from European mystery novels, including those of Mary Braddon and French writer Fortuné du Boisgobey. In doing so, he was following the lead of a number of well-established Japanese translators and editors who, in the decade before Henry achieved *shin'uchi* status, had been freely plagiarising, translating and adapting works by British, French and American Victorian-era sensation novelists. Among these translators were newspaper editor and novelist Kuroiwa Ruikō and writers such as Sudō Nansui (Nakajima 1964:20–22), both of whom helped popularise sensation fiction, especially detective novels, giving it a wider mass audience than pure fiction. Kuroiwa translated 75 Western novels, including works by Braddon, Victor Hugo, Alexandre Dumas and du Boisgobey.

Sensation fiction reached the height of its popularity among the British middle classes in the 1860s and 1870s, encouraging the examination and reflection of new psychological states and ways of relating to others that were associated with the dislocations of the Industrial Revolution. Among the genre's most popular writers were Mary Braddon, Wilkie Collins, Charles Dickens and Arthur Conan Doyle. Ian Ousby's description of the genre as showing 'a preference for the striking and unusual situation or series of events and for characters in the grip of strong or extreme emotion…combined with an interest in fact and topicality, creating an air of contemporary verisimilitude' (Ousby 1976:80) is one of the most comprehensive. Henry Black's choice of material reflects the genre's common themes, which Ousby (1976:81–82) identifies as 'a world of missing wills, long-lost heirs, mistaken identities, relatives who disappear to be reunited with their families in the final volume or installment, and illegitimate children who live in ignorance of their true parentage'.

Another reason for the popularity in Japan of sensation fiction was the debt it owed to English contemporary stage drama which used what Lyn Pykett lists as 'stylized dramatic tableaux, heightened emotions and extraordinary incidents of melodrama', including 'spectacular "special effects", involving dioramas, panoramas, elaborate lighting systems and machinery of all kinds' (Pykett 1994:2). These were precisely the devices found in Japan's own melodramatic *kabuki*, whose playwrights also relied on the same themes used in sensation fiction, such as frustrated love, poisonings and mistaken identity. It was not unusual for storytellers to attend *kabuki* performances to study the facial expressions and movements of actors so they could incorporate them into their own performances. Many plots were also shared by *kabuki* playwrights and storytellers. The synergies between drama and print in sensation fiction, and the cross-cultural borrowing from sensation fiction by Japanese authors, editors and storytellers assume importance in shedding light on Henry's *kabuki* performances and his choice of works by Mary Braddon, who had also been an actress. Henry's elaborate 1891 adaptation of Braddon's short story 'Her Last Appearance' (Eikokujin 1891), whose central character is an actress, is a prime example.

Another factor that boosted the popularity of sensation fiction in Japan was the growth in newspaper circulation. By the 1890s, canny editors had begun to increase their circulations by printing sensational accounts of court proceedings, which replicated many of the themes in mystery fiction. As already noted, Black also sourced material for his narrations from the Tokyo courts.

As in Europe, sensation fiction became a target of criticism in Japan, where purists considered it a cut below pure fiction. In May 1893, Kuroiwa found it necessary to mount an editorial defence of the genre in his newspaper *Yorozu chōhō* against claims that it would ruin the literary novel. Kuroiwa argued the need for a distinction between the literary novel (*shōsetsu*) and the detective novel (*tantei shōsetsu*), enumerating the distinctive features of detective fiction (Itō 2002:16–17). Recent scholarship supports Kuroiwa's claims that the genre played an important role. In the West, sensation fiction enabled the 'modern subject to criticise the system in which it also functions as an integral part', enabling it to both reinforce and resist 'the disciplinary regime it represents' (Thomas 1999:13). This was also the case in Japan, where the genre's 'combination of storytelling and social awareness' enabled its exponents to cleverly use its 'narrative and conceptual resources' to 'depict and critique contemporary Japanese society' (Seaman 2004:1). Consequently, editorial campaigners like Kuroiwa and former Freedom and People's Rights Movement activists like Henry Black were quick to realise the ideological potential of the genre.

For Henry Black, sensation fiction proved the perfect vehicle for conveying 19th-century notions of European modernity to curious audiences. All of the stories he produced in 1891 contain features that render them modern. In contrast to the earlier *Kusaba no tsuyu*, the 1891 adaptations of which the originals can be identified depart further from the original plots, attesting to Henry's increased confidence as an innovative storyteller. In theme, structure and the frequency of humorous and didactic digressions devoted to explanations of Western customs, the narrations dating from 1891 are the creations of an artist confident in the knowledge that he was supplying a product that was much in demand.

By the 1880s, Henry's adaptations followed a tried and true formula. For about two decades after 1880, a large number of European mystery novels were published as adaptive translations, known as *hon'an mono*, in book form or serialised in newspapers. By blending European and Japanese sensibilities to overcome barriers created by the direct translation of unfamiliar concepts, these cheap and widely read novels held an important place in popular culture in late 19th-century Japan. The capacity of audiences and readers to absorb edifying information had already been used by intellectuals, such as the Meirokusha members, who had displayed a propensity for including commentary and explanations on Western traits in the translations from Western sources published in their journal *Meiroku zasshi* (1976:xxi). In the 1880s, a new generation of translators and adaptors of European stories were at work, freely altering the original texts by changing names of characters and places, as well as tone and plot, to familiarise readers with European cultures, geographies and notions of modernity within a Japanese psychological framework. The extent of the translators' originality in their adaptive translations was often ambiguous, but as a genre, the intertextual transformations that the translations represent are useful tools in assessing how the mass media facilitated intercultural transaction in early modern Japan. Here, the concept of 'transaction' most appropriately reflects what J Scott Miller has identified as the role of adaptive translations during this period – 'to tame and modify the foreign to fit domestic sensibilities, usually in the service of art or entertainment' (Miller 2001:13).

In many instances, the altering of placenames to Japanese ones in *hon'an mono* gave new mnemonic significance to erstwhile European sites of action or characters. The practice of using *kanji* enabled sophisticated wordplay and puns in choosing or adapting the names. Japanese names of characters and places were often chosen because of the similarities between the sounds of *kanji* characters, which usually have at least two pronunciations, or even because of the meanings in the *kanji*. A clever writer could even choose *kanji* which both reflected the sound of the original French or English name and the personality of the character. In Henry's stories, this strategy resulted in characters with common surnames like Yamada and Ito, as if to emphasise their ordinariness. These characters read *The Times* and rode in omnibuses, but returned home to dine on *miso* soup. In at least two instances, Henry also appears to have commemorated friends by giving their names to key characters. Henry's contemporary, editor and publisher Kuroiwa Ruikō, was also a master at the construction of names for eponymous purposes. A prime example is Kuroiwa's use of the name Kawabayashi Ikudō for the scheming pharmacist and killer originally known as Victor Carrington in the adaptation of the Mary Braddon murder-mystery *Diavola*. Braddon's choice of the name Victor reflects the character's desire to dominate his victims. But Kuroiwa creates a new surname by combining *kanji* characters signifying skin (*kawa*) and grove (*hayashi*) to give the character macabre overtones that suggest an intention to kill (McArthur & Bryce 2007).[68] Hybrid characters and liminal worlds such as these permitted readers to feel an affinity with their characters while vicariously experiencing exotic locations such as Paris or London.

This form of adaptive translation was also known as *gōketsuryū* (heroic style). It was replaced in mainstream literature around 1886 by *shūmitsu buntai* (minute style), which purported to be an accurate rendition of the original.[69] But, while a better educated public began to seek more faithfully rendered versions of foreign literature by the mid-1880s, Henry's

---

68 It helped that the phonological significance of *kawa* also evoked the meaning of 'river', allowing the name to share the overall watery motif in his version of the story, entitled *Sute obune* (Abandoned small boat).

69 For a fuller discussion of Meiji-era adaptive translation, see J Scott Miller (2001), especially p. 74.

adaptations and their publication in book form and as serialised versions in newspapers indicate a residual (and numerically significant) demand for a medium able to interpret Western subject matter and give meaning to the transition to modernity experienced by audiences in the 1890s.

The age of reform

Henry Black's narrations during the 1890s show that modernity was as contested then as it is now. Modernity was both disturbing and exciting. It disrupted people's lives, but it also provided opportunities for personal improvement. Henry's 1891 stories therefore served as blueprints for survival in Meiji Japan.

The Japanese had grounds for mistrusting many reforms aimed at achieving modernity. By the 1890s, many had tired of the government's unrelenting series of reform edicts aimed at inculcating civilisation and enlightenment in the populace. Henry's stories played to this sense of frustration by sometimes targeting the overzealous and bothersome instigators and perpetrators of the reform agenda – the bureaucracy. He got away with satirising the bureaucracy because he sugar-coated his warnings about the downside of modernity with humour, enabling the stories he told to serve as antidotes to his audiences' resentment and fatigue at the pace and nature of change.

The word *kairyō* (reform) was used to encompass the changes. It appeared at least as early as 1873 in a petition composed by Maejima Hisoka (1835–1919), an official interpreter to the *bakufu* and subsequently founder of Japan's postal service. Before the 1868 Meiji Restoration, Maejima had petitioned the *shōgun* for the replacement of *kanji* with a style closer to the spoken language. Then in 1869 and 1873, he directed similar petitions at the Meiji government (Kornicki 1982:4). The word *kairyō* appeared in the title of the 1873 petition. Pleas for *kairyō* were 'legion' in the *Tōkyō nichi nichi shinbun* newspaper during the 1880s, rendering it a 'shibboleth' associated with Westernisation (Kornicki 1982:4). It is interesting that the word should have been initially linked to the reform of the language. Language reform was soon to become an issue close to the hearts of many writers who, as noted earlier, were inspired by the vernacular used by the oral storytellers at a time when the difference between spoken and literary Japanese was comparable to that between today's spoken English and the language of Shakespeare. *Kairyō* very quickly expanded to accommodate all manner of reform targets. Pleas in *Tōkyō nichi nichi shinbun* included calls for reform of dress through the introduction of Western-style clothing, because it was more suited for working in, and even calls for the genetic modification of the Japanese race through intermarriage with European and American women. *Kairyō* appears frequently in Henry's narrations, reflecting the contemporary discourse of the phenomenon. In *Eikoku Rondon gekijō miyage*, for example, Henry even used the word in reference to the persistent calls for reform made by Fukuchi Gen'ichirō, editor of *Tōkyō nichi nichi shinbun* from 1874 to 1888, in a remark to audiences on the differences between Western and Japanese theatre:

> Types of theatre in my country Britain, and in Japan, are fairly different. Above all, there are gentlemen such as Fukuchi Gen'ichirō doing their utmost to reform the theatre. One of the issues is whether it is better to reform by adopting the Western approach, or whether the Japanese theatre is better reformed while retaining its unique look entirely (Eikokujin 1891:12).

To carry out its reforms, the government relied heavily on its agents in the bureaucracy as mediators, interpreters and enforcers of its regulations, and the bureaucrats were by no means universally popular. Many of them, at least in the first decades after the Restoration, came from the same *samurai* class and had been the oppressors before the Restoration. Their inclusion in the bureaucracy reinforced and prolonged the divide between bureaucrats and ordinary people during the early Meiji years (Garon 1997:18).

As citizens of the new Japan, everyone, including, of course, theatre audiences, was the subject of an ongoing experiment in which the Meiji elite, to which the country's bureaucrats belonged, sought to mould minds as they created a new society. Sheldon Garon, who argues that the Meiji government was even more interventionist and centralised than the preceding administration of the Tokugawa shogunate, has characterised this experiment as 'social management' to distinguish it from Western theories of social control (Garon 1997:xv). Indicative of the hands-on role the bureaucracy played in the Meiji years was the 1870–1885 Kōbushō (Ministry of Industry), which constructed railway and telegraph networks to support economic growth and provided tangible, nationwide evidence of the government's commitment to bringing the entire nation within its aegis (Morris-Suzuki 1994:73). Not even individuals could escape the reforming hand of the state. Ordinary citizens became the target of a constant stream of edicts from above, including edicts banning urination in public and restricting public bathing.

Little wonder then that, in enforcing these edicts, the bureaucracy became a target of resentment. Nishimura Shigeki, writing in *Meiroku zasshi* as early as 1875, summed up the resentment in his complaint that 'high regional officials are like territorial lords of old, and even the lower, unranked clerks trifle with the people oppressively. Legislation is entirely in the hands of officials who cause the people to obey the law whether they agree or not and who punish those who disobey' (*Meiroku zasshi* 1976:522). Capitalising on this, the press soon took to lampooning bureaucrats and attacking them whenever they were seen to be corrupt (Lehmann 1982:199).

Some of the criticisms were allayed when the bureaucracy was rationalised in 1885 to cope with the increased intricacy of its administrative load (Lehmann 1982:199–200). New regulations also ensured that more university graduates entered the bureaucracy, reducing its dominance by those who gained their posts by virtue of *samurai* descent. For these reasons, historians place the birth of the modern Japanese bureaucracy in the mid-1880s (Beasley 1989:649–651). After the introduction of the merit-based system, the bureaucracy grew in prestige and influence throughout the rest of the Meiji period (Lehmann 1982:201). But this did not stop many zealous bureaucrats fuelling resentment by jailing their critics. In the early 1890s, for example, Home Ministry officials jailed many journalists and suspended hundreds of others (Huffman 1997:259). These were precisely the years when Henry Black was making his mark as a *rakugoka*. He too, together with newspaper cartoonists and editors, indulged in occasional lampooning and criticism of bureaucrats.

Henry Black had no particular fondness for conniving bureaucrats. His father had lost his job as a newspaper editor through the machinations of bureaucrats dissatisfied with his criticisms of them. Henry's *Shachū no dokubari* (The poisoned pin in the coach) contains a prime example of his lampooning of the Meiji-era bureaucracy. In the tale, Henry shows he was aware of the intricacies of government regulations that governed the conduct of high-ranking bureaucrats in public places and reinforced their social standing, setting them apart from other citizens.[70] In a scene

70 For a sample of disciplinary measures pertaining to bureaucrats in 1876, see 'Rules for Disciplinary Punishment of Officials' and 'Instructions to be Observed in Inflicting Disciplinary Punishments' (McLaren 1979:II,264–265 and 266–268), especially Item II

indicative of popular resentment towards the bureaucracy's prestige, he alleged, tongue-in-cheek, of course, that, if a *sōninkan*, a bureaucrat ranked just below a government minister, was seen entering a lowly sake bar, he would later have to produce paperwork explaining his actions to his superiors:

> It is no loss of status for anyone to enter an ice seller's stall and enjoy ice cream or lemonade, even if it's a gentleman out walking with his wife. In my country Britain there are no ice sellers, but there are places where you can get a drink. These places have customers of not just poor social standing (*mibun no warui mono*) but also of quite high standing. It is said that it's not a bit unbecoming or bad mannered for someone to have a beer or a wine of one's liking and then leave.
>
> Customs are different depending on the country. In Japan, what would happen if a *sōninkan* went into a bar (*sakaya*) and doffed his hat? If such a thing were to appear in the newspapers, he would either issue a *shintai ukagai* [a document requesting a decision on one's course of action from a superior after one had made an error on the job], or would have to quit his job (Kairakutei 1891b:48–49).

Miso soup with *The Times*

Buffeted by reform and hectored by the government and its agents in the bureaucracy, Henry's audiences sought respite in the theatres. In 1891, Henry provided them with a diet of stories which transported them to another more exotic world in which people rode in coaches, attended the opera and had their *miso* soup while reading *The Times*.

One of Henry's more popular works that year was a complex and entertaining adaptation of French author Fortuné du Boisgobey's 1881 murder mystery *Le Crime de l'omnibus*,[71] to which Henry gave the title *Shachū no dokubari* (The poisoned pin in the coach). It was later published by Sanyūsha. In the original, du Boisgobey tells how his two heroes,

---

of Imperial Decree No. 35, 14 April 1876, which notes that 'those persons, who by not regulating their behaviour bring discredit upon the service, shall also be considered as guilty of a "fault" and shall be liable to a punishment'.

71 Published by Feuilleton in *Le Petit Journal* 13 March to 1 July 1881; also published as *The Mystery of an Omnibus* (Munro, New York, 1882) and *An Omnibus Mystery* (Vizetelly, London, 1885). I am indebted to Terry Hale of the University of Hull for pointing out the origin of the tale.

artist Paul Freneuse and his companion Binos, uncover the reason for the mysterious death of a beautiful young woman on an omnibus travelling between Jardin des Plantes and Place Pigalle. To cut the plot to 14 short narrated episodes, each with a cliffhanger ending, Henry considerably abridged and simplified the story. For example, Du Boisgobey plants a fragment of a letter with the murder weapon, a poisoned pin, on the coach floor, but Henry dispenses with the letter fragment in his version. Du Boisgobey's large cast of characters included prostitutes, artists and the many denizens of cabarets and cafes around Montmartre. In Henry's version, extraneous characters are almost completely eliminated, but he retained the essential elements. Both stories rely on a poisoned pin and a series of improbably coincidental encounters between several Parisians whose lives are linked.

Henry's tale begins as a mysterious woman begs to board a full, late night coach in Paris. The coachman refuses her a seat, but when a male passenger offers to give up his seat and sit outside with the coachman, the coachman relents and lets the woman board. When the coach reaches its terminus, the woman and a young artist, Kanō Motokichi, are the only remaining passengers. But when Motokichi and the coachman attempt to wake the woman, they realise she is dead. When Motokichi finds a pin of the type women use in their dress on the coach, he souvenirs it and takes it home. Later, when his art student Itō Jirōkichi teases Motokichi's cat with the pin, accidentally pricking it, the cat dies instantly. They deduce that the pin is poisoned. Itō persuades Motokichi not to go to the police, but to let him find the killer because his hobby is detective work. Ito keeps the pin and departs.

Plots involving an unidentified person found dead on a vehicle were a novelty. Australian novelist Fergus Hume used a similar plot in 1886, five years after du Boisgobey, in his extremely popular novel *The Mystery of a Hansom Cab*. Hume took the unusual step of acknowledging du Boisgobey's plot at the end of the first chapter, using the conceit of an editorial in the Melbourne newspaper, *The Argus*, which questions whether du Boisgobey 'would have been daring enough to write about a crime being committed in such an unlikely place as a hansom cab'. This places Henry together with Hume among a select number of people who used the device. The timing of Henry's effort, ten years after du Boisgobey's novel, provides further insight into the early development of the detective novel in Japan.

Henry appears to have acknowledged his male lover, Takamatsu Motokochi, in using the name Kanō Motokichi for the central character

(Paul Freneuse in du Boisgobey's version). Henry and Motokichi were living together in the year he published *Shachū no dokubari.*

The cover of the Diet Library's copy of the 189-page *Shachū no dokubari* shows a European woman regally posed with her arms resting on the back of a plush chair. A horsedrawn coach traverses the middle distance and there are turreted buildings in the background. Occasional illustrations in the book show key moments in the story. All of the characters are in Western dress, with women wearing fashionable crinolines and hats and the men wearing top hats and carrying walking sticks.

In Henry's version of the story, Motokichi attends the opera with retired businessman Mr Yamada and Yamada's daughter, Otaka. At the opera, Motokichi recognises a man and woman in the audience as having been passengers on the coach. Yamada acknowledges that he once had business dealings with the man, whom he describes as a shady lawyer, and that he thinks his name was Tsuchiya. Motokichi recognises him as the man who gave up his seat on the coach for the dead woman and the woman with him at the opera as the one sitting beside the dead woman in the coach. But when an aide to Yamada brings a telegram advising him of the death of his brother Ichizō in Germany, Yamada immediately leaves the opera. After the performance, Motokichi attempts to follow the two people spotted in the audience, but they cannily evade him.

In an attempt to locate the two people, Motokichi's friend Itō Jirōkichi visits a pub to seek the assistance of a drinking acquaintance, who is coincidentally Tsuchiya (see figure 14), whom Motokichi had seen at the opera. He gives Tsuchiya the pin. Tsuchiya later takes Itō to the boarding house where the dead woman lived and urges him to find out her name from the occupants. Itō informs the landlady of the woman's death and together they visit the morgue where a doctor has pronounced the woman dead from a heart ailment. Itō learns that the dead woman was Suzuki Okatsu from Italy.

In Part Six, we learn that Tsuchiya has been hired by Yamada to determine whether Yamada's dead brother had descendants. Tsuchiya advises that the brother had a daughter named Okatsu by a mistress called Suzuki Otomi in Turin 20 years before. He tells Yamada that the brother's will stipulated that his fortune, amounting to at least a million yen, should go to Okatsu. But Tsuchiya explains that the fortune can now go to Yamada, as Okatsu has been found dead. Tsuchiya obtains a promissory note from Yamada stating that, if Tsuchiya can obtain proof of Okatsu's death, Tsuchiya will get a 20 per cent share of the fortune. He explains to Yamada that this will satisfy French law, which stipulates that if a will's beneficiary cannot be located or proven dead, other family claimants cannot receive the money until 30 years have elapsed.

In Part Seven, Kanō consoles his life model Onobu who fears for her sister Okatsu, who has not visited her for three days. When Itō arrives and informs them that the dead woman was also called Okatsu, the distraught Onobu faints. Coincidentally, Yamada and Otaka arrive at the studio, where Yamada surmises from Itō's tale that his brother had two daughters. Yamada later receives a visit from his brother Ichizō's clerk, Inoue, who informs him that the two daughters are from the same former mistress and that the will gives Ichizō's fortune to both of them.

There follow a number of plot twists that frequently rely on coincidence, during which Itō deduces that the woman who evaded Motokichi on the night of the opera has abducted Onobu and may be contemplating killing her. Itō enlists the aid of a detective, Kimura, who informs him that Tsuchiya is not to be trusted. He says Tsuchiya had known all along that the dead woman was Okatsu, but needed to use Itō to visit the morgue to obtain proof of Okatsu's death so that he could get a share of Yamada's inheritance. Kimura disguises himself as a coachman and offers to take Tsuchiya's wife and Onobu to the graveyard where Okatsu is buried, but, on the way, he stops outside Motokichi's house and insists that Tsuchiya's wife go in. When she refuses, he forces her out of the coach and into a dramatic confrontation with Motokichi and Itō. There, he removes his disguise and tells her that he knows she is Okatsu's killer. He demands that she hand over the poisoned pin. The woman stabs herself with the pin and dies.

In the final episode, Onobu has married Motokichi. Onobu is in the living room doing embroidery when Motokichi enters and kisses her. He has come back from Tsuchiya's trial. Tsuchiya has been sentenced to death for killing Okatsu. Yamada has been sentenced to life imprisonment after the promissory note was found during a police search of Tsuchiya's home. 'That all happened three years ago', Black concludes. 'I have heard that they have since had a baby boy. I do not know what will happen to the couple, but I join with you, dear readers, in wishing them a long and happy life together.'

Like du Boisgobey, Henry takes us on a tour of Paris, in which he introduces his audience to the theatre, a morgue, a graveyard and the down-at-heel home of the dead woman's former landlady. But the significance of the story lies not just in its tour of Paris. A close study of Henry's version suggests that he designed it as an opportunity to showcase modern life in a Western European metropolis. Modern touches are the telegram received by the villain Yamada at the opera and the notion of speedy, long-distance travel exemplified by Tsuchiya's plan to mount a cross-border escape to Italy by train. In the spirit of the Meirokusha journal writers, Henry included his didactic explications of French law as it pertained to a woman's right to inherit property and the notion of the statute of limitations. Each of these examples reflected popular Japanese interest in contemporary aspects of modernity associated with the West.

Stories for the times

Shachū no dokubari was but one of several stories Henry narrated or published in 1891. Among his other works that year was the 42-instalment *Nagare no akatsuki* (Dawn at the river), which appeared in *Yamato shinbun* from January to March (Morioka & Sasaki 1983:142) and was also published in book form by San'yūsha. This was a tragic romance dealing with the French aristocrat, Baron Sawanabe, who flees France for London during the French Revolution. It contains elements reminiscent of the French teacher Charles Darnay in Dickens' *A Tale of Two Cities* and relies on the stock sensation fiction device of identical twin brothers, one intrinsically good and the other dissolute. In London, Sawanabe becomes a teacher of French and marries a farmer's daughter called Osen. Shortly after this, Napoleon takes over in France and the baron returns to his home country without Osen. Osen bears twins, but faced with financial difficulties, throws one of the twins, Jōji, into the Thames. Jōji is rescued by a fisherman and becomes an honest clerk for a moneylender, until 20 years later he encounters his good-for-nothing brother. Pressed for money by his twin, Jōji begins embezzling from his boss. His crime is in danger of being discovered, so while his boss is convalescing in the country, Jōji poisons his brother and makes it appear as if he himself has committed suicide over the embezzlement by faking a will and substituting his own body with his brother's. He takes 10,000 *yen* and makes his escape. The moneylender returns and, unaware of the ruse, holds a funeral. A detective notices that the skin on the body's hands and feet are tough and thinks this is unusual for a clerk. Jōji goes to France, where he falls in love with his half-sister not realising who she really is. This becomes the catalyst for his arrest and confession of his past misdemeanours, whereupon he is sentenced. He meets his father and reproves him for abandoning his mother, Osen. His remorseful father reunites with Osen and they live as husband and wife once again.

Another work produced in 1891 was *Eikoku no otoshibanashi* (The beer drinking contest). It appeared in the journal *Hyakkaen* in March 1891. This humorous tale, set in England, has subsequently entered the *rakugo* canon and is still occasionally narrated in theatres, although most people in the audience are unaware that Henry Black created it. The story is of a colonel who offers to pay a large sum to any of his men who can drink 15 bottles of beer. John, nicknamed 'Wine Barrel', accepts the challenge but requests an hour's delay. When he returns, he promptly downs the 15 bottles. In his absence, John had drunk the same amount of beer to confirm that he could win the bet.

In 1891, *Yamato shinbun* also published Henry's *Setsunaru tsumi* (The pitiful sin) in 39 instalments between 8 May and 21 June. This murder mystery involves a double love triangle. Ohana wants to marry actor Saitō Eizaburō, so kills his good-for-nothing wife, Omatsu, by feeding her powdered glass. But Eizaburō flees and changes his name to Saitō Kōzō. By the time Ohana locates him, she has contracted tuberculosis. Kōzō takes pity on Ohana and decides to die with her. During a court trial, he attempts to confess that he was guilty with Ohana, but after being persuaded by Okiku, the daughter of the detective Takayama, he testifies that he is innocent. Saitō then marries Okiku (Itō 2002:175–176).

San'yūsha also released Henry's *Bara musume* (The rose girl) in 1891 (Morioka & Sasaki 1983:144). It was a detective story, set in Paris, and involved a plot to assassinate the French crown prince. The anarchist Ohana plans to disguise herself as a flower girl to lure the prince and kill him with poison gas. When the Chief of Police in Paris, Kawamichi Shō, learns that German political offender and scientist, Nishino Takeshi, has entered the country with the intention of assassinating the crown prince, he puts Detective Ōmura on the case. Ōmura learns that the prince has become enamoured of the beautiful flower-seller, Ohana, but that she is really Nishino's younger sister. Ōmura apprehends Ohana and gains her confidence. The information he gains from Ohana enables him to arrest several accomplices, but Ohana escapes.

The story is full of action, contains accounts of nightlife in 19th-century Paris and introduces brandy, morphine, an attractive flower girl and a duel with swords. It was later published 'as a translation' titled *Kokuji tantei* (Affairs of state detective) by Kikuchi Yūhō in 1898 in the *Ōsaka mainichi shinbun*. The source of the story remains unknown (Itō 2002:174–175).

As well as performing in Tokyo's theatres, Henry Black visited Kyoto in 1891 to perform at the Shōfukutei where he narrated *Nagare no akatsuki* in afternoon shows and *Eikoku Rondon gekijō miyage* in the evenings (Kurata 1981–87:V,114). The latter shows Henry in his element, giving extended and colourful descriptions of the theatre in London, English marriage customs, and even an amusing anecdote about the British prime minister, none of which were in the Braddon original. Seventeen-year-old Gātsurudo, daughter of a wealthy farmer called Beniyūeru, is visiting her aunt in London. When her aunt takes her to the Adelphi Theatre, she falls in love with a spendthrift actor Sumerurī.

They marry and Gātsurudo's father disowns her, frustrating Sumerurī's attempts to live off his wife's dowry. Sumerurī gambles their money away, obliging Gātsurudo to train as an actress. She is very successful and begins to live apart from her husband. But when an admirer, John Brown, proposes marriage, Gātsurudo declines the offer because she is already married. Knowing that Sumerurī is dissolute and treats Gātsurudo badly, Brown kills him. He persuades Gātsurudo to marry him by threatening to commit suicide if she refuses his hand. When the police close in on Brown, the couple leave for Paris, where Brown begins to waste their money, obliging Gātsurudo to again return to England to resume her acting career. In a delectably gruesome scene, Brown takes out a pistol and blows his brains out when confronted by a British detective in a gentlemen's club in Paris.

Yet another of the tales Henry narrated in 1891 was *Iwade ginkō chishio no tegata* (The bloodstained handprint at the Iwade Bank). In the opening scene, sleet falls as Iwade Yoshio, president of the Iwade Bank, leaves the bank and hurries toward the station by London Bridge to catch his regular train home near the town of Chīsubikki. Just short of the station, he encounters a filthy, shivering urchin, Yamada Matashichi, who picks the banker's pocket (see figure 8). Iwade realises he cannot pay for his train ticket and returns to the bank to get some cash. The following day, the police inform him that Matashichi has admitted to the crime.

When Iwade meets Matashichi, he confesses, adding that his mother had died of cold and hunger on the night of the theft. Iwade offers to look after him and give him a job in his bank. At the age of 20, Matashichi and Iwade's only daughter Omasa fall in love and make a secret vow to marry. Itō, the bank's manager, learns of the couple's love for each other and informs Iwade, who accuses Matashichi of duping his daughter so that he can marry her for her inheritance. Iwade angrily dismisses Matashichi, ordering him never to come to their house again, but gives him 200 *yen* to help him make his way in the world. Matashichi humbly thanks Iwade for all he has done for him and promises to repay the money. A few days later, the normally punctual Iwade fails to return home for his evening meal and is found stabbed to death in his office (see figure 9). Matashichi is arrested in Liverpool while attempting to board a ship for the United States. Omasa insists that Matashichi is innocent and visits her father's brother, Iwade Takejirō, a lawyer, for help. Takejirō uses a magic lantern (see figure 7) to match a bloodstained handprint found near the corpse to the handprint of the bank's janitor, Katō Torakichi, who confesses to the murder. Takejirō persuades Omasa's mother to consent to Omasa's marriage to Matashichi. Takejirō overcomes the mother's objections by arguing that Oliver Cromwell, Napoleon, General Ulysses Grant and Japan's great feudal-era unifier Toyotomi Hideyoshi all rose from humble origins to eventually contribute to their country. The couple live happily ever after in England.

Henry Black's prolific list of titles represents a remarkable achievement in terms of performance and publication. It is testimony to his fertile imagination and creative ability. It is even more remarkable when we consider that, in addition to his regular performances in Tokyo, Henry spent some of 1891 offering narrations at theatres in Kyoto and Kobe in the Kansai region and appearing in several plays, known as *kōdan shibai* (plays by storytellers).

In March 1891, for example, he appeared in *kōdan shibai*, performing the *kabuki* roles of Kumagai in *Heike Monogatari* and Rochishin in *Suikoden* (Morioka & Sasaki 1983:144). There is also evidence that in April, he 'threatened to quit San'yūha unless given in *kōdan shibai* one of the major roles in *Chūshingura*' (Morioka & Sasaki 1983:144). This play, known in English as 'The treasury of loyal retainers' details a revenge killing by 47 *rōnin* (masterless *samurai*) and is one of the *kabuki* repertoire's most popular offerings. It is based on events in Edo in the years 1701–1703. Henry demanded the part of Yuranosuke, leader of the 47 *rōnin*, or at least the role of Kampei, or his wife Okaru (Morioka & Sasaki 1983:144). Both Kampei and Okaru are part of the household of *daimyō* Enya Hangan, whose enforced suicide is the reason for the eventual act of revenge. Henry's demands hint at an egocentric nature that caused friction between him and other guild members throughout his career. Accounts cited by Morioka and Sasaki (1983:144) show that, in June 1891, Henry also played the female role of Omura in *Ibaraki Dōji, Sōzaburo no Imōto Omura* at the Nakamura-za Theatre.

Participation in *kabuki* performances required an ability to memorise complex dialogue, mimic the requisite stylised gestures and facial expressions, and carry them out with split-second timing. The effort required to play so many roles in one year and in front of demanding audiences would have been tremendous, especially for someone like Henry Black who was not a professional *kabuki* actor. In the midst of a very busy year, Henry also managed to publish a book on cosmetics with his male lover, Takamatsu Motokichi, whose name he used for the central character in *Shachū no dokubari*.

Stories as texts for shaping history

Henry's narrations from 1891 suggest that he was motivated by the sense of mission to civilise that he had already displayed years earlier as a speaker at meetings of the Freedom and People's Rights Movement. While the scarcity of eyewitness comment on Henry's performances and of newspaper reviews of his stories and performances make it difficult to gauge his impact, it can safely be assumed that his success had its basis in popular demand and that, once he had narrated his stories and had them printed, they entered the public domain where they were received by audiences who were free to act upon the ideas conveyed by his stories.

The French hermeneutic phenomenologist Paul Ricoeur famously noted that once initiated 'our deeds escape us and have effects which we did not intend'. Ricoeur was convinced that our actions can 'contribute' to the emergence of patterns of human action which he described as the 'social imprint' (Ricoeur 1973:101). Applying the language of intertextuality in assessing the 'social imprint' of Henry's narrations as texts, it is also useful to combine Ricoeur's approach with that of popular culture historian John Storey. Storey considers that such texts 'do not simply reflect history, they make history and are part of its processes and practices' (Storey 1996:3). In this way, we see that culture can 'constitute the structure and shape of history' (Ricoeur 1973:101). In the language of intertextuality, this amounts to saying that *rakugo* 'texts' – the stories as told by the narrators, especially the more innovative ones, and the ideas they contained – were a medium which could shape opinion and events in the Meiji era.

Statements made by Henry Black in interview (Nyorai 1896) and in comment in the printed versions of his narrations indicate that he recognised the importance of the audience and understood them to accept him as a moderniser. Francis McCullagh's observation that Henry's choice of European material for his Japanese audiences was 'almost inevitable…in order to meet the continual demand for novelty' (McCullagh 1902:219) helps us to appreciate Henry's understanding of what audiences wanted. What they wanted, it seems, was tales in which they could vicariously experience modern Europe as a precursor of their own future. For audiences listening to Henry in Meiji Japan's variety halls, the future held the prospect of a world of fast trains, international travel, great metropolises which served as transport hubs, a legal code that guaranteed equality for all, and amazing scientific discoveries.

Above:

Figure 1. Henry Black, middle, with Gaisberg's assistant, Mr Addis, at an entertainment quarter in Tokyo in 1903.

Photo courtesy of EMI Group Archive Trust, UK.

Left:

Figure 2. Henry Black posing as Omiwa in a New Year greeting card promoting the *kabuki* play *Imoseyama* (Mt. Imo and Mt. Se).

With permission from Mr Kanō Hisashi.

Left:

Figure 3. An imprint of Black's insignia with the intertwined initials HJB for Henry James Black.

With permission from Mr Kanō Hisashi.

Below:

Figure 4. Gunji was the boy whom Henry took into his household in the early 1900s.

With permission from Mr Kanō Hisashi.

Facing page:

Figure 5. Section of an article about Henry Black (Ishii Burakku) in *Miyako shinbun*, 12 January, 1902, p. 6.

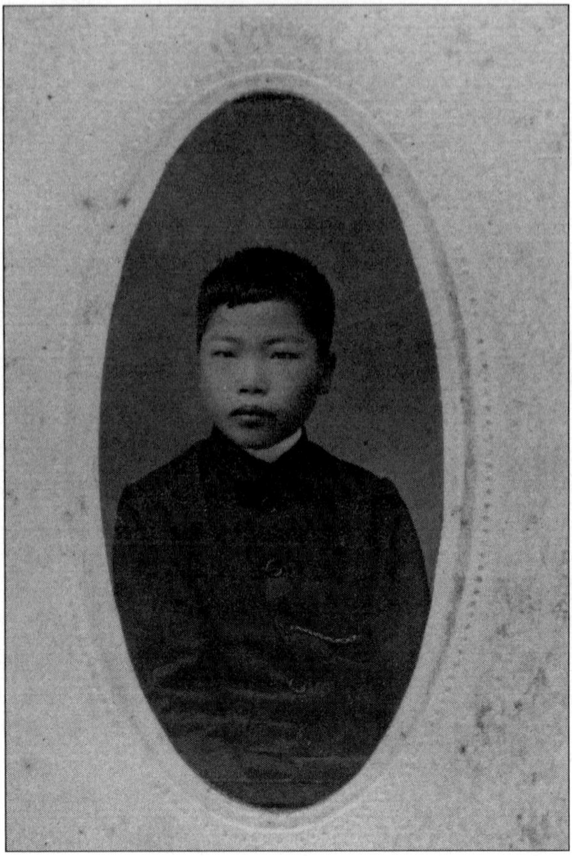

英國へ歸ッた併し日本で育ッた男ですから矢張り日本が好いたと見え、再び渡航して來たのハ當人十六才の時です夫れから何かな文明的の事を日本へ廣めんと殊勝な考へを起した、すると此の頃自由民權の説などが追々八釜敷くなッて來て、演説よ新聞と頻りに論議を始めたのです、政府でも驚いたのゝ呆れたのゝ知らねが、少しく過劇な論をすると直ぐと演説ハ中止解散新聞ハ發行停止と云ふ樣な状況であつた、恰ど此の頃ブラックハ築地の万年橋の待合福田屋で演説會を開きしが、隨分過激な事を云ふ處から打捨て置られないとて警視廳でハ頻りに心配をしたが、何分英國人であるから日本の警察權で何する事も出來ません、夫れから警視總監より外務省へ照會をして英國公使に談判をするなど、大分手數を掛けたと云ふ事を聞いて居るが、夫からやッと落語家の鑑札を受けて寄席へ出る事となり、故人伯圓の前で例の血染の手形を演ッた、これが日本藝人となッた手解きです、

石井ブラック

合名會社三井銀行第拾七期決算公告

（明治三十四年下半季）

貸借對照表

負債

諸預金	貳九、〇四八、四九〇・七壹參
支拂送金手形	七八、六九六・六六〇
再割引手形	貳、〇壹九、貳壹壹・八八〇
他店より借	六壹、九參八・九〇〇
雜勘定	七八八・壹〇〇
資本金	五、〇〇〇、〇〇〇・〇〇〇
積立金	四、九〇〇、〇〇〇・〇〇〇
當期純益金	參五壹、壹〇八・九貳四
前期繰越金	壹壹五、貳五壹・六七壹
合計	四壹、五八五、四八六・八四八

資產

貸附金	五、〇八九、〇九貳・九參〇
當座預金貸越	貳、四九四、壹〇九・參貳〇
割引手形	壹〇、八壹壹、貳五四・八貳〇
荷爲替手形	七四、七六八・八九〇
預ケ金	貳九、參八〇・五七〇
他店へ貸	五九、〇七壹・六四〇
國債、地方債證券	壹四、九六壹、五七〇・四〇六
會社債券及株券	參貳、壹八壹・八四〇
雜勘定	壹、五四四、八〇七・四〇〇
營業用地所建物及什器 地所及建物	四、壹〇四、壹八六・貳六〇
金銀在高	貳、參八五、壹貳貳・七七貳
合計	四壹、五八五、四八六・八四八

損益勘定

當期純益金	參五壹、壹〇八・九貳四
前期繰越金	壹壹五、貳五壹・六七壹
合計	四六六、參六〇・五九五

三菱合資會社銀行部第十三期實際報告

貸借對照表

負債に屬する分

資本金	壹、〇〇〇、〇〇〇・〇〇
定期預金	五、貳九八、四九五・四壹
當座預金	八、七九貳、五貳參・貳六
別段預金	貳〇九、〇參壹・八九
振出手形	八參六・貳貳
支拂手形	貳七九・壹五
他店より借	參貳參、七九七・六參
前半期繰越高	壹、壹九六、參七六・參七
當期純益金	貳參六、壹八七・〇參
合計	壹七、〇五七、五貳七・貳六

資產に屬する分

貸附金	壹、九四七、五七貳・八貳
當座預金貸越	四五五、貳五八・壹參
割引手形	八、七貳貳、參七四・壹貳
買入證券	四八〇、七五貳・七五
國債證券	貳、壹七八、六參四・六參
會社株券及社債券	壹、壹八〇、六〇〇・〇〇
金銀有高	貳、〇九貳、參參四・八壹
合計	壹七、〇五七、五貳七・貳六

財產目錄ハ資產の分と同一に付寄す

損益勘定表

一　金九拾參万五千九百六拾四圓八拾錢　當期總益金

一　金壹百拾九万六千參百七拾六圓參拾七錢　前半期繰越高

合計金貳百拾參万貳千參百四拾壹圓拾七錢

內

金六拾九万九千七百七拾七圓七拾七錢　當期利息及諸經費

差引

金壹百四拾參万貳千五百六十參圓四拾錢

內

金五万圓也　利益金として本社へ繰込

金壹百參拾八万貳千五百六拾參圓四拾錢　後半期へ繰越高

右之通候也

明治卅五年一月

明治廿六年設立

三菱合資會社銀行部

落語の名家

（此の書の口演者）

（兩國藥研堀　玉水館上野撮影）

呂利新左衛門　　桂文治　　三遊亭遊三　　橘家圓喬
亭圓遊　　柳亭燕枝　　快樂亭ブラック　　橘家圓蔵
三遊亭小圓朝　　桂文左衛門　　三遊亭圓橘

Facing page, top:

Figure 6. Portrait of Black, mid row, second from left. The presence of Black among portraits of colleagues described in the title as '*rakugo* luminaries' testifies to the prominence he achieved.

Facing page, bottom:

Figure 7. Illustration from Black's *sokkibon* version of *The Bloodstained Handprint at the Iwade Bank*: magic lantern.

Above:

Figure 8. *The Bloodstained Handprint at the Iwade Bank*: urchin Matashichi asks for money from Mr Iwade.

Figure 9. *The Bloodstained Handprint at the Iwade Bank*: Mr Iwade, dead.

Facing page:

Figure 10. *The Orphan*: the beating of Seikichi by the wife of the undertaker. Note barrel-shaped Japanese-style coffins in the background.

Courtesy of National Diet Library, Japan.

Above:

Figure 11. *The Orphan*: Bunroku slays Omine.

Courtesy of National Diet Library, Japan.

伊藤次郎吉
長嶋千代

Facing page, top:

Figure 12. ***The Orphan*****: Seikichi arraigned before the court on a charge of pick-pocketing.**

Courtesy of National Diet Library, Japan.

Facing page, bottom:

Figure 13. ***The Poison Pin in the Coach*****: Itō Jirōkichi meets Nagashima Chiyo, the landlady of Suzuki Okatsu, to explain the circumstances of Okatsu's death.**

Courtesy of National Diet Library, Japan.

Above:

Figure 14. ***The Poison Pin in the Coach*****: Itō Jirōkichi meets Tsuchiya in a pub.**

Courtesy of National Diet Library, Japan.

Above:

Figure 15. Black in the role of Banzuiin Chōbee.

Source: *East of Asia Magazine*, Vol 1, 1902.

Below:

Figure 16. Formal portrait of Henry Black in Western dress.

Source: *East of Asia Magazine*, Vol 1, 1902.

Chapter 9

Sensation fiction as modernity

> The oddest thing was that nothing belonging to Mr Iwade was missing. Gold watch and chain in chest pocket, diamond ring on finger – everything was there. And the contents of the safe did not appear to have been tampered with, so robbery was ruled out as a motive. But the only person suspected was Yamada Matashichi, who although he was greatly indebted to his patron, had not been around at the time of the death. The police took details of his height, clothing, and body shape and these were sent by telegram and telephone from London Police Station to all police stations in Britain (Kairakutei 1893:51).

Henry Black's audiences were intensely involved in the modernisation process. Catering to their involvement, Henry's stories vividly portrayed characters experiencing the sorts of vicissitudes and benefits of Western European modernity which his audiences could anticipate experiencing or were already encountering. Not everything in the stories painted an optimistic picture. They also served as warnings of some of the more detrimental outcomes of modernisation, such as slum life. But, on the whole, there emerges from his adaptations of European sensation fiction a picture of a Europe in which human beings benefited from scientific discoveries and from civil and criminal codes which meted out justice in an equitable and civilised fashion.

As Henry's joke about needing eyes in the back of their heads implied, if people were to survive the new era, they would have to adapt by adopting their own strategies. Henry's response to the problem of survival was to propose strategies that involved a reinvention of the self. The new self was a hybrid of European and Japanese elements, similar to the characters portrayed in his adaptive translations. By applying the storyteller's knack of interweaving humour and suspense, Henry offered blueprints for survival in his stories. They implied far-reaching alterations on both a psychological and a physical level. As a result, his stories represent a point of contact between modern Europe and modernising Japan. They brought the idea of modernity, as it was variously understood in Europe, to the hearts and minds of his Japanese audiences.

Speed – transport and communications

In his mapping of the locations of events or residences of characters in canonic British and French novels of the 19th century, Franco Moretti found a steady widening of 'literary geography' as technologies and social conditions altered to permit greater mobility. Using Jane Austen novels, Moretti has shown how the geographical spaces within which her characters moved were greater than those portrayed by previous authors. Although Austen's characters are limited mainly to southeast England, the ability of her heroines to get on a horsedrawn coach and travel at least a day or so increased the range of choice of their romantic attachments, or allowed marriages to more distant suitors in other counties (Moretti 1998:206). Austen's books demonstrated an expansion of the geographic limits of the marriage market. By the 1890s, Henry's characters, both male and female, based on the characters of modern sensation novels, extended the limits beyond counties to traverse national borders. And in the cities of Henry's stories, fast, efficient modes of transport and communication abetted the smooth functioning of a modern metropolis and even served as the scene of crimes. The cities in Henry's tales are traversed by networks of horsedrawn coaches, mail delivery services, fast trains and telegraph lines. Rail networks link them to other cities or villages within their orbit.

As a result, many of the protagonists in Henry's stories exhibit a degree of social and geographic mobility linked to modes of transport only just becoming known to his audiences. This mobility was linked to emancipation during the Meiji period, particularly for Japanese women. As early as 1871, the government had sent five girls to study in the United States, but such experiments were abandoned as the Meiji years wore on, rendering the extended geographic mobility of Henry's female protagonists subversive. For many Japanese women, the most geographic dislocation they experienced was a move from the country to a nearby town or textile factory, often in a rural location. In many of Henry's narrations, modern modes of transport at relatively high-speed and over long-distances facilitate the development of plots and relationships. Women of independent means use coaches and trains to travel across borders or between widely separated cities. In *Shachū no dokubari*, Suzuki Okatsu dies in Paris shortly after coming from Italy to locate her lost sister, and her sister Onobu contemplates returning to Italy by train after learning of Okatsu's death. At a time when it was highly unusual for Japanese women to travel overseas, the fact that such mobility was taken for granted in Henry's stories enhances the impression of emancipation.

Faster modes of transport had also revolutionised communications and facilitated new jobs and lifestyles. In *Minashigo*, Henry's adaptation of Dickens's *Oliver Twist*, the home of the silk merchant Fukuda Zenkichi is in the tranquil environs of the town of Hyanden, said to be a short train commute from London (Ishii 1896:144). Henry made it clear to audiences that the speed and convenience of modern train travel enabled the wealthy to escape the pressures of the city and live in tranquillity and comfort in its more rural outskirts. Like London, Tokyo was developing its suburbs, which exacerbated class divisions. The wealthy could choose to live the rural idyll away from the slums.

There is a dramatic demonstration of the speed of rail transport toward the end of *Minashigo* when Fukuda Zenkichi's father travels by train from London to Leeds, a distance Henry says is 60 *ri* (235.6 kilometres or 146.4 miles).[72] Henry informs his audience that where Seikichi walked the distance in 14 days, Fukuda traversed it by train in just 'two or three hours' (Ishii 1896:164–165). In *Iwade ginkō chishio no tegata*, Iwade Yoshio works in a bank a short walk from the station near London Bridge (Kairakutei 1893:6). From the station he can easily reach his comfortably palatial home in the rural village of Chiisubikku three *ri* away at the end of a day's work. After leaving the bank at around 5 pm, this new mode of transport whisks him back to the village in time to unwind before beginning his evening meal punctually at 7 pm. The swiftness of the journey is compared elsewhere in the tale to the much longer time it takes a servant on a well-bred Arab stallion to reach the bank from the Iwade home during a late night emergency when trains no longer run.

In *Shachū no dokubari*, Henry claimed that rickshaws in Japan, China and India were more convenient since they were available 24 hours a day. Much horsedrawn transport in Europe, he noted, stopped running after about 9 or 10 pm because 'the horses have to be fed and looked after or they collapse' (Kairakutei 1891b:9). Henry cleverly capitalised on audiences'

---

72 One *ri* is 2.44 miles or 3.9273 kilometres. The distance by road between London and Leeds is about 195 miles or 316 kilometres.

interest in the then topical horsedrawn omnibus. In an aside to his audience in *Iwade ginkō chishio no tegata*, intended to explain how extremely filthy the desperately poor urchin Matashichi was, Henry says that he was dirtier than the *yakko* who rode on a small platform on the front of omnibuses hawking for passengers and announcing their destination (Kairakutei 1893:25). Exposed to the elements, including mud from poorly kept roads, the familiar figure of the *yakko* was the definitive image of grime. The *yakko* symbolised the plight of the child worker in a dirty, poorly paid occupation made possible through the introduction of a modern mode of transport.

The first horsedrawn omnibus in Tokyo was operated from 1872, by entrepreneur Yuri Narimasa, between Kaminarimon in Asakusa and Shinbashi (Ogi et al 1987:376–377). To attract customers to the omnibus and warn pedestrians of their approach, Yuri placed a man blowing on a trumpet on board. In 1874, Yuri imported from Britain a double-decker omnibus for the route, but the service was suspended that year after the omnibus struck and killed a woman at Kotobuki-chō in Asakusa. Soon afterwards, other entrepreneurs began operating smaller horsedrawn omnibuses on the same route and between Shinagawa and Shinbashi. Since the roads were poorly maintained, they developed a reputation as an uncomfortable mode of transport, attracting the nicknames *gata basha* and *gatakuri basha*, onomatopoeic terms suggesting they rattled and shook their passengers.

In *Shachū no dokubari*, Henry empathised with audiences over the mortal danger posed by the omnibuses in a humorous scene in which amateur sleuth Itō Jirōkichi informs Okatsu's landlady that Okatsu's death involved a horsedrawn coach (see figure 13). The landlady becomes agitated and assumes Okatsu has been run down by a horsedrawn omnibus, itemising the forms of horsedrawn transport then available in Tokyo. Although the story is set in Paris, the scene humorously demonstrates the hybridity of adaptive translations by superimposing well-known Tokyo landmarks, including its bridges, on a map of the French capital.

> Really the roads are such a danger, what with horse-drawn trams, red omnibuses, Entarō buses and the like. Women and children really have to have their wits about them when they go out. Why, in the old days they used to have the attendant walking at the front of the carriage! But these days the attendants've gone up in the world and gone to Yanagihara or some place and got themselves some old clothes and all they do now is get off at every intersection looking like the ghost of a

> Chinaman, so it's got even more dangerous! Oh dear! Where did she get struck down and killed? Was it at Shinbashi Bridge? Manseibashi Bridge? Or was it Nihonbashi Bridge? (Kairakutei 1891b:67–68).

Fifteen years later, by 1906, most of the horsedrawn omnibuses had been withdrawn from service and replaced by electric trams (Ogi et al 1987:378–379). The landlady's fear of omnibuses presages similar reactions towards the electric trams as Tokyoites adjusted to new forms of public transport. Smith (1978:57) notes that the trams were also 'a powerful symbol of the problematic threat of change'.

The woman's reference to 'Entarō buses' evoked performances by the popular *rakugoka* Tachibanaya Entarō, who in 1877 began incorporating into his performances imitations of the sound of the trumpet used to attract customers and warn pedestrians of their approach. The popularity of Entarō's imitations led to the omnibuses becoming known as *Entarō basha*, or simply, *entarō*. Near the beginning of *Shachū no dokubari*, where Henry sets the scene for the mysterious killing of Okatsu, he jokes as he describes the coach setting off on its night journey across Paris that 'had Entarō been there, he would have blown his trumpet to warn the pedestrians' (Kairakutei 1891b:13).

Equality before the law

Since his days as a speaker with the pro-democracy movement, Henry Black had had an interest in law reform. Many parts of his narrated stories reflect that interest. In his version of Dickens' *Oliver Twist*, Henry's interest in the law and criminology shows in the scene where Nancy attends the court to try to find out what has happened to Oliver (see figure 12). In Henry's version, the incognito visit of Nancy's Japanese equivalent, Omine, to the court affords Henry an opportunity to inform his audience that in Britain the public is permitted to attend police committal hearings (Ishii 1896:64–65). At this point in the narration, Henry's ideologically motivated elaborations are more detailed than anything Dickens wrote:

> So Omine went. But Britain is different from Japan in that the public is allowed to attend police hearings. Not that police hearings are especially interesting. When it comes to a hearing in a court of capital offence, not only is just hearing the opinion of the public prosecutor (*kensatsukan*) and the argument of the defendant interesting, it could be quite a useful academic exercise. The police investigations involve

> a lot of trivial things hardly worth listening to – like a drunk getting admonished after sobering up and then getting fined for arguing, or someone going out for a bargain, getting taken into custody with a woman and then being handed over to his landlord or his wife.
>
> But in any case, you can usually listen in on a police investigation. There is nothing in the world as cheap as something you can listen to for free. Even with a particularly uninteresting matter, when it comes to what is seen and heard, I think it's better than not listening at all.
>
> For that reason, no matter when you go, there's always room in the police gallery seats and they hardly ever put up the full-house sign.
>
> Anyway, Omine went to the police, and once she had sat behind other people and made herself as small as possible so she would not stand out, all sorts of people were called out and underwent investigation with some being acquitted and others being handed down their punishment, and some being sent off to the courts.
>
> Eventually out came Takahashi Seikichi. But having been beaten up on the streets, he had met a terrible fate. He was muddied and had blood on his face. He was altogether a sight for sore eyes.

Henry Black's note-taking in the Tokyo Court of Petty Sessions (Kurata 1981–87:III, 81) has already been referred to. It is a pity *Jiji shinpō* the newspaper reporting his attendance in 1884 did not give more information on the cases then before the courts, given the propensity for *rakugo* to turn any event into an interesting story imbued with humour. Henry's note-taking at the courts indicates a burgeoning interest in crime reporting, a prerequisite for the creation of sensation fiction.

Charles Dickens had championed the role of police detectives as a modern innovation in the 1850s, going with them on their beats and writing approvingly of their work (Ousby 1976:85). Henry had shown an interest in juries and reform of the prison system and criminal code when he had addressed meetings of the Freedom and People's Rights Movement adherents in mid-1879. Now, like Charles Dickens, he was taking his notebook and observing at close quarters what legal practitioners were doing, in order to tell others about it. In the 1890s he maintained his interest in legal reform, using his *rakugoka* status to promote it among his audiences by introducing detectives and legal code reform issues into his narrations. That Henry, a European, was able to observe a Japanese court in this manner was possibly one of the reasons why his presence there attracted the attention of the newspaper. Given the long struggle by reformers to introduce a Western-style penal code as justification for eliminating the unequal treaties, the interest of a foreigner in the processes of Japanese law was a sensitive issue.

Law reform was an important plank in Meiji-era Japanese government attempts to revise the terms of unequal treaties signed between Japan and Western powers, including the United States and Britain, between 1858 and 1869. The treaties subjected Japan's external trade to tariffs imposed by the foreign signatories. They also gave foreigners extraterritoriality in a limited number of ports, guaranteeing them immunity from Japanese judicial control (Hoare 1994:1–17; Jansen 1995:283–285).

As far as the Western powers were concerned, no revision of the treaties could occur until Japan modernised its laws and legal codes. Among perceived deficiencies in pre-Meiji Restoration legal practice was the lack of the profession of attorney.[73] A neo-Confucian state philosophy meant that many *daimyō* had used Chinese models for their codes, but, although they had to ensure statutes did not contravene those of the central government (*bakufu*), legal procedures and penalties for crimes were not standardised across the country. Moreover, punishments differed depending on rank (Steenstrup 1996:121–123). In spite of the inconsistencies, however, some Tokugawa regime practices and institutions may have facilitated the post-1868 modernisation of Japan. In law and legal practice, for example, American scholar of Japanese law John O Haley suggests that 'the existence of analogous institutions, processes, and even norms in Tokugawa law' ensured that 'for the most part, Western legal institutions, processes, and even derivative legal rules proved to be easily integrated into the Japanese cultural and institutional matrix' (Haley 1991:70).

Nevertheless, the process of reform and integration entailed several decades of trial and error as interested parties debated, legislated, annulled and rewrote relevant laws and legal codes, with help from foreign experts, including Georges Bousquet, a French lawyer from the Paris Court of Appeal, who arrived in 1872, Gustave Boissonade, a professor from the Faculty of Law in Paris, and German constitutional expert Hermann Roesler. Boissonade, whose daughter danced at the Emperor's Birthday ball at the Rokumeikan in November 1884, remained in Japan for 20 years,

73 According to Noda (1976:145), attorneys were not needed because 'individuals were not then considered as proper subjects of rights'.

helping to draft the penal and criminal procedure codes, 'the first modern codes to be applied in Japan' (Noda, 1976:44–53). In the early Meiji years, many judges were trained in English and French law so that, even before the new Japanese codes came into force, French or English law became benchmarks for handing down rulings (Noda 1976:53; Young & Hamilton 2001:2–10).

The introduction of codes from Britain and France compounded debate over the extent to which newly framed laws and codes should reflect indigenous Japanese morality. Symptomatic of this was the mixed reception accorded the new civil code, which Boissonade had helped compile. Promulgated in 1891, Henry Black's most prolific year, it was due to come into force in 1894, but in 1892 its detractors succeeded in postponing it (Noda 1976:45–49). Haley's assessment of the matter acknowledges a number of likely factors, including that it was a factional dispute between proponents of 'English' and 'French' schools of Western jurisprudence, that it was a reaction by traditionalists to the prospect of the loss of 'traditional values and patterns of behavior', and that it was a symptom of a struggle between 'progressive internationalists' and 'ultranationalist political reactionaries'.

The evidence indicates that by the 1890s 'esteem for French law had waned in Japan as in Europe as deference to German legal science (and German economic and military power) grew' (Haley 1991:10).[74] In the event, it was not until 1896 that a new civil code covering general principles, real rights and obligations was enacted, and not until 1899 that a code covering family law and succession was enacted. Young and Hamilton suggest that the Japanese proceeded with caution in relation to family law because it represents a set of legal rules which 'govern perhaps the single most important element that secures social stability over time and defines the persistence and continuity of an inherently indigenous identity' (Young & Hamilton 2001:7).

In the long run, penal code reform amounted to a radical reorientation away from a pre-Meiji neo-Confucian morality toward a Western morality based on individual rights of the kind emphasised in Henry's narrations. The changes affected rights to property, with consequent implications for definitions of family, marriage and citizenship within the nation-state. An indication of the extent of the changes is the fact that even the language

74 Haley (1991:70) also notes that this 'first phase' of legal reform did not really 'culminate until the enactment of the second Criminal Code in 1907, by which time all but the already predominantly German procedural codes had been redrafted along German lines'.

of the law 'was almost completely rewritten' so that 'in definition hardly a single term of Japanese legal language survived the transformation' (Haley 1991:69). Pre-Restoration terminology was simply incapable of expressing many of the newly introduced concepts. It is hardly surprising, therefore, that *rakugoka*, whose art was intrinsically linked to the Japanese language, should also have engaged in the debate over the changes.

The debate also reflected concern that Western legal codes were not necessarily a panacea, as demonstrated by the reception in 1881 of Takahashi Kenzō's translation of Samuel March Phillips' *Famous Cases of Circumstantial Evidence*, a collection of cases in the West, many involving a miscarriage of justice that culminated in a death sentence. While the book was printed by the Justice Ministry for purely utilitarian reasons, it soon found a ready market in non-government book shops (Nakajima, 1964:17–18).

One early campaigner who addressed this concern was Kuroiwa Ruikō (Silver 2003:853), whose *Yorozu chōhō* soon became the largest selling newspaper in Tokyo. In 1894, Kuroiwa serialised *Hito no un* (People's luck), which had sufficient plot and character similarities to suggest it was an adaptive translation of Mary Braddon's *Lady Audley's Secret* (Silver 2003:853). Kuroiwa timed *Hito no un* to coincide with an editorial campaign against the court ruling in the Sōma Affair, an inheritance scandal that had entertained the public for a decade. Both *Hito no un* and the real-life Sōma Affair featured 'murder, money, bastardy, insanity, forensic medicine, and the reputation of an aristocratic family, all focused into the drama of a courtroom confrontation' (Silver 2003:853). While the court exonerated those accused of poisoning Viscount Sōma, Kuroiwa maintained that the court had been bought and justice had not been done.[75]

Kuroiwa immediately followed *Hito no un* with *Sute obune*, an adaptive translation of Braddon's *Diavola*. The plot, featuring a woman wrongly accused of attempting to poison a baron, duplicates the themes of *Hito no un*. Intertextually speaking, these two adaptive translations demonstrate how Braddon's works supported the case in Japan against wholesale adoption of Western legal codes.

---

75 Kuroiwa's extension of the campaign fitted with his conviction that a newspaper should be used as a political tool and with his campaign against capital punishment. Kuroiwa was keen to show that in spite of Japan's recent borrowing from the Western, particularly French, legal code, it was still possible to have a miscarriage of justice. Silver (2003) has pointed out that, in this context, Kuroiwa's use of *Hito no un* indicates a degree of creative 'resistance' within Japanese popular culture sufficient to question the notion that Western versions of modernity were all-encompassing and dominant.

Another storyteller who sided with Kuroiwa in the debate was Henry's mentor San'yūtei Enchō, whose 1895 tale *Meijin chōji* (Master Cabinet-maker Chōji), an adaptation of de Maupassant's *Un Parricide,* is a nostalgic look back at some of the benefits of Tokugawa legal practice. Both versions begin with a protagonist, a cabinet-maker, at the peak of success and fame. Both portray his encounter with a seemingly married couple who befriend him and become his benefactors. In Enchō's version, when Chōji suspects that the couple are his own parents who abandoned him as a baby, he entreats them to admit that they are his parents. But when the couple deny they are his parents, Chōji kills them in a fit of righteous rage. Whereas de Maupassant's version ends abruptly at that point by asking readers to make their own judgement, Enchō elaborates at considerable length on the trial and the judge's decision. In a sensational end to the trial, Enchō has Chōji go free on a technicality. In the final stages of the trial, the judge, an appointee of the *shōgun*, reveals evidence that the woman, Oryū, whom Chōji killed, was indeed his birth mother. But the judge finds that Oryū had earlier forfeited any right to be considered his mother as she had left his father for her lover, the man whom Chōji had killed believing he was his father. Oryū and her lover had arranged the proxy murder of Chōji's father. Thus, Chōji learns his real identity. The judge rules that the killings were not patricide, but were instead Chōji's justifiable revenge for the death of his father. In de Maupassant's version, there is no suggestion that either of the two might not be the killer's parents. That complication is entirely Enchō's invention.

Enchō set his story in the late Edo period, dating Chōji's apprenticeship to a cabinet-maker in 1803. There were interesting parallels between Chōji's actions and the revenge killing in December 1880 by ex-*samurai* Usui Rokurō of his father's killer and Judge of the Tokyo Superior Court, Ichinose Naohisa. Saiga Ryūkō's novel of the incident elicited considerable public sympathy for Usui, who in real life was sentenced to life imprisonment, rather than death, and released from prison ten years later. In a study of the incident, Mertz concludes that 'whether Rokurō would live or die for his crime…was implicitly symbolic of the fate of Tokugawa Confucian ethics within the modernising Meiji state' (Mertz 2003:117). Similarly, Enchō's imbuing of his story 15 years later with Tokugawa Confucian ethics positions it as part of the debate over the merits or otherwise of the new legal codes. Under any strict interpretation of the new codes, both Rokurō and Chōji would have been sentenced to death, but the appeal of their stories derived from sympathy and support for a still-popular Confucian ethic. In Chōji's case, Enchō garnered audience sympathy for the aggrieved son whose act served as retribution for the murder of his father in the same manner as Usui Rokurō. Enchō's choice of a pre-Restoration setting makes his tale an exercise in nostalgia and caters to proponents of the case for incorporating Japanese morality in the framing of new codes of law.

In contrast, Henry Black's use of European works invariably emphasised Western legal practice as the model for a modern, civilised country. One of the best examples of this is his 1891 adaptation of Braddon's 1877 tale 'Her Last Appearance' as his narrated story *Eikoku Rondon gekijō miyage* (Story from a London theatre). In this story, the nobleman John Brown, who has escaped to Paris to avoid detection for murdering the actor, Sumerurī, is confronted by the detective Shiberia Deboa at a gentleman's club. The detective urges Brown to give himself up, reassuring him that he will have legal representation in a court trial. But, in one of Henry's more graphically gruesome scenes, Brown seizes a pistol and spectacularly blows his brains out in front of his genteel onlookers (Eikokujin 1891: 216–217). Similarly, Henry's 1891 *Shachū no dokubari* concludes with the businessman Mr Yamada jailed as an accessory to the death of his niece Okatsu, in spite of his social standing as a wealthy, opera-going gentleman. The tales illustrated the theme of equality which had been spelled out in the new penal code the previous year.

The true benefits of science

In keeping with the sensation fiction genre and its use of detectives, Henry's narrations contain numerous accounts of the benefits of science and modern technology to solving crimes. In *Shachū no dokubari*, for example, the audience learns of the importance of the morgue in modern forensic investigation. When Itō and the landlady visit the Paris morgue to identify Okatsu, Henry explains the use of unclaimed bodies as cadavers for medical scientists (Kairakutei 1891b:69). In *Iwade ginkō chishio no tegata*, Henry shows how swiftly the police can track Yamada Matashichi from London to the Liverpool docks 100 *ri* away, using the telegraph and telephone to instantly convey information about him throughout the country.

In its application of the science of fingerprinting, *Iwade ginkō chishio no tegata* stands as one of the finest examples of Henry's use of science to solve a crime. Henry Black may have been made aware of the forensic potential of fingerprints by the work of Henry Faulds, a British missionary doctor who lived near Tsukiji and worked at Tsukiji Hospital in the 1880s. Henry was living near Tsukiji by 1885, in a house shared with Motokichi. In a letter to the British journal *Nature* in 1880, Faulds stated that he was inspired to embark on his investigations after learning that Japanese potters frequently left their fingerprints on clay pots to identify their provenance.

> When bloody finger-marks or impressions on clay, glass, &c., exist, they may lead to the scientific identification of criminals. Already I have had experience in two such cases, and found useful evidence from these marks. In one case, greasy finger-marks revealed who had been drinking some rectified spirit. The pattern was unique, and fortunately I had previously obtained a copy of it. They agreed with microscopic fidelity (Faulds 1880:605).

Faulds speculated that fingerprints might help in 'medico-legal investigations, as when the hands only of some mutilated victim were found', and mentioned that

> Chinese criminals from early times have been made to give the impressions of their fingers, just as we make ours yield their photographs...There can be no doubt as to the advantage of having, besides their photographs, a nature-copy of the for-ever-unchangeable finger-furrows of important criminals. It need not surprise us that the Chinese have been before us in this as in other matters (Faulds 1880:605).

Although Henry Black gives only cursory treatment in his narration to the reason for the killer's leaving of a bloody handprint on a piece of paper at the crime scene, the device must have enthralled audiences at the time. In the story, Henry stressed the link to Japan, which supports the theory that his information came from Faulds. When the detective who shows Iwade Takejirō the bloodstained piece of paper found at the crime scene states that he does not consider it a vital piece of evidence, Takejirō retorts that he considers it the key to finding his brother's killer:

> Four or five years ago, when I went around the world I stayed for a short time in China and Japan. In these countries, unlike in Britain, when one draws up a contract they always use a thing called an *ingyō* (seal). These are made of boxwood, gold or silver, or other metals, and they engrave their name in it and press it on an inkpad and then add it to below their name. But sometimes they do not use the seal,

> and instead put ink on their index finger and press it to below their name. In other words, it's called a *boin* (imprint made with a thumb) or *tsumein* (imprint made with the tip of the index finger). Even where they normally have a *jitsuin* (a legal, registered seal), if they have to be very particular about it, as when they are undergoing an investigation and evidence is sought, they will give a fingerprint. But in China, when someone becomes a soldier, he has ink put on his whole hand and presses the hand to the bottom of the certificate of induction.
>
> If that soldier deserts, they use the handprint and find him. But why did something as unusual as this come about? If there is a seal, you never know who used it and it is no proof at all. How is it that even if you put a handprint at the bottom of a certificate of enlistment you can find the whereabouts of a soldier when he runs away? If you carefully look into the origins, it is a custom dating from a very long time ago. The lines and patterns in the skin of a human hand differ from person to person. If you get 100 people together, or a thousand people, and compare their hands, you will never find the same lines (Kairakutei 1893:71–73).

Henry's reference to fingerprinting appears to have been a world first in detective fiction. It preceded Mark Twain's 1893 reference to it in *Life on the Mississippi* (Morioka & Sasaki 1983:159).

Conclusion

Henry's characters are not always at home in their landscapes. His tales portray the daily struggle with the appurtenances of a modern nation-state: industrialisation, bureaucratisation, increased speed and mechanisation of transport and communications and legal reform. Many of his characters are confused, lost, resentful, or still trying to adjust. His comments on reform, addressed in asides to his audience, indicate the persistence of ambivalence toward reform and change.

Nevertheless, an analysis of Henry Black's narrations between the mid-1880s and mid-1890s demonstrates that, although historians have concluded that a new generation had begun to reappraise the place of indigenous culture by the late 1880s, European prototypes of modernity still aroused the curiosity of *yose* audiences and readers of the printed versions of the narrators' tales at least until the mid-1890s. Henry's humorous examples of persons unable to cope with the trappings of modernity (such as the elderly landlady complaining of the roads made dangerous by passing omnibuses in *Shachū no dokubari*) are reminders of the human cost of modernisation during this period and of the problems ordinary people experienced because of the rapid and indiscriminate nature of the modernisation process. While the humour may have helped allay anxiety over the unfamiliar or threatening trappings of modernity, these characters are an indication that modernity was contested and that opinion over the purpose and nature of reform was by no means unanimous. The tales indicate that, although Henry Black demonstrated an affinity for his target audience, his foreign origins afforded him an additional perspective as an outsider willing to comment and criticise. His portrayals of the benefits and demerits of modernity in print and on the stage show that dissent and debate over reform and modernity found a receptive audience well into the 1890s, in spite of state attempts to control dissent through legislation and social management.

Chapter 10

Adapting Dickens

Dystopia and modern life

> At last he entered Rondon town, but at the very outskirts, even though the houses were dirty and many of the roads were narrow, people were hurrying about as if they didn't have a moment to spare compared to country folk. While he was trying to consider what to do on being surprised at all this confusion of coming and going, he rested by leaning on the railing of a bridge over a small stream and wondered what he could do. When from the other direction there came a small round-faced urchin about the same stature as Seikichi, but sinister looking with a flat nose, a big mouth, thick eyebrows and small eyes (Ishii 1896:36).

Some time in the 1890s, Henry Black formally adopted a Japanese boy named Seikichi. Henry had known Seikichi's parents, both of whom were in the entertainment business. They had both died within a short space of time, leaving Seikichi without support.[76] As Henry was by now a Japanese citizen with the surname of Ishii, the boy became Ishii Seikichi. In 1894, Henry embarked on an adaptation of Charles Dickens' *Oliver Twist*, which he gave the Japanese title *Minashigo* (the orphan). As with his other adaptive translations, Henry chose Japanese names for his characters: Fagan became Tōgoro; Sikes became Bunroku; and Oliver became Seikichi. Henry's choice of the name Seikichi was undoubtedly deliberate. The parallels between Oliver and the real-life Seikichi are obvious. Both were orphaned and both were about the same age. Henry's choice of the name Seikichi in this story was similar to his use of the name of his live-in lover Motokichi two years earlier for the central character of *Shachū no dokubari*. Seikichi was to remain with Henry for much of the rest of his life. He and Henry both studied conjuring and performed together on

[76] Author's interview with one of Seikichi's grandsons, Mr Sudō Mitsuo, Tokyo, 3 May 1991.

stage. Seikichi later married a French woman named Rosa. The couple, together with their children, formed the household in which Henry was to spend his final years in semi-retirement.

Minashigo was Henry's last major serialised work. It was published in 57 instalments from May 1894 in the *Yamato shinbun* (Morioka & Sasaki 1983:145, fn56) and collated in book form in 1896 (Ishii 1896). In *Minashigo* Henry had the perfect prototype for warning audiences about the dangers of unquestioning acceptance of Western-style industrialisation. It was, as Dickens had intended in *Oliver Twist*, a grim picture of inequality and injustice in the newly industrialising cities of capitalist Europe.

> The story I will perform here is about something which truly occurred in Britain. So that everyone can better follow it, I have, for the sake of convenience, altered the names to Japanese ones. It occurred about 20 years ago in a place called the town of Rīzu about 146 miles from Rondon. It is not such a big place. But it has about 10,000 homes, which for the countryside makes it a somewhat prosperous region. Here, there is an orphanage established by the government. Although since it is in the countryside, we can say the number of people receiving assistance is few compared to the city, there is an unequal distribution of assets (*zaisan fuheikin*), and some seven or eight hundred people are being looked after by the authorities (*okami*). The head of this orphanage, a man called Tanaka Seiemon, is a government official whom I wish I could describe as upright. But unfortunately he is very greedy and is the sort of cold-hearted type who siphons off the supplies for those he is charged with looking after and lines his own pockets (Ishii 1896:1–2).

The atmosphere of the Dickens original is retained, although Henry used the opportunity to comment on current social issues peculiar to Japan, as in this scene in which Oliver (Seikichi) meets The Artful Dodger (Chibikichi):

> The boy had a ruddy face and hair so long it looked as if he hadn't had a trim for ages, on top of which he wore a torn hat with a huge overcoat with its overly long sleeves turned back.
>
> One of his hands was hidden, while the other held a long wooden pipe with a huge bowl on it which he was smoking as he approached. A minor smoking on the streets is really not a pleasant sight. The boy was intent on behaving like an adult. These days, one occasionally sees primary school children smoking on their way home from school, but

I do think it is good if parents and teachers effectively admonish them over it. Most of all, parents and teachers ought not to smoke in front of them. This urchin noticed Seikichi leaning on the railing and went over to him and tapped him on the back.

URCHIN: Hey, what are you doin'?

SEIKICHI: Uh, is it bad to stand here?

URCHIN: What? Who said anything about it being bad to stand here?! Stand, sit, sleep, whatever you do it's your business. But I was wondering why you were standing round looking blank so I asked ya what ya were doin'.

SEIKICHI: It's just that I haven't had anything to eat since last night so I'm hungry.

URCHIN: What? Haven't eaten since last night? You sure must be hungry! I'm out of luck too today. I don't have any money on me, but there should be something for you to eat.

SEIKICHI: Thank you so much.

URCHIN: You don't have to speak so politely. People might get something from you when they don't have anything. Maybe you'd better come with me.

So saying, he led Seikichi to a beer hall. When they entered it, because it was a pub on the outskirts of town, it wasn't a tidy establishment, and the food didn't seem tasty. But there was a long table with chairs on each side of it. A waitress of about 18 or 19 years came over to them.

WAITRESS: What would you like?

URCHIN: Miss, bring us a serving of that meat, and three thick slices of bread, and then two beers. Make it snappy will you. If you're away too long, I won't fall in love with you.

He played it like an adult giving the order. The waitress chuckled as she brought the things over to them.

URCHIN: So, you go ahead and eat. I've eaten just a while ago, so I'm not hungry. I'll just drink the beer so you have the meat and bread. Then you can have that beer.

SEIKICHI: Thank you.

> He'd been told to drink, so he took up the cup and took a gulp, but he screwed up his face and stared, coughing, at the cup.
>
> URCHIN: What's the matter? Doesn't it taste good?
>
> SEIKICHI: Thank you, but it is not so delicious.
>
> URCHIN: What? You don't like beer?
>
> SEIKICHI: It's as if it's a bit bitter and sour. Hasn't it gone off?
>
> URCHIN: What! Gone off? You'd have to be joking! It couldn't possibly be off. It's the finest on offer! Haven't you ever had a beer before?
>
> SEIKICHI: That's correct. I have never had any till now.
>
> URCHIN: Where on earth have you come from?
>
> SEIKICHI: I have come from the country.
>
> URCHIN: Don't they have beer where you come from?
>
> SEIKICHI: There is beer, but I have never drunk it.
>
> URCHIN: So, how old are you?
>
> SEIKICHI: I am fourteen.
>
> URCHIN: Fourteen! Hang on. You mean to say you've never had beer? (Ishii 1896:36–40).

Between 1886, when Henry Black cooperated in the compilation of *Kusaba no tsuyu*, and the 1894 serialisation of *Minashigo*, his works reflected a growing awareness in audience and readers of the darker side of modernity. The city increasingly emerges as a central metaphor for the future. The semiotic transition moves from the Arcadian idyll shared by Bess and Lucille at Ingleshaw Castle in *Kusaba no tsuyu* (Dew by the graveside), through the Paris flophouses of the 1891 *Shachū no dokubari* (The poisoned pin in the coach) and slums of London in *Iwade ginkō chishio no tegata* (The bloodstained handprint at the Iwade Bank), culminating in the filthy robbers' den of the 1894 adaptation of *Oliver Twist* as *Minashigo*.

Whereas *Kusaba no tsuyu* portrayed the healing effects of the countryside on a young woman traumatised by slum life, *Minashigo* reversed the hero's progress, by bringing the innocent Seikichi into a monolithic and foreboding city. In *Minashigo*, the countryside is something the innocent hero Seikichi merely traverses on his way from one grim provincial town to the even grimmer and dysfunctional city of London.

The London of *Minashigo* is the bleakest of the cities in Henry's narrations. It is a grim, crime-ridden landscape full of poverty. London's evils even extend to the countryside as the story's malevolent characters flee there to escape justice or pillage the houses of the innocent in towns on London's fringe. In *Kusaba no tsuyu*, it is the country estate that offers hope for Bess. Bess's main salvation is her flight to the country where, safe within the castle and its beautiful grounds the compassionate Lucille attempts to educate her and provide her with a brighter future. There is only a hint of the city visiting its evils upon the country when, at the end of the story, Bess's estranged husband, who has come from the city finally locates her and accidentally kills her when he thrusts a knife meant for Bruno into her. By contrast, in *Minashigo* Seikichi must flee from the hardships of Leeds to the even larger city of London in which he experiences an unrelenting series of betrayals and hardships until he finds his grandfather in the final episodes. In *Minashigo*, the city clearly dominates the tale as a metaphor for danger. *Kusaba no tsuyu* retained echoes of Austen's expanded marriage market, which was facilitated by an efficient network of horsedrawn coaches. *Minashigo* has nothing of this, reflecting instead Dickens' robbers' market as the thieves use modern means of transport, including trains, to extend their reach into the countryside.

Throughout the transition, Henry's tales offer an increasingly bleak vision of the city as labyrinthine and alienating, substantiating Franco Moretti's observation that developments in the social geography of the 19th-century novel paralleled developments in industrial capitalism (Moretti 1998:17). Although Henry worked in Japan and not in 19th-century Europe – the focus of Moretti's inquiries – the social geography of Henry's narrations similarly reflected the more negative outcomes of modernity in Meiji-era Japan, particularly the growth of urban slums and poverty in the nation's larger cities. In *Minashigo*, the negative aspects of modernity include urban poverty, a venal and corrupt bureaucracy, unemployment and the abuse of women's rights. These concerns were a continuation of Henry's 20-year interest in themes first mentioned at speech meetings in the late 1870s. His portrayal of the bureaucracy in *Minashigo* also reflects his own experiences and those of his father at the hands of officials of the Meiji government.

City and hinterland

Reflecting the Dickens original, *Minashigo* deals with the simple goodness of a boy from a country town who enters the city, reconciles with it and, ultimately, witnesses the defeat of urban evil in the murderer Bunroku and his accomplice Tōgoro's robber gang. Henry Black's version follows the adventures of the orphan Seikichi from the workhouse in a provincial English city to his encounter with Tōgoro and his gang of thieves and eventual meeting with his real grandfather.

As with all his adaptations, Henry's *Minashigo* is considerably simpler than the original. Minor characters and subplots are eliminated. We do not, for example, find the celebrated Little Dick, Oliver's workhouse companion. Readers of *Oliver Twist* are familiar with Little Dick as the orphan who urged Oliver to ask for more porridge, but Henry omits reference to that well-known and pivotal incident. What is retained in Henry's version is a picture of the widespread poverty and injustice of industrial England and slum London. *Minashigo* was entertainment, but it was also a warning to audiences.

The high degree of departure from the original Dickens plot in *Minashigo* confirms that by 1893, Henry had become more confident in his ability as an adaptor. The dialogue is in the vernacular and there are many didactic digressions. It appears that Henry has completed the process of his experimentation with adaptation. Where Dickens has the robbers making off with Oliver after he is wounded during an attempt to rob Mrs Maylie's house, Henry has Seikichi shot by Bunroku when the occupants of the house of silk merchant Fukuda Zenkichi realise there is a robbery in progress. Bunroku attempts to kill Seikichi as a precaution, because he fears that he would divulge details about them to the household. The incident is told in graphic detail:

> Seikichi begged them not to make him do it. Bunroku shoved him through the window, but he stalled so Bunroku pointed his pistol at him. Seikichi walked across the room, but stopped and thought that if he did what they were telling him to do, he would become an accomplice.
>
> Seikichi stalled, frozen with uncertainty and fear. Bunroku put his head through the window and threatened him with the pistol again. Seikichi wanted to cry out, but feared being heard. He took some more steps. Over there, he saw a small corridor but half way along it was a hinged door which was shut. He could not escape that way. Here, there was a wide carpeted stairway, so he considered fleeing that way. He decided it would be better to do so and get shot and even die than to be branded a robber. He made a show of getting a chair to open the door,

> but just as he reached the bottom of the stairs, he shouted 'ROBBER' and ran up three steps.
>
> Bunroku swore. Then, afraid that they would have to flee leaving Seikichi to blab, he shot at him. Seikichi fell on the stairs in pain when the bullet struck his thigh. Bunroku shot at him twice again as he lay on the floor. Then the two robbers fled to Tōgōro's place (Ishii 1896:121–124).

In Dickens' version, this shooting incident sets off a convoluted chain of events that takes at least the second half of the novel to unravel. Henry Black's version places the shooting near the end of the story. Despite its grim picture of the city, *Minashigo* resolves the tension between country and city in the final vanquishing of evil, which served Henry's dramatic purpose and may have satisfied his audiences' need for at least a vicarious sense of resolution in the face of their own continuing real-life difficulties in the metropolis.

The tensions between city and country, together with the mingling of Western and Japanese elements, portrayed in Henry Black's narrations served as metaphors for the debate over the direction of modernisation. In reality, there was resolution of the tensions as the debate over modernity instigated by the advent of industrial capitalism continued, but the issues of nostalgia for an idealised and agrarian past, which is lost when one enters the city, and the alienation of the individual in the industrialised city, are all raised in Henry's stories. They were issues that preoccupied his audiences, particularly those in the metropolis of Tokyo.

Henry Black's choice of material in the 1890s shows that he assumed a role as social critic by disparaging aspects of the impact upon city dwellers of industrialisation and commercialisation which were visible by the late 19th century in urban centres in Europe and North America. Henry depicted modern 19th-century metropolises, most frequently London and Paris, as centres of transport and communications and as home to burgeoning bureaucracies and institutions, such as banks, which underpinned the development of an industrialising, capitalist economy.

The images of the metropolis shed light on late 19th-century Japanese understanding of the city at a time when Westernisation was challenging past assumptions about the nature of urban life in Japan (Smith 1978:46). This was particularly apparent in Tokyo. Eager to emulate the West, Meiji governments were determined to turn Tokyo into a symbol of the nation's prosperity. This process was well under way in the last years of the 19th century. The government's Municipal Improvement Act of 1888 had already inspired the adoption of principles of city design pioneered in Haussmann's Paris, turning Tokyo into what Fujitani Takashi (1996:98) has described as a city of mnemonic sites constructed as 'material signs on the physical landscape'. Low, wooden structures in central Tokyo were razed and replaced with grandiose brick edifices, particularly around the showcase districts of Ginza and Tokyo Station. The new red brick Tokyo Station was designed to impress with its position directly facing the imperial palace, obliging the emperor to parade in state from the palace to the station on his journeys to provincial areas. While the refashioning of Tokyo impressed foreigners, it also provided sightseeing destinations for Japanese citizens visiting the city from the countryside. The new buildings were tangible evidence of modernity, but in the minds of many the new city landscape also represented a confusing break with the past.

Henry Black's descriptions of exotic cities were also evocative of a genre established by earlier travel writers who penned stories about the new Tokyo for domestic audiences beginning between 1874 and 1876. A prime example was the compilation by Hattori Bushō of *Tōkyō shin hanjōki* (A chronicle of the new prosperity in Tokyo).[77] Following this precedent, Japanese audiences were conditioned to accept voyeuristic accounts of city life, much of which was perceived as exotic and providing 'a backdrop for the pageant of *bunmei kaika*' (civilisation and enlightenment) (Smith 1978:54). Smith notes that this new-found willingness to reshape Tokyo suggests it was 'viewed less as a city than as a symbol of the nation' (Smith 1978:55), with little thought given to the consequences of its reshaping on the residents.

Henry's stories, on the other hand, gave audiences some insight into the consequences through his more realistic images of Western cities as home to both vast riches and grinding poverty. By the time Henry was presenting his visions of the city as a hybrid entity, Tokyo's citizens were eager for answers to the question of how to cope with the changes, or at the very least to know how others were coping with the same problems. Henry offered them better insights than the planners of the new metropolis did with their utopian visions and imposing new edifices. He also offered them entertainment and a cathartic dose of humour to relieve the strain of city life.

To establish the modern city as the crucible of change, sensation fiction required a binary divide between the metropolis and the surrounding

77 Smith (1978:54) describes the work as a 'spicy description of customs in the city… modeled after a late Edo guide…and focused on the new and curious, and set the tone of wide-eyed journalistic wonder that characterized the several *hanjō mono* that followed'.

countryside. In *Minashigo* Black exemplifies this divide in faithfully imitating Dickens' original in his Oliver equivalent, Seikichi, whose progress from country town to city encapsulated the debate among foreign residents and Japanese themselves over the replacement of an agrarian, feudal and slower-paced 'Old Japan' with an industrialised and modern 'Young Japan'. The New Japan–Old Japan debate was essentially a debate about modernity. Its resolution in the late 19th century with the re-emergence of Confucian and *samurai* values among the new generation occurred at the time Henry Black narrated *Minashigo.*

In this context, *Minashigo* can be understood as a warning to audiences that modernity came at a price. Reflecting Dickens' original, Seikichi quickly has his expectations dashed on entering London. The citizens of the overcrowded city are indifferent to his plight and move at a more frenetic pace than country people, making the city a less compassionate space. It is also home to fabulous wealth contrasted with extreme poverty. When Seikichi is taken to the Strand (Sutorando) in London, he is dumbfounded when he sees shops selling the finest watches, tobacco, bags and imported luxury goods. Henry invites his listeners to imagine the scene by likening it to the area between Shinbashi and Kyōbashi, then home to newly built Western-style brick edifices synonymous with the rebuilding of Tokyo as a modern, Western-style metropolis.

> In London, it is where the finest of the shops are. But of course it is a place where things are expensive, where you'd get a shock if you so much as ask the price. Seikichi was speechless with amazement at the sight of the wide street, the huge houses, and the beautiful objects arrayed in the shop fronts (Ishii 1896:49).

Dwellings in Henry's cities vary from the narrow, filthy tenement-lined alleys of Tōgorō's hideout in the London of *Minashigo* and the flophouse used by Onobu and the Italian beggar Kinzō in *Shachū no dokubari*, to the plush apartments overlooking The Strand. Glass windows, still a novelty to many in Japan, are described in great detail in *Minashigo* in Henry's version of Dickens' thieves' break-in at Fukuda Zenkichi's home (Ishii 1896:118). He uses the incident to expound on the diamond cutter and rubber suction cup which European robbers used to cut and remove glass windows soundlessly:

> Robbers hate glass windows. They break and bits of glass fall making a noise. But they have a thing made of rubber in the shape of a morning glory. Wet it with spit, place it on the glass, and cut with a cutter fitted with diamonds (Kairakutei 1896:118).

Dickens' original gives no such detail, as glass windows were taken for granted by Europeans.

In Henry's narrated landscapes, the settings also become parables of how human nature is conditioned by the new industrial and commercial milieu. The protagonists' responses to opportunities and pressures provided by these environments were, for contemporary audiences, a metaphor for the transformation of their own lives within the newly evolving, newly constructed Meiji state. Just as in the new Meiji state there were winners and losers, narrations such as *Minashigo* show glittering riches as well as dire poverty. *Minashigo* portrays vividly the manner in which the city provided opportunities for betterment in its image of the rich merchant banker Fukuda Zenkichi returning by fast train each evening to his country mansion in time to dine punctually at 7 pm. The symbolism of the incursion of this wealthy banker into the rural landscape is particularly indicative of Black's message that Meiji modernity did not bring equality; rather, it brought opportunities and personal success for some and not for others.

Although modern cities offered the prospect of jobs and variety of choice, *Minashigo* taught that modernity did not end the struggle for equality begun by many of the adherents of the earlier Freedom and People's Rights Movement. The narration offers proof that, years after the movement's demise, Henry had still not given up his efforts to enlighten audiences about the struggle.

The story is also a metaphor for the contemporary migration of population into the cities. Just as Oliver Twist gravitated to the city, so too in Japan the rural unemployed, the second and third sons and the daughters unable to inherit the family's land, went to Tokyo to seek work or a new life. Most of the surplus sons and daughters who migrated to the cities, causing the population of many rural towns and villages to fall, found work in small-scale manufacturing, retail and construction enterprises. The majority of these enterprises applied work techniques and technology that differed little from pre-Restoration norms (Waswo 1996:60). Workers in these small production units would have easily identified with Seikichi's status as a lowly helper for a small-time undertaker. Mass production had been slow to take off in Japan after the Restoration. Even in the early 1880s, just before Henry Black began his *rakugo* career, only about 400,000 of some seven million people in non-agricultural enterprises were in the modern sector of the economy. More than half of these were government employees and less than 200,000 were in the modern private sector (Waswo 1996:60).

Of Henry's stories, *Minashigo* was his most dire warning that a move to the city did not guarantee riches and happiness. But the privations of urban poverty are also brought home to the audience forcefully in other earlier works. In *Iwade ginkō chishio no tegata*, for example, even the normally kindly banker Iwade Yoshio momentarily contemplates giving the cold and shivering beggar Matashichi some money, but then hurries to the station, afraid that he will miss his train. Later, in a fit of remorse, when informed that Matashichi's mother has perished from hunger and exposure to the cold, Iwade cries out: 'Aaah! In London, the capital of this so-called enlightened country Britain (*bunmei kaika to iwaseru Eikoku*), can there be such miserable people?' (Kairakutei 1893:7).

Black's presentation of slum-dwellers in a number of his stories, beginning with Bess in the 1886 *Kusaba no tsuyu*, reflects growing contemporary concern about an urban underclass. As Sheldon Garon (1987:24) notes, 'it was the slum, the most visible sign of inequality, that provoked the first public discussion of the Social Question in Japan'. In the year Henry Black presented *Kusaba no tsuyu*, the *Chōya shinbun* reported on the existence of three large slums in Tokyo in an exposé that prompted similar investigations by other newspapers (Garon 1987:24). In *Kusaba no tsuyu*, Bess urges her husband-to-be, Bruno, to take up the cause of the slum-dwelling poor as a social obligation when he enters parliament. Her plea accorded well with a growing awareness of the presence of slums in some of the larger Japanese cities, which coincided with nascent campaigns by Japanese Christians to alleviate the urban poverty exacerbated by the drift of population from the countryside.

As always, Henry's adaptations are important, as much for the elements of the original they retain or amplify upon, as for what they omit. In Braddon's original and in Henry's *Kusaba no tsuyu*, Lucille's act of charity toward Bess epitomised the developing social conscience of the English middle and upper classes and Henry used this as an example of English charity and benevolence. He paints a vivid picture of Lucille's privileged upbringing, describing the vast gardens surrounding her home, Ingleshaw Castle, her luxurious life cosseted by servants, and the custom of presenting young debutantes to the queen. But Henry also tells his audience that such aristocrats make it a practice to visit poor households within their community to distribute largesse, particularly to poor families stricken with illness. Commenting on Lucille's decision to treat Bess by taking her back to the castle, Henry addresses his listeners and readers directly, saying he can understand how they might question whether in Britain 'a princess from a noble family could take in a woman she did not know who appeared to be a beggar and treat her kindly'.

> Readers reading the above might doubt that. In counties or towns within one's jurisdiction, if there are poor people, the noble lady calls at each poor household two or three times a week, and if in the poor household there is a sick person, she offers medicine or treats them for their illness, and everyone regards this as her normal role. Since, possibly on such an occasion, they spare no effort to bring money or goods, the respect the poor have for the aristocracy increases greatly and thus the power of the aristocracy is still considerable (Buradon 1886:45–46).

By 1881, three years before the *Chōya shinbun* report and Black's description of slum life in *Kusaba no tsuyu*, during the economically harsh deflationary period of the Matsukata administration, three slums in Tokyo – at Samegabashi in Yotsuya, Shin Ami-chō in Shiba and Mannen-chō in Shitaya – contained an estimated 10 per cent of the city's population (Uchida 1987:164–165). By the time the campaigning journalist Yokoyama Gennosuke collated his observations of the slums in 1899 in his book *Nihon no kasō shakai* (Japan's lower class society), each of the three slums was estimated to contain populations varying between 5000 and 32,000 people (Uchida 1987:164–165). Most of the occupants were blue-collar workers, including day labourers, rickshaw drivers, ragpickers, physiognomists, persons who specialised in replacing the bamboo pipe sections of the *kiseru* (*rao no sugekae*) and street entertainers. They also housed fallen *samurai*, poverty-stricken artisans and merchants. Many people listening to or reading Henry's references to slums would have immediately understood what he was talking about, even if they did not live in a slum.

There were many other similar sections of the city where residents lived in very crowded conditions with little privacy. In 1898, more than 40,000 rickshaw pullers were said to be living in slum conditions. In 1891, there were slums in Nihonbashi, Kyōbashi, Kanda, Shiba, Asakusa and Koishikawa. Slum clearance became a matter of government policy when, in 1880, Tokyo Governor Matsuda Michiyuki issued a plan for a Chūō-shiku, which called for Nihonbashi, Kanda and Kōjimachi to become the business and administrative heart of the city, following the removal of the slum housing because it was a fire hazard (Uchida 1987:164–165).

The poor health of many of the poorly paid workers living in slum conditions, of whom Bess in *Kusaba no tsuyu* and Seikichi in *Minashigo* are representative, began to concern governments around this time. As the 19th century drew to a close, Japan's industrial revolution offered a steadily increasing number of women the opportunity to go beyond the confines of the village and earn wages (Waswo 1996:60–61). But many had to work long hours in substandard conditions and their health suffered as a result. Women in cotton-spinning factories worked shifts of at least eleven hours, often without a break for meals and frequently obliged to spend time outside their shift hours tending the machines they worked (Morris-Suzuki 1994:87; Tsurumi 1990:especially 43–44, 49–50, 141–144, 162–163).

Henry Black's narrations therefore serve as palatable, but timely warnings about the opportunities and pitfalls of the Industrial Revolution. In *Shachū no dokubari*, for example, Okatsu and Onobu are illegitimate and poorly educated sisters who attempt to forge new identities by leaving Italy and seeking work in Paris. Okatsu meets her death in a coach and Onobu is only able to earn a pittance as an artist's model. In *Kusaba no tsuyu*, Henry's female victim of modern industrial development is Bess, a slum-dweller unable to rise beyond a cycle of sporadic poorly paid employment until she encounters Lucille's aristocratic charity. When the orphan Bess confesses to Bruno that at one stage she had been very ill and that her husband Tom had been the only one to comfort her (Buradon 1886:140), it is clear that the illness was a result of her poverty. Marriage was Bess's only way out of the poverty trap. A subtext here is Lucille's pleas to Bruno that once he enter parliament he work to help poor people (*kyūmin*) like Bess. (Buradon 1886:56)

Henry's portrayals of Bess, Okatsu and Onobu, or Omine in *Minashigo* are cautionary tales about the hardships women might endure during the early stages of modern industrial growth, such as that experienced by Japan between the mid 1880s and the mid 1890s when factory production took a sharp upturn (Duus 1976:136). The lives of these fictional women portend how industrialisation and commercialisation would alter the physical and psychological landscape of Japanese cities, as well as human relationships. The growing unease over workers' conditions evolved in the first strikes by factory workers in Japan in the late 1880s (Tsurumi 1990:50–58).

In the late 1890s, Yokoyama Gennosuke had worked as a temporary employee of the survey office of the Ministry of Agriculture and Commerce. His findings contributed to a 1902–1903 publication of a survey of factory workers' conditions put out by the Ministry (Shokkō 1998). The survey's revelations and the consequent publicity given to workers' conditions led to the overhaul of labour and health laws. The survey revealed that the most common diseases among textile factory workers were 'diseases of the respiratory tract and digestive system, followed by the eyes, joints, and reproductive organs' (Shokkō 1998:140). The report noted that workers were 'engaged all day at their machines in extremely monotonous and meaningless work' with 'few holidays and little time for rest, and are required to work as soon as they have finished their meals, with the result that many of them suffer digestive ailments and lack of nutrition' (Shokkō 1998:140–141). Most of the workers at such factories were women. Patricia Tsurumi notes that the motivation for the review was the creation of 'healthy industries' more than 'healthy workers', Home Ministry and Ministry of Agriculture and Commerce bureaucrats behind the review 'believed that short-run profits gained from hazardous working conditions would in the long run cost the nation too much in diminished efficiency on the part of weakened workers, who might also produce sickly offspring' (Tsurumi 1990:6–7).

The monitoring of social conditions reflected the social management in which the government and bureaucrats were engaged, which was taken to greater extremes in later years. The concern for social problems such as urban poverty identified by Henry Black in his narrations was shared by social planning bureaucrats under the government's 'leading spokesman for social policy', Soeda Juichi of the Finance Ministry (Garon 1987:26). By the late 1890s they were closely monitoring developments in Europe and warning of the possibility that Japan would experience the same labour movement agitation brought on by the terrible conditions inflicted on workers in the factories of Industrial Revolution England. Henry's cautionary tales of conditions in Europe, together with the work of Yokoyama Gennosuke, preceded even the earliest official acknowledgement of the problems by the bureaucracy, making them a valuable resource in documenting the development of labour rights in Japan.

A venal bureaucracy

Some of Henry's most trenchant criticism of bureaucrats is to be found in *Minashigo*. His description of Tanaka Seiemon, the venal head of the orphanage from which Seikichi flees, mirrors Dickens' treatment of the equivalent character in *Oliver Twist*. The passage also contains a hint of the dependence by the poor on state welfare, which Britain was then pioneering and for which Japanese social activists were pressing their government. But Henry's description of Tanaka diverges from Dickens to include a characteristically Japanese understanding of the Meiji-era bureaucracy. Here, Henry addresses his audience directly, drawing upon a contemporary Japanese image of small or middle-ranking bureaucrats as catfish. The metaphor was quintessentially Meiji Japanese and his audiences were in on the secret. Referring to Tanaka, Henry tells his audience of a 'British saying' that 'small fish are bony (*honeppoi*)', a Japanese euphemism for 'hard-to-deal-with'. While asserting that he was sure there were no such bureaucrats in Japan, Henry proceeded, tongue-in-cheek, to criticise Japan's low-ranking bureaucrats as equally *honeppoi* (Ishii 1896:2). The significance of the remark lies in the Meiji political satirist's convention of likening such persons to catfish.

> There is a British proverb that says that small fish are bony (*honeppoi*). Indeed, when one thinks about it, it is a clever turn of phrase. The small catfish (*konamazu*) is invariably bony. Even if you cook it in mock turtle soup (*suppon ni*), the bones get stuck in the mouth and it's not a bit delicious. All top bureaucrats often toil away honestly, showing compassion (*awaremi*) and not discriminating against those below them, but when you get down to the lower ranks, they are apt to be oppressed and there are some who are quite unreasonable. I very much doubt that such a disgraceful thing would happen in Japan. Needless to say, all the bureaucrats [in Japan] are the epitome of integrity and absolute incorruptibility. To Britain's shame, however, there are unfortunately among my countrymen, a number of reprehensible types, such as Tanaka Seiemon, in the bureaucracy (Ishii 1896:2).

It is worth noting that seven years before the publication of *Minashigo*, the *Mesamashi shinbun* had reported on 6 April 1887 that Henry was taking painting lessons from Kawanabe Kyōsai, an artist noted for his satirical representations of bureaucrats as catfish. Kyōsai made a name for himself as a painter of comical frogs, demons and humans with grotesquely elongated necks and noses. He also painted satires of faddish Japanese obsessed with the superficial symbols of modernity such as Western-style umbrellas and silk hats. His bewhiskered catfish became the Meiji satirist's symbol of a conceited bureaucrat who aped Western sartorial style by sporting fashionable sideburns or moustache resembling the whiskers on a catfish.[78]

---

78 One of the finest examples of this theme is Kawanabe's painting 'Fuji koshi no neko to namazu' (Cat and catfish flying over Mt. Fuji) in 'Kyōsai no giga, kyōga' (Oikawa 1996:127). The painting, which dates from 1881, is a double parody on the popular Kanō School of painting theme of a dragon flying over Mt. Fuji and Kinkō-sennin, 'the

Although no records at the Kyōsai Museum just outside Tokyo substantiate the *Mesamashi shinbun* account of Henry studying under the great artist,[79] the possibility is consistent with his taking a number of foreign students, including the *yatoi* architect, Josiah Conder.[80] Kyōsai had already become a favourite of residents in the foreign concession of Tsukiji following his receipt of an award for his work 'Crow on a bare branch' at the 1881 Domestic Industrial Exposition.[81] The possibility that Henry did learn painting from Kawanabe Kyōsai is intriguing in view of his discourse on the differences between Japanese and Western styles of painting in his 1891 work, *Shachū no dokubari*. The main character in that story, Kanō Motokichi, is a portrait artist and Henry was able to expound on the differences between Japanese and Western painting, explaining to audiences that, whereas it took between 10 and 11 days to complete a Japanese-style painting, it could take between six and 10 months to complete a Western-style oil painting. He also noted in the story that, unlike Japanese-style paintings, a Western-style oil painting can be painted over if the artist makes a mistake (Kairakutei 1891b:88).

A number of characteristics would have endeared Henry to Kyōsai. For one thing, Henry shared Kyōsai's reputation as 'a drinker and teller of tall tales' (Jordan 1997:111). Kyōsai's work was also known for its comicality, caricature and satire, all important elements in *rakugo*. Like Kyōsai's works, many *rakugo* stories attribute human characteristics to animals[82] or depict animals that become humans but cannot free themselves of their animal

---

Chinese immortal who flies on the head of a dragon'. Kyōsai has turned the dragon into a catfish and with a cat riding on it, which in many of his pictures symbolised a geisha. The image depicts the philandering bureaucrat lording it over the new, modern Tokyo. Below the flying catfish are the high-rise towers of the modern city of Tokyo.

79 The article is reproduced in Shogei (1977:4). Dr Kusumi Kawanabe, granddaughter of the artist and director of the Kyōsai Memorial Museum, could shed no further light on the *Mesamashi shinbun* report of Black studying under Kyōsai. There is no entry in a diary kept by her grandfather to substantiate the report. I am indebted to Dr Kawanabe for the details from the diary.

80 Kyōsai was known to several contemporary foreigners, including collectors resident in Japan such as French archaeologist Emile Etienne Guimet and his travelling companion, artist Félix Régamey, British doctor William Anderson and the 'father' of Tokyo University medical studies department Erwin von Baelz (Oikawa 1996:5).

81 After receiving the award, Kawanabe Kyōsai 'was invited to the foreign settlement in Tsukiji, where he is said to have created some two hundred crow paintings at the request of the foreigners resident there' (Oikawa 1996:37).

82 Kyōsai's work is part of a long Japanese tradition of comic paintings and prints that began with Toba Sōjō (1053–1140) and the work partially attributed to him, the *Chōjū giga* (frolicking animals scrolls). Kyōsai was a student of Utagawa Kuniyoshi (1797–1861) who was known for his wood-block depictions of humanoid cherries and chess pieces and of human faces consisting of many small figures. Kyōsai's depictions of frolicking animals,

habits. (An example is the story of a dog who realised his wish to become a man, but continued lifting one of his legs whenever he urinated.) In addition, as 'one of the first satirists of modern political and social conditions', Kyōsai portrayed real-life events for popular consumption (Jordan 1997:111). Similarly, Henry illustrated his awareness of the humorous consequences of rapid modernisation, frequently synonymous with Westernisation, in references to human foibles and contemporary fashions and mores, as well as to the questionable behaviour of members of the bureaucracy in Japan and in the West.

The derogatory comment about the 'bony' Tanaka Seiemon in *Minashigo* was far more scathing and critical than anything in *Shachū no dokubari*, in which Henry lampooned the Meiji-era bureaucracy with his tongue-in-cheek reference to high-ranked bureaucrats facing dismissal unless they could produce volumes of paperwork to explain their visit to a bar. Tanaka Seiemon was clearly venal and corrupt compared to the browbeaten bureaucrats smothered in red tape in the earlier story. He was an essential element in the dysfunctional human landscape of *Minashigo*.

---

including frogs, bats, cats, catfish, rats and turtles, drew inspiration from the *Chōjū giga* and from Kuniyoshi's works.

Chapter 11

Face creams and tooth powder

> Just as the Japanese praise foreigners with the words 'So lovely!' much of the softness and lustre of the skin of Westerners is due to the effect of cosmetics.
>
> (Burakku & Takamatsu, 1891:1).

On 12 May 1891, during his most productive year, Henry Black published a book with his partner on beauty and hygiene.[83] The 85-page *Keshōhō: danjo seibi* (Beauty and Makeup Methods for Men and Women) cost 35 *sen*.[84] The publication of this book by a person specialising in *rakugo* is not as bizarre a development as it might appear. Several factors were at play.

For one thing, Henry had a collaborator in the form of his partner Takamatsu Motokichi. The *Yamato shinbun* advertisement promoting the book stated that it was available through Motokichi of the company Eidendō at Irifune-chō 8-chōme, 1-banchi in Kyōbashi, which was also Henry's address. 'The Briton Burakku' is listed in the book as editor and Motokichi as translator. Henry cross-promoted Eidendō in another narration around this time. In *Eikoku Rondon gekijō miyage*, when the nobleman John Smith (Jon Sumisu) dyes his hair to alter his appearance, Henry urged his listeners to obtain the product he used through Eidendō: 'If you don't have the ointment, then try at Eidendō for blue or black' (Eikokujin 1891:116). Sumisu also put on makeup to make himself look darker.

Henry acknowledged his friendship with Motokichi by giving his name to the central character in *Shachū no dokubari*, published in the same year as

83 An advertisement for the book appeared in the *Yamato shinbun*, 23 May 1891 (cited by Asaoka 1988:13).

84 The cover carries the English words: 'Beauty, how to increase and preserve the beauty of the complexion, hair and teeth'. The authors' address is given as 'Irifune-chō 8 chōme, 1 banchi in Kyōbashi'. Asaoka Kunio located a copy of book at the National Diet Library in Tokyo (Asaoka 1988:13).

Keshōhō: danjo seibi. We know that Henry and Motokichi lived in Irifune-chō until at least 1893, when a police dossier, compiled as part of paperwork required for Henry's marriage, mentioned that he was living there with the 'well known homosexual' Takamatsu Motokichi.

Publication of the book should also be considered within the context of the Meiji-era state-sponsored promotion of public health and hygiene, as well as state interest in refashioning the role of women. The book has three sections, 'Skin', 'Hair' and 'Mouth', each with an introductory explanation. The first of these urged readers to emulate foreigners and to take personal hygiene and cosmetics seriously:

> It is human nature for men and women alike to want praise for taking pride in having one's body, hair and skin as beautiful and glossy as possible. One can say that if one uses a cosmetic suited to one's body, one can certainly enhance one's beauty, but such people who do so are few in this world. Normally, things which are whitish coloured lose their gloss due to the sunlight and take on a darker hue, or things which have had a dark hue to begin with become so dark it is difficult to see them. Take soap for example. Bathing by using things like rice bran should ensure the skin attains its natural colour and lustre. This is through one's own efforts, by effectively removing dirt and softening the skin, so that the original colour returns and one looks lovely at a glance. What's more, moles, pimples, hardened skin, rough spots and other sorts of sores are quite easily fixed. Just as the Japanese praise foreigners with the words 'So lovely!', much of the softness and lustre of the skin of Westerners is due to the effect of cosmetics (Burakku & Takamatsu 1891:1–2).

Henry went on to explain that methods for making the products in their book came from Britain, France and America, but that all ingredients were available locally. This suggests that he culled information for the book from a range of overseas sources and translated it for Motokichi who transcribed the details. Henry was good at self-promotion, claiming that persons who were already good-looking and used the cosmetics would enhance their appearance and that 'even those who are not good-looking will acquire a beauty and lustre and will certainly meet with praise from others' (Burakku & Takamatsu 1891:2–3). The book listed ways of preparing beauty aids, including face whitener, toothpaste, mouth deodorant and eau de Cologne. In the introduction to the section on mouth hygiene, it promised that the recipes for mouth deodorants and tooth cleaners would help eliminate mouth odour, give clean teeth and relieve toothache (Burakku & Takamatsu 1891:60–61).

Meiji governments eagerly promoted Western-style chemical cosmetics as adjuncts to hygiene and modernisation. An example of this was a campaign by governments through schools to encourage children to clean their hands and brush their teeth. Henry also promoted soap in *Shachū no dokubari* in 1891, when he referred to the landlady of the dead Okatsu as having a face so grimy (*kao ni aka ga kobiritsuite iru*) that it needed a wash with the popular Kaō brand soap available in Tokyo's Bakura-chō district (Kairakutei 1891b:65). Soap was a relatively early post-Restoration innovation, having been the subject of domestic research from pre-Meiji times, leading to the establishment of soap factories in Kyoto in 1873 and in Yokohama in 1874 (*Meiji* 1986:14). Bakura-chō, in Nihonbashi, was the site of the soaps, cosmetics and household goods firm Nagase Shōten, which was using the Kaō brand name by 1891. Kaō brand soap is still popular in Japan today. Cholera outbreaks in the late 1880s, just before Henry and Motokichi's book was published, had spurred the promotion of soap as a health aid (*Meiji* 1986:16). It should also be remembered that 'cholera prevention' had been one of the topics Henry addressed at speech meetings with his father and their associates in the Freedom and People's Rights Movement between June 1879 and January 1880.

Another early starter in the cosmetics business was the now well-known company Shiseidō, established in 1872 by Fukuhara Arinobu as Japan's first Western-style pharmacy. One of the company's products, sold from 1888, was tooth powder and paste, which were among the earliest products the company promoted. Shiseidō began selling cosmetics in 1897.

Henry and Motokichi's book was also a natural adjunct to a growing interest in fashion and appearance, stimulated in part by government decrees affecting the very appearance of women. For example, in 1868, the year of the Meiji Restoration, the government issued a decree that married women need no longer blacken their teeth. The custom had continued from earlier eras when aristocrats, including men, had blackened their teeth.

Frequently associated with Westernisation, campaigns to refashion Japanese women were fuelled by constructs such as the Rokumeikan, the government-built pavilion for Western style balls and concerts at which upper-class citizens dressed principally in European-style clothes and adopted European hairstyles. The example set by the wives of prominent government figures at these functions fuelled demand for information on how to attain Western-style beauty and dress (*Meiji* 1986:14). Itō Umeko, wife of elder statesman Itō Hirobumi, set her own example. She actively promoted the cultivation of Western-style feminine accomplishments through the formation of women's groups dedicated to the improvement of etiquette and conversational skills (Sievers 1983:93). Contemporary magazines devoted considerable space to informing readers, particularly women, of fashion changes, as well as of newly available cosmetics and methods of achieving a fashionable look.

Henry even chided audiences at times for their uncritical adoption of Western customs. As one of the more tangible expressions of modernity, fashions in clothing were a superficial target for his critical eye, particularly women's fashion. Meiji Japanese exhibited considerable interest in Western clothing and Henry found himself obliged to explain that such fashions altered rapidly in the West. In *Shachū no dokubari*, for example, he used the poor fashion sense of Okatsu's landlady to explain the rapidity of change in European fashion: 'But she seemed to be someone who didn't care about appearances. Even with her dress, she had quite a strange style. She was done up in a lady's hat that appeared to have been the fashion fourteen or fifteen years ago, and a drab shawl' (Kairakutei 1891b:70).

In *Oliver Twist*, Dickens made no detailed mention of the position of the pockets on the back of Mr Brownlow's 'bottle-green coat with a black velvet collar' as his readers would have taken their position for granted. But, aware of audience interest in such matters, Henry spared no detail, telling audiences that the elderly man was wearing a long, black *mantoru* (coat) with a pocket in the rear 'such that when one sits down, the pocket is positioned underneath the backside'. Henry then gave a humorous aside about those who carry a sweet home in the pocket from a visit to friends, having to be careful not to sit on it while travelling in a horsedrawn trolley. He explained that handkerchiefs were the most sought after things among British pickpockets 'because they were good little money earners' (Ishii 1896:50–51).

Indicative of Henry Black's familiarity with the discourse on beauty is a passage in *Shachū no dokubari* which refers to the custom of Western artists using live models. Here, Henry says this is a seemingly straightforward task, but that unless a male model is good-looking 'like Zaigo Chūjō Narihira, Hikaru Genji, or a handsome man such as myself, an artist will not make a decent living' (Kairakutei 1891b:24). Zaigo Chūjō Narihira was a reference to Ariwara no Narihira (825–880), the fifth son of Prince Abo and a noted *waka* poet of the early Heian period. Narihira was said to be 'famous as the model of the courtly lover, and numerous legends surround his name'.[85] Hikaru Genji is the amorous central character in *The Tale of Genji*, an 11th-century novel whose authorship is attributed to the court lady, Murasaki Shikibu. Henry then describes the ideal female beauty, noting that in the case of a woman, 'her look must have eyes like a lotus flower (*fuyō no manajiri*), lips like a red flower (*tanka no kuchibiru*), and the blushing charm (*chingyo rakugan*) of a bashful flower under the hidden moon (*heigetsu shūka*)' (Kairakutei 1891b:24).[86] The passage is packed full of allusions, some of which may have been familiar to readers of advertising copy at the time. Listeners might have known, for example, that the lotus flower was a simile for a beautiful woman. They might also have known that the notion of bashfulness implied in the *kanji* of the expression *chingyo rakugan* originally derived from the notion that fish and birds flee from humans, even if humans find them beautiful to behold. Later the expression altered in nuance to signify the shyness of animals in the presence of humans. By Henry's time, it implied the bashful charm of a beautiful, but modest woman.

What the book shows

Keshōhō: danjo seibi joined a growing selection of publications about health and hygiene that contributed to the discourse on modernity and women. The book is an indication of the timing and extent of Japanese interest in Western cosmetics and of the development of the average citizen's understanding and appreciation of the importance of personal hygiene. It sheds light on Henry Black's role as a facilitator of modernisation and proves that, long after his cooperation with members of the Freedom and People's Rights Movement, he maintained an interest in disseminating to ordinary people an understanding of hygiene in the years just prior to the mass production of cosmetics.

---

85 For more information, see 'Ariwara no Narihira' (Hisamatsu 1976:54) and 'Ariwara no Narihira' (*Dai jinmei* 1953–56:I,123–124).

86 'Onna nareba fuyō manajiri, tanka no kuchibiru, chingyo rakugan heigetsu shūka no yosooi de nakereba ikemasen.' The passage contains these meanings: *fuyō* (a cotton/ Confederate rose) is also an alternative name for the lotus flower and a simile for a beautiful woman (Niimura 1992:2269); *manajiri* (eyes); *tanka* (red flower), making *tanka no kuchibiru* a simile for the lips of a beautiful woman (Niimura 1992:1624); *chingyo rakugan* (fish and birds flee [at the sight of such beauty]) (Niimura 1992:1695); *heigetsu shūka* (sometimes written as *shūka heigetsu*). On exposure to a beautiful countenance, even a flower is bashful and the moon goes into hiding. Signifies a beautiful woman (Niimura 1992:1209): *yosooi* (toilet/ makeup/ attire).

The book is also a window onto his personal life, the depth of his knowledge of Japan and his aesthetic sensibility. If Henry had not previously known about historical figures such as Zaigo Chūjō Narihira or Hikaru Genji, or allusions to bashful flowers under a hidden moon, he must have been receiving good advice on such matters, which may have come from Takamatsu Motokichi. Very little is known about Motokichi other than the police reference to him living with Henry. His co-authorship of the book suggests that Henry's partner was at least familiar with the making or use of cosmetics, which raises the possibility that Motokichi was in some way involved with stage makeup and met Henry through their involvement in theatre. He may also have been a beautician. These conclusions are, however, no more than speculation.

Chapter 12

Narrating the Meiji woman

> You marry and might regret it for life. Morally speaking, it is assumed that the wife you marry will be the one for life until death do you part. Since in Britain divorce is not permitted, a lot of people have problems. In Japan, changing a wife is as easy as changing the *tatami* matting (Eikokujin 1891:61).

In *Eikoku Rondon gekijō miyage*, Henry Black told of a woman, Gātsurudo, disowned by her father for falling in love with and marrying an abusive and dissolute actor. The story was adapted in 1891 from Mary Braddon's 'Her Last Appearance' (Braddon 1877), but in Henry's version Gātsurudo's fate is altogether more positive. Braddon's actress does not marry again, move to Paris or inherit an estate. Instead, she dies alone, weak and miserable after a performance, leaving her admirer disappointed. Henry's adaptation has a central female character who is strong-willed and displays considerable independence. His additions to the story and transformation of its central character were in keeping with his participation in the Meiji-era debate over women's rights.

Women and their status were often at the heart of Henry's stories. A typical example is his 1892 narration *Tsurugi no hawatari* (The sword's blade), in which the father of the heroine Oshizu is killed by an acrobat called Kanda Taketarō. Oshizu is duped into marrying Taketarō, but at the last minute is saved from the marriage by Shimada Ichitarō, who has been in love with her all along. Between the moment of her father's murder and her ultimate marriage to Ichitarō, Oshizu endures all manner of trials and tribulations which toughen her (Itō 2002: 180–181).

A major theme in Henry's 1891 tale, *Shachū no dokubari*, dealt forthrightly with the right of a woman to inherit from her father even when illegitimate. For this story, Henry adapted material from du Boisgobey's mystery novel, *Le Crime de l'omnibus*, set in Paris, which allowed him to participate in the discourse of legal reform, including the Japanese adoption of elements of French Napoleonic legal codes and their impact on the status of women.

Tsurugi no hawatari appears to be an adaptation of the Fortuné du Boisgobey mystery novel *Le Pouce crochu*, which was published in English as *Zigzag the Clown*.[87] Henry's adaptation was variously published under the titles *Kanda Taketarō*, *Kuruwaza Taketarō* (Acrobat Taketarō) and *Kyokugeishi* (The acrobat) and has many of the classic elements of sensation fiction.

Like Oshizu, Henry's heroines were drawn from the 'women's sensation fiction' sub-genre of Victorian sensation fiction. In the main, this sub-genre portrayed two types of women: 'active assertive women, who convey a sense of the threat of insurgent femininity trying to break out of the doll's house of domesticity, and passive dependent women, who are imprisoned by it, unable to articulate their sense of confinement, and driven to desperate measures' (Pykett 1994:49). Lyn Pykett (1994:45) characterises the popularity of the women's sensation novel as 'both a response to and part of social change and a changing conceptualisation of women'.

Henry's female characters were as varied as those in the genre from which he borrowed. In many of the plots chosen or constructed by Henry, women are the perpetrators of or the inspiration for action. In *Shachū no dokubari*, the beautiful artist's model Suzuki Onobu, who stands to gain a large inheritance, is the target of fortune-hunting killers, but is rescued by the painter Kanō Motokichi. In *Bara musume*, the central female is the anarchist flower seller Ohana, who plans to assassinate a French prince. And in *Minashigo*, Henry follows Dickens' *Oliver Twist* storyline faithfully, with Fukuda Yūkichi confirming in the final few pages that his deceased daughter, Seikichi's mother, had married a man called Itō after eloping with him. Fukuda's sorrow at the loss of his daughter is tempered by the thought that she loved Itō enough to marry him and produce Seikichi, his grandson. A subplot in *Iwade ginkō chishio no tegata* is the pledge between Matashichi and Omasa that they will marry once Matashichi is able to make his way in the world. This is in spite of Matashichi's origins as a homeless orphan and Omasa's as the daughter of a wealthy banker. Despite the odds, the two finally receive permission to marry in what could be seen as a vindication of the right to marry for love.

In remaining true to the women's sensation fiction genre's presentation of alternative and nonconformist female role models, many of Henry's

87 I am indebted to Terry Hale of the University of Hull for pointing out the origin of the tale.

female protagonists exemplified initial gains made by women immediately after the Restoration. They were often the antithesis of the 'good wife, wise mother' ideology subsequently promoted by the state. Oshizu was one of Henry's typical heroines. Battered by misfortune and frequently misunderstood, Oshizu finally sees justice done and wins her man.

In Henry's tales, many of the female protagonists struggle with the issues of the day and seek solutions to the problems which society throws at them. Their struggles are necessitated by their lack of education, absence of gainful employment, or enforced domesticity through a dull marriage. Emancipation and education of women were topics of debate in Japan when Henry presented his sensation fiction-inspired narrations. Although women were by 1890 the 'backbone of the Japanese economy', outnumbering men in light industry, especially in textiles, where a predominantly female workforce produced 40 per cent of the gross national product and 60 per cent of foreign exchange, they did not have the vote and only a little more than 30 per cent of those eligible to attend school did so (Nolte & Hastings 1991:153).

Nevertheless, by the 1890s, the Meiji Restoration and its subsequent reforms had wrought far-reaching changes to the role of women and to the manner in which men and women related to each other. The status of women was also intrinsically linked to the national debate over law reform. Given Henry's continued interest in legal issues, it is therefore not surprising that his choice of material for adaptation portrayed evidence of the impact of social change on women. In Britain, debate over prostitution and educational and employment opportunities for women before and after the introduction of the English Divorce Act of 1857 had contributed to the growth of women's sensation fiction. Similarly, in Japan, in the early years of the Meiji period, until around 1890, there was little government consensus, but much debate, over the nature of changes in the treatment of women. During these years, a number of elite women, whose reading of John Stuart Mill's *The Subjection of Women* inspired them to work through the Freedom and People's Rights Movement, addressed rural gatherings on women's rights (Nolte & Hastings 1991:155–156). But by the 1890s, the government – run by men – had won the debate, banning women from attending political meetings or even listening to political speeches through its promulgation in 1887 of the Peace Preservation Ordinance (Lehmann 1982: 299–230).

The ordinance marked the beginning of a systematic, government-sanctioned campaign to encourage middle-class women to serve the developing nation by remaining in the home as 'good wives and wise mothers'. In 1889, the government permitted propertied males to participate in the Diet, but banned women from similar political activity. But in the 1890s, when Henry Black was at his most active on the stage, women could attend *rakugo* performances or read *sokkibon*. The tenor and presence of the female characters in Henry's narrations suggest there was still a healthy and subversive questioning of the official version of femininity well into the 1890s.

The issue of women's property and inheritance rights, for example, figured prominently as a metaphor for female emancipation in these years. With regard to a woman's right to inherit and own property, the patterning of Japan's 1890 Civil Code on French laws embodying the notion of social equality effectively modified Edo period discrimination against wives. The earlier form of discrimination had placed the wife second to the husband and the changes ended the past practice of emphasising the male lineage (Yazaki 1968:360). Given the topicality of the issue of inheritance, whether for men or for women, and the manner by which one could gain or distribute an inheritance, Black devoted considerable effort in his 1891 tale, *Shachū no dokubari*, to explicating through the dialogue the intricacies of inheritance rights in France. In *Shachū no dokubari*, the audience learns of French law as it applied to kinship structure and property relations, particularly in relation to the rights of inheritance pertaining to women. In particular, the statute of limitations on the right to claim an inheritance is discussed in some detail. When Yamada, the retired and respectable businessman, wishes Okatsu dead because she is the illegitimate daughter of his brother's Italian mistress (*gonsai*), Henry explains the social stigma attached to having an illegitimate niece. Henry acknowledges that this is as much a source of shame for a family (*ie no haji*) in France as in Japan, but notes that in spite of being illegitimate and female, Okatsu and her sister Onobu are legal beneficiaries of their father's will.

Primogeniture owed its origins in Europe and Japan to feudalism. In Japan, military overlords had sought to maintain links to followers by allocating land to them (Macfarlane 1998:117). But there were important differences, which Henry's narrations elucidated. In England one could disinherit an heir by selling one's property or giving it to someone else in a will, so that not even the firstborn was assured of an inheritance. Japan had had its *ie* (household system) based on 'family farms', subjecting the *ie* to the vagaries of 'demography and genes' so that there developed a system of adoption to ensure succession.[88] This had resulted in the *ie* in many instances resembling a 'corporation'[89] or 'enterprise group'[90] thanks to the legal ability to recruit persons into it.

Pointing to differences between Japan and Europe early in *Shachū no dokubari*, Henry tells the audience that there are many women in Europe who are 'both young and rich':

> In Japan, one very much dislikes having a household name die out. People adopt if they have no child or if they have a girl, they take in a son-in-law (*muko*) who adopts their family name. In Britain, France, Germany and America, they do not worry about whether or not a household will die out. There are no laws there covering the taking in of adoptees and you cannot obtain a *muko* for a girl (Kairakutei 1891b:38).

Henry goes on to explain that daughters in Europe are married off with dowries and that, if a father dies, the daughter is quite within her rights to inherit the father's fortune and can then take the money with her when she marries.

It was this radical notion of inheritance, this ability to pass on property from a father to a daughter, rather than the restriction of inheritance rights to a firstborn son or a male adoptee, that was introduced under the new Meiji civil code. The new law ensured that, on paper at least, the passing of property from the *ie* to the firstborn son was not necessarily the natural order of things. The message Henry Black's audiences would have received from *Shachū no dokubari* was one of change in the power relationship between men and women. Onobu's example was a foretaste of what was to come.

Prior to the Meiji period, household members inherited property only with the permission of the household head.[91] The new civil code enabled household members for the first time to exercise their own, individual property rights. By the early 1890s, with Japan more than 20 years into an era of change, the right of the individual to dispose of property independent of the *ie* had become synonymous with modernity.

---

88 In Japan, certainly in the 19th century, adoption of persons who were not kin was not uncommon. Black took advantage of the system by being adopted in May 1893 into the family of his legal wife, Ishii Aka, and becoming Ishii Burakku.

89 The word is used by JJ Rein in *Japan: travels and researches* (1884) and by F Ratzell in *The History of Mankind* (1898), who are both quoted by Alan Macfarlane (1998:121).121.

90 Robert Smith uses this word in *Japanese Society* (1983) and is quoted by Alan Macfarlane (1998:121).

91 GB Sansom in *The Western World and Japan* (1950), quoted by Macfarlane (1998:122).

But these initiatives were short-lived. In 1898, seven years after *Shachū no dokubari*, a revised civil code responded to a conservative backlash and brought the family system back in line with feudal values (Yazaki 1968:360), reinstating the right of eldest sons to inherit family property. However, many of the limitations on Japanese women inheriting, owning property and becoming household heads, and the stipulation that they required their husband's permission to manage their own property or enter into a contract or profession were not unknown in Europe, as they were all contained in the Code Napoléon and, even more so, in the German equivalent (Lehmann 1982:231–232).

Tales like *Shachū no dokubari*, in which an uncle bequeaths a fortune to an illegitimate niece, and *Tsurugi no hawatari* , in which Oshizu has 5,000 *yen* from her murdered father, were integral to the contemporary debate over law reform as it pertained to women. They were also lessons in what British social anthropologist Alan Macfarlane cites as 'the development of individualised property relations as the central and decisive factor in the rise of modern civilisation, and in particular, capitalism' (Macfarlane 1998:104). The notion that ownership of private property and the accumulation of capital was a natural right was developed and defended throughout the 18th and 19th centuries by thinkers from political economist John Millar (1735–1801) to free-trade advocate Adam Smith (1723–1790) and political scientist, historian and politician Alexis de Tocqueville (1805–1859). In Japan, it found expression in the new laws of the Meiji period. And, as the example of Henry Black shows, it also found its way onto the *yose* stage and in the popular literature of the *sokkibon*. Thus, in *Shachū no dokubari*, the businessman Tanaka's musings on the appropriateness of allowing his daughter to marry a painter had considerable importance for Henry's audiences. That her suitor was a painter, whose uncertain income depended on the dictates of fashion and public taste, emphasised the importance attached to inheritance by demonstrating the extent to which 19th-century property relations determined status and social relations.

Bringing Mary Braddon to Japan

In her examination of the impact of European narrative styles on post-Meiji-Restoration Japanese literature, Kyoko Kurita has claimed that in pre-Meiji Japan, the narrative tradition lacked 'a sophisticated use of the romantic triangle' (Kurita 1997:229–230). This would explain why so many European sensation fiction works using the romantic triangle as a literary device were adapted by Japanese writers and translators in the 1880s and 1890s. Kurita has argued that the example of the romantic triangle in the West at this time showed Japanese writers how to increase the melodramatic potential of plots by involving society and other characters and even allowed them to 'assess the place of the individual and the nation in history' (Kurita 1997:230). But Kurita also argues that Meiji authors before Natsume Sōseki were unable to realise the full potential of the romantic triangle because they had first to outgrow an initial fascination with its symbolic potential (Kurita 1997:230). In this context, Henry Black's use of the romantic triangle prior to Sōseki suggests that he may have abetted the process of adapting it to Japanese conditions.

One of Henry Black's more favoured authors, Mary Braddon, was one of the sensation fiction genre's more accomplished exponents of the romantic triangle. Braddon had been an actress before turning to novel-writing in the 1860s. She was noted for her devious and inventive female criminals. Lyn Pykett characterises female criminals created by Braddon and other women writers of the genre as the 'most remarkable and remarked-upon criminals and wrong-doers' of the sensation fiction genre (Pykett 1994:49). Surveys of works adapted from European fiction by Japanese translators in the 1880s suggest that Braddon was one of the earliest female authors of European sensation fiction whose works were adapted in Japan (Miller 2001; Yanagida 1935, 1966). Her works attracted a coterie of translators and publishers who saw in them opportunities to participate in debates over the introduction of a Westernised set of legal codes and the nature of femininity. As mentioned already, at least four of Braddon's works were brought to Japan in the 1880s and 1890s at the height of the sensation fiction boom. Henry Black was responsible for two of these, using them to participate in discussion of several issues closely affecting the status of women, especially law reform, abolition of prostitution and equality of the sexes.

The performer in Henry found inspiration in Braddon's works. Her melodramatic works lent themselves to adaptation by a storyteller like Henry, who would have been keen to impress with cliff-hanger endings for every episode so that audiences would return the following night for the next instalment. As a former actress, Braddon had an eye for the melodramatic in her plots. That her *Diavola* was adapted by newspaper editor Kuroiwa Ruikō and adapted for the *kabuki* stage by playwright Kawatake Shinshichi III substantiates the theatrical appeal of her stories in Japan. Synergies between drama and print in sensation fiction also assume importance in the light of Henry Black's own appearances on the *kabuki* stage. It is not surprising, therefore, that the other Braddon work Henry chose to adapt was 'Her Last Appearance' whose central character, Gātsurudo, is an actress. Henry was in interesting company as a member of a select coterie who played a role in the process of translation, adaptation and transmutation into Meiji-era Japan of the European representations of modernity and popular culture found in Braddon's works.

Of Henry's narrations, *Eikoku Rondon gekijō miyage* exhibits an exceptionally high number of informative and amusing digressions. Although its basis, 'Her Last Appearance', with its short and overly melodramatic plot and dialogue, is not one of Braddon's better works, it obviously draws upon her experiences as an actress. In Henry's hands, the story becomes a lengthy 15-episode work of suspense, copiously interspersed with cultural comparisons and references to topical social reform issues that would have appealed to his audiences at the time. In Braddon's story, the actress Barbara Stowell is ill-treated by her actor husband Jack Stowell. Upon learning that she is married, an admirer, Sir Philip Hazlemere, urges her to divorce her husband and remarry. When the actress refuses his entreaties, Sir Philip disguises himself and murders her husband. The actress rebuffs Sir Philip and later dies backstage of an unexplained malady. Braddon deals in one sentence with the circumstances of the actress's marriage, stating merely that she was a 'country parson's daughter leading the peacefullest, happiest, obscurest life in a Hertfordshire village' who married in a ceremony 'which was solemnised before she had time to repent that weak moment of concession' (Braddon 1877:326). In his adaptation, Henry devoted considerable detail to his character's origins as Gātsurudo, the naïve daughter of a prosperous farmer named Beniyūeru, and takes four narrated episodes (58 pages of the *sokkibon*) merely to get to the marriage. In other sections he deals in detail with the treatment of crimes in Britain and laws pertaining to gambling and prostitution. None of these details are in the Braddon version. The Braddon work ends with the death of the actress, but in Henry's version Gātsurudo and her admirer marry and leave for Paris to avoid the police in episode 13. The resolution does not occur until episode 15 when Brown blows his brains out with a revolver at an exclusive gentlemen's club in Paris in a scene that is Henry Black at his inventive best.

The frequency of the many didactic diversions from the main storyline make *Eikoku Rondon gekijō miyage* one of Henry Black's more culturally instructive narrations and ensured that it was considerably longer than

Braddon's story. Henry used the tale as a vehicle for engaging in the debate about the abolition of prostitution, which preoccupied reformers and Christian activists throughout the Meiji period. As early as July 1879, Henry had spoken about it at a meeting sponsored by a pro-democracy organisation. In *Eikoku Rondon gekijō miyage* he used the opportunity provided by John Brown's attempt to lure Sumerurī, the dissolute actor husband of Gātsurudo, into a gambling den, to discuss British law and practices with regard to vices including prostitution and gambling:

> In Japan there is currently an argument for eliminating prostitution (*haishō ron*). There are many who take the view that if prostitutes are harmful to society, they ought to be immediately banned. In fact if one listens to their opinions, they would say that without a day's delay, without waiting even an hour or even a minute, they should be banned and the brothels should be burned. But if you listen to opinion on the other side, you cannot deny there is reason in it (Eikokujin 1891:132–133).

Henry then noted that in Japan, when police investigate cases of prostitution, they usually then withdraw without fining offenders:

> But on the surface it is forbidden to put out a sign advertising women. There is the argument that if people openly trade (in women) then there will be damage to society, so it cannot be tolerated. However, in London, there are many people who secretly operate gambling dens or brothels. If any of them are reported, the police enter the premises and it is immediately closed down (Eikokujin 1891:133).

He then addressed the problem of well-known red-light districts in Japan:

> Take the case of Tokyo and you'll see what I mean. Yoshiwara and Susaki are famous places. The streets are wide and the buildings are fine and beautifully decorated. When someone from the country comes to see the sights of Tokyo, if he doesn't go there to take a look, he can't claim to have seen Tokyo. He'll be stuck for something to talk about when he gets back to his hometown and will get laughed at (Eikokujin 1891:133).

There follows a joke about visitors who go to such places and find they cannot return home after losing their money by getting drunk. Finally, he warns his audience that such places are full of smooth-talking pimps who fleece customers and closes with a reference to the law in Britain (Eikokujin 1891:134): 'The British parliament has passed a law banning gambling dens and brothels, but Sumerurī goes to the door of a gambling den and knocks. Sumerurī gives the password and they are let in' (Eikokujin 1891:135).

Marriage customs

Henry uses the same Braddon work as a vehicle to discuss British marriage laws and customs. In Part Three of *Eikoku Rondon gekijō miyage*, when Gātsurudo and Sumerurī marry, he gives details about Christian wedding ceremonies and the necessity for a couple to register their marriage to ensure that offspring are legitimate and can inherit. He explains that this is mandated by British law. He compares such ceremonies in 'my Britain' with what he claims is the relative ease with which Japanese men take concubines and mistresses, adding that the Christian wedding ceremony represents a stronger commitment between the couple than that implied in the simple Japanese ritual of exchanging cups of *sake*:

> Even if citizens (*jinmin*) are upper, middle or lower class, no distinction is made, and when one takes a wife, one has to do so through this ceremony. So if people don't do it, for example if they live together and even call each other husband and wife, they are not a married couple in the eyes of the law. And a child born between them is illegitimate (*shisei no ko*) and has no right to inheritance. Even with people who have, or have not, a belief in religion, generally, when they take a wife, they go to the church and solemnly exchange vows in the presence of a minister (Eikokujin 1891:57).

Later in Part Five, after Gātsurudo and Sumerurī have married and begin to experience marital problems, Henry cites the British saying 'Marry in haste, regret it for the rest of your life' and explains that divorce is easy in Japan, whereas it is presumed that a couple who marry in Britain vow that they will remain married for life. He likens this to the Japanese tale of the sparrow whose tongue has been cut (*shitakiri suzume*). The tale depicts marital fidelity and the reference would have been instantly understood by audiences.

At the close of *Iwade ginkō chishio no tegata*, the hero Matashichi, the son of a poverty-stricken beggar woman, and the heroine Omasa, the daughter of a rich banker, are finally able to marry. Henry's key message here is that in Meiji Japan, people of any standing should be free to marry the partner of their choice. Omasa's uncle supports the match and persuades her mother that the marriage would be good for the Iwade household. When Omasa's mother asks the uncle why 'such a beggar' should be her daughter's husband, he reminds her that,

> even Oliver Cromwell, who briefly became the president of Britain was a herdsman (*ushiya*) once. Even Napoleon who became the emperor of France was of lowly birth (*umaretaru mibun ni atatte iyashi*). General Grant of the United States was the son of a brush-maker whose parents put him in primary school when he was an infant, but could not continue to do so and they spent their days in poverty. In Japan, the Taikō Hideyoshi[92] was a sandal carrier (*zōritori*) and became imperial regent (*kanpaku*). I could cite plenty of people who have risen up in the world to perform deeds for their country. I think that if he marries your Omasa I am sure he will perform deeds for the Iwade Bank (Kairakutei 1893:93).

Following this homily on the greater opportunities for social mobility in the Meiji period, Omasa's uncle reminds her mother of when she was in her teens and her husband-to-be was in his early twenties. They had loved each other and wanted to marry:

> Rather than someone who has status from the moment of birth, I think someone of previously lowly birth who has struggled hard, is honest, and has studied so that he has risen in the world, is precious. Someone who comes from the nobility, for example, these people receive respect thanks to the good deeds of their ancestors, but even if they are addressed as lord (*tonosama*) or as the imperial presence (*gozen*), when if you ask whether they can get so much as three meals a day, they can't (Kairakutei 1893:95).

After her uncle's speech, Omasa again begs her mother to let them marry. Persuaded by the logic of the argument in favour of equality of all people in Meiji-era Japan, her mother agrees to the marriage. Henry closes the tale by declaring that Matashichi and Omasa then live happily ever after 'in Britain'.

---

92 Toyotomi Hideyoshi received the honorific title of Taikō, which was 'applied in the Heian period (794–1185) to the grand minister of state or the regent of the realm and later used to refer to an imperial regent who had passed on his office to his son' (Japan, 1993:1497).

Omasa and Matashichi might have lived in an imaginary Britain, but they were integral to Henry's template for modern couples in Meiji-era Japan. Omasa was the new Meiji woman. She had overcome all the obstacles in her way and had married for love. In Henry's choice of material featuring characters such as Omasa and Gātsurudo and his ongoing affinity for Braddon's works, lies confirmation of the continuation of his earlier interest in the status of women in the New Japan. But his interest lay not only in the future of women in Japanese society. Henry also played female roles in a number of classic *kabuki* plays.

Chapter 13

Learning from the great Danjūrō

> On the fourth or fifth performance, people from the household of [Ichikawa] Danjūrō [IX] came to see the play and suggested I come next morning to learn from him because some of the gestures and lines were wrong. So I went to the Tsukiji home of Danjūrō and he was very pleased. He took me in hand and very kindly taught me this, that and the other, and I immediately carried out what he had taught (Henry Black speaks with journalist Nishūbashi Sei about acting the role of Banzuiin Chōbee [Nishūbashi 1905]).

In 1892, Henry Black played the role of Banzuiin Chōbee, a blustering townsman (*machi yakko*) hero to audiences through the ages. The sight of a foreign-born actor, especially in a role as famous as Banzuiin Chōbee, was an unprecedented development in the history of the Japanese stage (see figure 15). That Henry Black should receive tuition for the role from the great actor Ichikawa Danjūrō IX was further cause for comment. But this was not entirely surprising, since the Meiji-era urge for reform had by then extended to the *kabuki* stage and Danjūrō was one of the great reformers of the era. Co-operation between Danjūrō and Henry was a meeting of reformist minds.

Henry's 1892 Banzuiin Chōbee performances were not his first *kabuki* roles. He had already appeared in 1890 in the female roles of Omiwa in *Imoseyama* (Mt. Imo and Mt. Se) and Osato in *Senbon zakura* (The thousand cherry trees).[93] Both tales involve thwarted love and mistaken identity. In

93 According to Morioka and Sasaki (1983:142), reports of these performances appeared in *Asahi shinbun* on 17 September 1890. *Imoseyama* dates from 1771 and relates to Fujiwara Kamatari's defeat of Soga no Iruka in the seventh century. Omiwa, daughter of a *sake* shop proprietress, is in love with her neighbour Motome, whom she believes is a maker of ceremonial headgear. Motome is really Tankai, brother of the emperor's concubine. In one scene, described as 'superficially comic', but 'drenched in pathos', a love triangle leads to a confrontation between Omiwa and Princess Tachibana (Leiter 1979:217–219). *Senbon zakura*, also called *Yoshitsune senbon zakura* (Yoshitsune and the thousand

1891, he had played Kumagai in *Heike Monogatari*, Rochishin in *Suikoden*, and Omura in *Ibaraki Dōji*, *Sōzaburo no Imōto Omura* (Shogei 1977:4). The reception accorded Henry's *kabuki* performances appears to have boosted his ego. As mentioned earlier, in April 1891, he threatened to quit the San'yūha if he could not play the major roles in *Chūshingura* of Yuranosuke, leader of the 47 *rōnin*, or Kampei, or his wife Okaru (Morioka & Sasaki 1983:144).

While these performances were remarkable for the presence of a foreigner in key roles, the newspaper reports of his Banzuiin Chōbee performances at the Haruki Theatre in September 1892, which focus on Henry's co-operation with Ichikawa Danjurō IX, illustrate their importance to the debate over reform in the arts. In subsequent years, Henry performed other *kabuki* roles, including female ones, but Banzuiin Chōbee was to become his signature role.

Henry's performances attest to his ability to learn Japanese dialogue and deliver it like a native speaker, to his enthusiasm for the theatre and to his devotion to Japan. It had always been the practice for professional narrators to appear in extracts of *kabuki* plays, since this helped to promote narrators to their audiences. A remnant of this practice can still be seen today when well-known *rakugoka* appear in special new-year performances in theatres in Tokyo. The performances of today frequently involve comedy skits rather than the more serious *kabuki* extracts of earlier years, but the skits are often presented in the style of *kabuki*. One such performance I witnessed in the 1990s even included a thoroughly disrespectful and hilarious satire on the habit of the then ailing Emperor Shōwa (Hirohito) of saying '*ah, so desu ka*' (Is that so?) when talking to people at receptions and other formal occasions. In Henry's day, *kabuki* and *rakugo* enjoyed a symbiotic relationship (Ōta 1998:208), with *kabuki* often borrowing from *rakugo* for its storylines and *rakugoka* often attending *kabuki* performances to study the expressions and body movements of actors to incorporate them into their own performances. Gestures might include the pouring of *sake*, eating with chopsticks, or wielding a knife or sword. Duplicating these gestures and expressions in their *rakugo* performances helped *rakugoka* compensate for the lack of props.

In the absence of any established forms of Western drama, *kabuki*'s status as the only medium available for experimentation by reformist playwrights

---

cherry trees), relates to the legendary general, Yoshitsune. Osato appears in a scene set in a *sushi* shop. Osato is in love with Yasuke, whom she believes is the shop's apprentice, but Yasuke is really Koremori, a married novice priest on the run (Leiter 1979:708–711).

and actors at the time may have also facilitated Henry's entry into *kabuki*. From as early as the second decade of the Meiji period, Danjūrō IX had begun exploring more realistic acting techniques, incorporating them into *kabuki* to reflect the psychological states portrayed on stage with greater verisimilitude. In his zeal to try out new ideas, Danjūrō persuaded the playwrights Kawatake Mokuami and Fukuchi Ōchi to experiment with realism and to remain faithful to historical facts in their scripts (Leiter 1979:187). Danjūrō also pioneered a more naturalistic acting style to accompany such themes. The critic and playwright Kanagaki Robun coined the term *katsureki* (literally, 'live history') to describe it. The term quickly became associated with Danjūrō's unique style (Komiya 1969:198).

Kabuki and *rakugo*

Cross-fertilisation between *kabuki* and *rakugo* had occurred before the 1868 Restoration, most recently in response to edicts issued by the shogunate in the Tempō era (1831–1845). In Tokyo, the edicts had limited *kabuki* to a single theatre, prompting *yose* narrators to meet demand by incorporating elements of *kabuki* into dramatised narrations using a limited number of props.[94] San'yūtei Enchō's groundbreaking use of hand actions, facial expression and onomatopoeia to mimic a ghost wearing *geta* (wooden clogs) in *Botan dōrō* is a fine example of a combination of elements from the two genres. Since Japanese ghosts customarily do not have feet but appear to float, the sound of *geta* was at the time novel and horrifying to audiences.

Such borrowing between *kabuki* and *rakugo* was common during the innovative Meiji years, particularly in stories with a heavy *ninjō banashi* (stories of human feeling) content. Typical of the phenomenon was the play *Nezumi komon haru no shingata* written by Kawatake Mokuami (1816–1893). It featured Ichikawa Danjurō IX, but owed much to *Tenpō kaiso den*, a work by Henry's early mentor, narrator and orator Shōrin Hakuen.[95]

A further impetus for reform in *kabuki* was the fascination of foreigners for the genre. Accounts of visits to the *kabuki* by Clara Whitney in April 1876 attest to the fact that by the 1870s and 1880s, upper-class Japanese considered it an acceptable form of entertainment for their foreign guests (Whitney 1979). The visually appealing *kabuki*, with its revolving stage, liberal use of sound effects and lavish props, which could include falling snow, severed heads, dramatically instantaneous costume changes on stage,

94 Known as *shibai banashi* (see Ōta 1998:4).
95 See Nobuhiro Shinji in Yoshizawa (1976:1).

and recreations of running water in streams, was more accessible to foreign audiences than *rakugo* with its minimalist props and almost total dependence on understanding Japanese language. Since foreigners were the epitome of civilisation and enlightenment, it followed that *kabuki* ought to become a vehicle for impressing upon them that the Japanese, through their possession of a popular dance-drama genre, were capable of civilised behaviour. Consequently, *kabuki*, the *bunraku* puppet theatre and the aristocratic *noh* received generous state support in the Meiji years (Sanches 1975). These forms of drama were prioritised as more visual and more edifying. *Rakugo* did not receive such treatment.

In his book *Young Japan*, Henry's father, John Black, confirms that the Meiji government was sensitive to evaluations by foreigners of certain performance arts. However, he did not consider *rakugo* worthy of mention in *Young Japan*, even though, by the time he was compiling the book, his son had developed a close association with storytellers and had performed in *yose*.

In the early Meiji years, *kabuki* had image problems. It took the presence of approving foreigners at the *kabuki* theatres to bring it to the attention of the largely ex-*samurai* governing elite. *Kabuki* had for many years been out of bounds to the ruling *samurai* caste. Before the Restoration, *samurai* were only able to attend *kabuki* performances if they disguised themselves. Several classic *kabuki* plots rely on the prohibition to depict *samurai* heroes attending *kabuk*i incognito in order to kill or spy upon their enemies in the audience. As a result of the *samurai* disdain for *kabuki*, good *kabuki* actors, though often extremely famous and well-paid, were low on the social scale. Henry Black occasionally remarked on this to his audiences. In *Eikoku Rondon gekijō miyage*, he referred to *kabuki*'s lowly origins by lamenting the discrimination Japanese actors had suffered as *kawara kojiki* (riverbed beggars), a reference to the supposed origins of *kabuki* in performances by women on the dry bed of the Kamo River in Kyoto in the 17th century. Henry noted that, even though Danjurō had achieved recognition for his talents, earning more than a thousand *ryō* for a performance (Eikokujin 1891:98), 'the old barriers have not been withdrawn' (Eikokujin 1891:87).

> and even though entertainers are now able to hold their heads higher recently, there are still many instances of discrimination. In Europe and America, it was also like that but things are now very different and entertainers have become very respected by the people…In Britain, because a top actor is respected by the people, no matter what top

> bureaucrat or wealthy family he mixes with, he never bows his head or averts his eyes, but meets them as their equal. Last year, when the British crown prince's eldest daughter married into another family, presents came from the aristocrats they usually mix with, but on that occasion, Britain's top actor Irwin *sensei* sent a clock made of the finest marble. Since it is the custom in the West for those at the top not to receive a present from those beneath them, when one sees how Irwin *sensei* gives a present to the royal family with whom he is on familiar terms, then one can see just how much of a right to equality he has (Eikokujin 1891:88).

Henry pointedly used the honorific *sensei* (literally, teacher/master) after the actor's name to emphasise the respect in which he was held in Britain. To further reinforce the comparison, Henry told a tale about another famous actor at a banquet for newly inaugurated Prime Minister William Gladstone. When Gladstone suggested the actor deliver some lines from his latest play, the irate actor placed a coin on Gladstone's plate and left, telling the prime minister that he had come to enjoy a meal and not to perform: 'If you wish to see me perform, buy a ticket and come to the theatre! Here is the cost of my meal' (Eikokujin 1891:94).

Many in Henry's Japanese audience would have been aware of the interest in theatre reform even at a political level. They may have known of the formation in 1886 of the Society for the Reform of Drama at the urging of oligarchs Itō Hirobumi and Inoue Kaoru, the Foreign Minister. Reflecting the *samurai* disdain for *kabuki* as decadent, the society's instigators were determined to refashion it as an art form deserving of presentation to international audiences (Leiter 1979:187). To Itō and Inoue, the reform of *kabuki* was integral to their program for the creation of a modern Japan (Karatani 1993:55). As part of the campaign to raise the status of *kabuki*, Danjūrō was one of three leading players who in 1887 performed in the first presentation of *kabuki* to the emperor (Leiter 1979:187). The presence of foreigners among the invited audience at that performance, which took place under electric lighting in the grounds of Inoue's Tokyo residence, helped elevate the status of the art (Shively 1971:90).

In *Eikoku Rondon gekijō miyage*, Henry demonstrated that he was thoroughly conversant with the reform debate. When the heroine Gātsurudo attends her first performance at London's Adelphi Theatre, Henry went to some length to describe the main differences between theatre-going in Japan and Britain. Given the prevailing mood for reform of the theatre, Henry took the opportunity to cite the example of newspaper editor Fukuchi Gen'ichirō who had been running an editorial campaign for theatre reform. At this point, Henry wades into the debate over Westernisation of drama forms to make his own points about theatre reform:

> There are many women who, once married, cause bother to their husbands all because of their kimono. There are even women who have chosen their white silk kimono to wear in their coffin. Gātsurudo spent her first three days in London doing the rounds of frock shops and ordering some. After about five days the frocks arrived and she went with her aunt to see the sights. She went to see the Adelphi Theatre, the most famous theatre in London.
>
> Types of theatre in my country Britain, and in Japan are fairly different. Above all, there are gentlemen such as Fukuchi Gen'ichirō doing their utmost to reform the theatre. One of the issues is whether it is better to reform by adopting the Western style, or whether the Japanese theatre is better reformed while retaining its unique look entirely. In my narration, I will do my best to clarify the differences between the British theatre and the Japanese theatre. But above all, the big difference is in the length of time and the speed of scene changes. Firstly, in the old days in Japan, since the curtain rose as soon as the day dawned, the housemaid would be in a flap from the previous evening. What with having to put on white face powder (*oshiroi*), do up the hair, choose the kimono, and tighten the obi, dressing up took so much effort that there was no sleep the night before and they stayed up the entire time. People had to leave for the theatre at first light, so when they relaxed in their spectator's cubicle the fatigue of the previous night got to them and they often ended up nodding off, just when they'd been looking forward to it, and not even seeing the actors' faces.
>
> These days, we have become fairly well enlightened (*kaika*), and the Shintomiza Theatre and the Kabukiza Theatre do not raise the curtain until 12 o'clock tolls. But from the point of view of British theatre, the timing is still very early. The British are a crafty lot, so they are keen on making money, so no one wants to take time off from work to go to the theatre (Eikokujin 1891:12–13).

Henry then describes how British theatre-goers take their evening meal and then go to the theatre. 'Theatres in Britain start at 8 pm or 8:30 pm at the latest', he tells his audience. He even informs them that the British audience is summoned by a bell, unlike the Japanese use of wooden clappers (*hyōshigi*) which he says reminds him of the sound made by the wooden clappers used by residents patrolling city streets on fire alert (*hi no yōjin*). He explains that in Britain the final curtain goes down by 11 pm or 11:15 pm at the latest, adding that British audiences 'like to get home so that the next day they are not sleepy'. Henry also explained that, whereas in Japan audiences show approval by shouting the actor's *yagō* (hereditary stage name),[96] audiences in the West clap or throw flowers onto the stage (Eikokujin 1891:18).

Eikoku Rondon gekijō miyage is especially laden with comments from Henry about the theatre in Britain and Japan, suggesting that Henry chose this Braddon work as a platform for his participation in the theatre reform debate. For example, he indulged in detailed description of the Adelphi Theatre with its brightly gas-lit interior, 'the gorgeousness of the ceiling, the curtains on the boxes, and the decorations on the stage', all of which enthralled the village-raised Gātsurudo, and doubtless his audiences too. His comments do not have equivalent text in Braddon's story. The extent of his additions to the original attests to Henry's enthusiasm for the theatre and the reform agenda.

Henry was not the only foreigner who wanted reform. Writing in 1902, editor of the *Japan Mail* and correspondent for *The Times*, Captain F Brinkley, claimed that the theatre in Japan 'showed little vitality' because of the large sums of money extracted by 'capitalist' theatre owners from the theatre lessees and actors. In writing that 'the theatre, in fact, has not shared the general progress of modern Japan', Brinkley shared Henry Black's concern about the detrimental impact of performances that could drag on for a full day.

> The waste of time thus entailed and the unwholesome effects of sitting for so many hours in a crowded, ill-ventilated building are not the only evil features of the habit. People who spend the day looking at a play must be provided with meals, and out of that necessity there springs up around the theatre a little city of restaurants and tea-houses, all adding to the costliness of the entertainment and subtracting from the productive capacity of the nation (Brinkley 1904:120–121).

96 For an explanation of the origin of this term, see Leiter (1979:692).

Driven as it was by political and diplomatic imperatives, the reform of *kabuki* was thorough. What once had been out of bounds to *samurai* was now opened even to politicians and foreigners, so that by 1904, the work of the Society for the Reform of Drama was complete. In that year, the British diplomat Basil Hall Chamberlain confidently declared that the makeover of *kabuki* as suitable for foreign eyes had been accomplished. In a compendium of things Japanese, Chamberlain wrote that, whereas *noh* actors 'were honoured under the old regime', *kabuki* actors were once 'despised' as 'outcasts'. Chamberlain acknowledged that a viewing of a *kabuki* play 'will be of greater interest to most foreign spectators' because of the accessibility of the material 'as pictures of manners' (Chamberlain 1984:463). As in John Black's book, *rakugo* was notably absent from Chamberlain's ostensibly comprehensive roundup of the theatre arts in Japan.

Henry Black and Shakespeare

In the absence of alternatives accessible to a broad audience in the immediate aftermath of the Restoration, *kabuki* emerged as the form entrusted with absorbing Western influence, including the influence of Shakespeare, whose impact on drama and literature at the time was electrifying and far-reaching. Shakespeare's 'realistic personages who spoke a language alive with individualistic character and philosophy' influenced writers like Tsubouchi Shōyō and other initiators of the contemporary movement to promote the use of the vernacular in the modern Japanese novel (Minamitani 1990:181).

Excerpts of *Hamlet* were introduced to Japanese theatre piecemeal until Tsubouchi presented a full outline of the plot in 1885. The first fully-staged adaptation of a Shakespeare play occurred in May 1885, with a *kabuki*-style performance in Osaka of *Sakuradoki zeni no yo no naka* (Money Makes the World Go Round), an adaptation of *The Merchant of Venice* based on Charles and Mary Lamb's *Tales from Shakespeare* (Minamitani 1990:181). The following year, a musical *jōruri*-style (ballad-drama style) adaptation of *Hamlet* by the storyteller Kanagaki Robun (1829–1894) appeared in the *Tōkyō e-iri shinbun*. Tsubouchi Shōyō maintained his interest in Shakespeare and was in the audience at a staging of *Hamlet* on 1 June 1891, at the Gaiety Theatre, the main entertainment venue for foreign residents of Yokohama. This was one of the earliest recorded unadapted performances of Shakespeare in Japan. It was also the year when Henry was at his most active on stage as a *kabuki* performer and narrator.

There is evidence that Henry used this interest in Shakespeare to include the playwright in his early repertoire.[97] His renditions of Shakespeare would have been an important means for the Japanese public to experience the bard's works. The sight of the manifestly European Henry declaiming Shakespeare in Japanese would have appealed to many educated Japanese at the time. Accounts of Henry performing extracts from Shakespeare suggest that these performances met a demand and supplemented his income.

Mary Braddon at the *kabuki*

Experimentation was common in the 1880s, with innovative playwrights seeking material elsewhere. An outstanding example, the adaptation of Mary Braddon's serialised novel *Diavola* as a *kabuki* play by Kawatake Shinshichi III, has already been mentioned. This was a response to the popularity of the editor and translator Kuroiwa Ruikō's publication between October 1894 and July 1895 of a serialised adaptive translation of *Diavola* as *Sute obune* in his newspaper *Yorozu chōhō*. The Kuroiwa version was commissioned as a *kabuki* play by Kawatake for special New Year performances at the Kabukiza Theatre in Tokyo in 1898. Eight years later, in 1906, the story was again adapted as a play in more modernised form at the Hongōza Theatre.[98]

The *kabuki* version of *Sute obune* is an interesting case study in light of Henry's reference in *Eikoku Rondon gekijō miyage* to the ongoing debate over the need to westernise aspects of *kabuki*. The *kabuki* version of *Sute obune* appears to have had a mixed reception among the critics. Their reaction suggests that the debate was by no means resolved. Summing up the performance, *Kabukiza* manager Tamura Nariyoshi wrote that the actors Kataoka Ichizō, as the naval captain Kobuishi, and Bandō Shūchō, as the woman Konami, had turned in 'quite excellent' performances, but

97 My evidence is a letter to myself from Gilbert George, Australia-Japan Foundation director, August 12, 1987. Mr George wrote that Mrs Gertrude F. Williams had told him that her husband, the Australian-born businessman Harold S. Williams (1898–1987), knew Henry Black and 'went to Shinkai-ichi to hear him give a Japanese rendition of Shakespeare in his fine speaking voice, inherited from his father'. (Letter to Ian McArthur, Ref. 3/1/26-87T, ZT-II (L0723) 12 Aug. 1987.) Given Williams' age when he arrived in Japan, it is likely the performance he witnessed was early in the 20th century when Henry Black was certainly middle-aged. I also have a letter sent to me from Mrs Williams in which she states that Henry Black 'translated English novels and particularly Shakespearean plays and held his audience spellbound by his dramatic renditions'. Letter, Nov. 19, 1987.

98 For a detailed account of the transition of the Braddon novel to *kabuki* and beyond, see McArthur (2007).

that the main audience drawcards, Onoe Kikugorō's dual roles of the evil chemist Kawabayashi Ikudō and Baron Tokiwa, were lacklustre and failed to provoke interest, with the result that the play ended in failure (*shippai ni owaritari*) (Tamura 1922:73). The *Waseda bungaku* critic opined that the play did not epitomise *kabuki*. The critic said a major factor in the play's lack of success was Kikugorō's lack of sensitivity and technique required for 'this sort of realistic play'. Another critic, probably Nomura Mumeian,[99] wrote that the complications in the original story had been simplified so much that the result was insipid and prosaic (*bosshumi*) and without any highlights (*miseba naku*).

These harsh criticisms illustrate the problems playwrights had in trying to adapt Western material to the *kabuki* format. The transformation of this Braddon story is just one of many examples of intertextual transmutation of Western material via the stage at the time. In a written greeting on the occasion of the opening of the Saruwaka Theatre in Tokyo on 16 November 1884, Henry's collaborator Danjūrō captured the spirit of the times in this expression of his views on the purpose of theatre reform:

> It is right that in civilized countries the theatre should be considered a means of education. Our intercourse with the outside world becomes ever more intimate, and we live in an age when there is scarcely time for all the reforms that must be made. It is in keeping with the age that the structure of our theatres should change (Komiya 1969:199).

The experimentation of the 1880s paved the way for Henry Black's participation in *kabuki*. His *rakugoka* mentors actively encouraged it as a means of reviving their art form.

Performing Banzuiin Chōbee

Henry Black's signature *kabuki* role was to be that of the popular Banzuiin Chōbee, a figure somewhat equivalent in the pantheon of national heroes to Robin Hood in England. Henry performed the role to much publicity and acclaim in 1892. The real Banzuiin Chōbee lived from 1622 to 1657. His adventures gave rise after his death at the hand of the *samurai*, Mizuno Jūrōzaemon, to many legends which are still portrayed in *kabuki*. Chōbee was a popular figure and a good fighter, but also had many enemies. Jūrōzaemon killed him out of revenge over an insult.

---

99 Tamura (1922:74) gives the name only as Mumeian, but Nomura Mumeian is known to have been a contemporary theatre critic.

On 5 August 1892, *Tōkyō asahi* noted that Henry was preparing for the role. The paper wrote that 'the renowned English-born Black' was memorising dialogue for the role of Banzuiin Chōbee, 'that true-born citizen of Edo' (Kurata 1981–87:V,154). Henry told a *Yomiuri shinbun* interviewer that he took the role at the suggestion of his mentor Shōrin Hakuen. He at first protested to Hakuen that he could not act, but was persuaded to give it a try (Nyorai 1896:1). Hakuen was also a member of the cast. In another account, Henry told the journalist Nishūbashi Sei that the idea for the performance came from a comment made to fellow *rakugoka* Shōrin Hakuchi when they attended a performance of the role by Ichikawa Danjūrō IX. Henry recalled that he had admired Danjūrō's portrayal and joked to Hakuchi that he would like to try the role, adding that a Chōbee with different coloured eyes and hair to the usual 'might be interesting'. According to Henry, his wish later came true when Shōrin Hakuchi and Shōrin Hakukaku visited and urged him to take on the role in *Suzugamori*. The result was that 'in any event, when it came to the performance, the fact that my Chōbee was different was much talked about and drew a full house' (Nishūbashi 1905:299).

As Henry could not read Japanese, he had the script transposed phonetically into roman letters and memorised it with the help of 'experts in the art form' (*michi no hito*) who visited his residence for lessons in 'how to raise and lower my voice, how to link the words, how to handle the script'. It would appear that one of the experts was San'yūtei Enryū, an expert in *shibai banashi* (dramatised narrations), whom he mentioned in the Nishūbashi interview. Henry claimed that he memorised his lines so well that his surprised colleagues praised him for his fluent rendition during their first practice session:

> [W]hen it came to actually reading it in rehearsal, everyone gathered on the second floor of a tea house and the script writer was there and at last I did it. While all the others were using their script and dictionaries and looking at each others' faces, I had already memorised it so that I didn't bring my script, and everyone thought it odd and said they were sure I must have been given a script (Nyorai 1896:1).

Henry told the *Yomiuri shinbun* that on that occasion his dedication impressed the actor Nakamura Kangorō who offered to coach him in dialogue. Contrary to other accounts, the *Tōkyō asahi shinbun* said Henry originally sought the help of *kabuki* actor Ichikawa Danjūrō but, since the actor was away on a trip into the country, he ultimately trained under

Danjūrō's protege Ichikawa Shinzō. The newspaper praised Black's handling of the role, mentioning his 'fine declamation, foot stamping, stance, and forceful gaze' (Kurata 1981–87:V,154). This style, known as *aragoto*, had been associated with the Ichikawa family line since it was pioneered by Ichikawa Danjūrō I (1660–1704) (Leiter 1979:18). The performances, which Henry Black gave at the peak of his creative ability, caught the eye of a reporter for the English-language *Japan Weekly Mail*. The report, which was full of praise, appeared in the paper on 3 September 1892.

> Mr Black, a son of the author of *Young Japan*, and already favorably known as one of the *hanashika* or story-tellers of Tokyo, made his debut a few days ago as Banzuiin Chōbee, in a scene taken from the 'Story of the Otokodate of Yedo'... Hakuen, the noted *hanashika*, a stout-built man apparently on the wrong side of fifty, as the maiden Yaegami Hime in the drama of 'Nijūshikō' was a ridiculous spectacle, but after the first shock of surprise, the audience listened to him with sympathetic attention. Black's acting, however, was far removed from any suspicion of caricature; it was a clever and conscientious rendering of a difficult part and has been deservedly praised by the play-going public.
>
> The unique spectacle of an Englishman essaying such a role drew large audiences, who showed their feelings in ways thoroughly characteristic of the people. Black had evidently made a study of Danjūrō in the part, and every successful imitation of that popular actor evoked a spontaneous burst of applause; on the other hand, any marked lapse from the stereotyped rendering caused the house to shake from end to end with irrepressible mirth (*Japan Weekly Mail* 1892).

Reviews in the Japanese-language press were good. The *Chūō shinbun* of 20 August 1892 said the performances were 'unexpectedly well received', adding that 'a Westerner donning Japanese garb and taking to the stage is unprecedented' (Kurata 1981–87:V,156). The *Tōkyō asahi* of 5 August praised his bombastic *aragoto* style of acting for its 'fine declamation, foot stamping, stance, and robust glare' (Kurata 1981–87:V,154). Recalling the event some years later, the *Yomiuri shinbun* journalist Yamamoto Shōgetsu, also described Henry Black's performance.

> Black appeared after lifting aside the curtain on the *kago* (palanquin), and suddenly stood up with a gesture that looked as if he might be about to shake someone's hand. When he spoke his lines with that

characteristically familiar foreigner's manner of speech, the theatre erupted in applause. It was an accomplished Black-style performance (Yamamoto 1936:96–97).

Despite Henry's good intentions, word of the occasional 'marked lapse' soon reached the ears of the very actor who virtually owned the role. Several days after the premiere performances, Ichikawa Danjūrō IX, the actor whose performance had sparked Henry's interest in the role contacted him to offer assistance. The co-operation extended by Danjūrō IX ensured that the newspapers noticed. The correspondent for *The Times*, Francis Brinkley, wrote in 1902 that Danjūrō, who was 'incomparably the greatest actor of his era', had an estimated annual income of 'from ten to fifteen thousand gold dollars' (Brinkley 1904:119).

Another well-known male role Henry played in 1891 was that of Kumagai in *Heike Monogatari*. This role, one of *kabuki*'s greatest, depicts Kumagai Jiro Naozane, a warrior of the Genji clan, whose enemies were the Heike clan. Kumagai falls in love with Sagami, a member of the retinue of Fuji no Kata, who is a leading lady-in-waiting to the emperor. Sagami falls pregnant to Kumagai and, with the help of Fuji no Kata, the couple flee to western Japan. All this occurs 17 years before the play opens. The content of the play focuses on the battle of Ichi no Tani and its terrible aftermath. In the battle, Kumagai reluctantly kills a young man whom he thinks is Atsumori, the son of Fuji no Kata. In reality, it is his own son Jiro disguised in Atsumori's armour. The play ends with Kumagai becoming a Buddhist priest to atone for killing his own son. One of the highlights of the play is Kumagai's monologue in which he describes to Fuji no Kata and Sagami the battle in which he killed the person he thought was Atsumori. In 1891 Henry also played the role of the fierce priest bandit Rochishin in *Suikoden*.

Henry's performances in female *kabuki* roles in 1890 and 1891 have already been noted. He played the part of Omiwa, a merchant's daughter, who appears in the second act of *Imoseyama* (see figure 2). The role required Henry to become the distraught lover of Motome, who is really the young lord Tankai, betrothed to Princess Tachibana. When Omiwa realises that Motome is in the nearby palace, she goes looking for him, but is blocked by Princess Tachibana's ladies-in-waiting. In 'one of the most tragic passages in kabuki', Omiwa, unable to enter the palace and taunted by the ladies-in-waiting, constantly turns her eyes toward the palace door, hoping her lover will emerge. Tankai doesn't appear and one of the ladies-in-waiting strikes Omiwa. She falls to the ground and the ladies tie a wooden stand to a thread on her spindle. Aware now that her lover is Tankai and that he is at that very moment marrying the princess, she revives and drags herself toward the palace. But Kanawa Imakuni, a retainer of Fujiwara Kamatari, the enemy of Soga Iruka, who now owns the palace suddenly emerges from the palace, recognises Omiwa and strikes her with his sword. Thinking the thread is attached to Tankai's kimono, Omiwa struggles to wind it in, in the vain hope that Tankai will be at the other end. She dies on stage as she winds in the thread (Halford 1990:100–103).

In *Senbon zakura* Henry played Osato, who appears in Scene Five, entitled 'The Sushi shop'. She is the daughter of the sushi shop owner Yazaemon, who is protecting Koremori, a fugitive devotee of the Taira clan. Yazaemon has convinced Koremori to pretend he is his apprentice with the name of Yasuke. As part of this ruse, Yazaemon wants Osato to marry Yasuke. Osato, unaware of Yasuke's real identity as Koremori, falls in love with him and cannot understand why he does not appear to love her. When she overhears Koremori's wife talking with him, she realises that she can never marry him (Halford 1990:366–368).

Henry's performances of female roles in *kabuki* made him something of an authority on the subject. He made good use of his experience and knowledge in *Eikoku Rondon gekijō miyage*. When Gātsurudo auditions to become an actress, Henry takes the opportunity to inform the audience that *kabuki*'s exclusive use of male actors can cause problems.

> But in Britain, women and men act together. The men play male roles and the women play female roles. In Japan there are places where there are very skilled *oyama* playing female roles, but no matter how much Shinkoma or Taganojyō plaster the whitener on their faces and don wigs and long sleeves and mimic women with tender voices, no matter their skill, if you know they are men, then somehow there are parts where the feeling isn't conveyed. And even when you watch the play, it's not so interesting.
>
> Then when you go to an all-female play, the performance of Kumehachi is quite accomplished. There is the half-shaven head, the fluent speech, and the appearance of chivalry, but it is a woman and if you think that would not be as good as one's husband in the evening, then you get the feeling that Nezumi kozō[100] or Nipponzaemon wouldn't be worth it.

[100] This is an abbreviated title for the Kawatake Mokuami play *Nezumi Komon Haru no Shingata*. It is also the nickname of the thief Inaba Kozō or Konezumi Jirōkichi, the play's central character, who was executed in 1832 (Leiter 1979:466–467).

> Most of all there is more interest in having a man play a man's role and a woman play a woman's role.
>
> According to the program, a male actor will appear with Kumehachi the female actress at the Azumaza in Asakusa, but till now, they have built modified theatres, changed the storylines of plays and tried various drama reforms, but for the first time, in the twenty-third year of the Meiji era [1890], men and women will act together at the Azuma Theatre. This is a major reform. Three cheers for that. I am sure it will get a full house (Eikokujin 1891:77–78).

Henry ended the monologue by mentioning that, because women in Britain are reluctant to become actresses, theatre owners are eager to find good actresses.

Engagement in the reform debate

Henry Black's sympathies had been with Danjūrō and his attempts at reform even before he became a full-time *rakugoka*. As already mentioned, two sentences in his 1886 English primer show that he had long admired Danjūrō and knew of his interest in reform for some years before their meeting. Referring to European acting styles, Henry stated in Conversations Section, Lesson 14 of his English language primer (Burakku 1886) that 'everything is more real than in Japanese plays', and in answer to the question 'Whom do I consider the best actor in Tokio?' the text responded that 'Danjūrō is certainly the cleverest.' The sample conversation concluded with one speaker stating that 'actors are very much despised in Japan'.

In the 1880s and 1890s, *rakugo* and *kabuki* were caught in the wider debate over reform. Henry Black's co-operation with Danjūrō was a meeting of reformist minds. Danjūrō would have been aware that Henry's status as a foreigner lent legitimacy to the campaign to elevate the art form from a degenerate to a civilised one. For the government, the successful resolution of the debate had diplomatic implications. As Danjūrō and government ministers pointed out, the theatre – and they meant *kabuki* – was a tool for civilising the masses. But for *rakugoka*, including Henry, and for *kabuki* playwrights and actors, theatre reform held the prospect of their continued survival. While politicians, intellectuals, and practitioners responded by urging changes in the higher art forms, including *kabuki*, the low status of *rakugo* as an entertainment form ensured that it remained comparatively free from government reform efforts. Ironically, this allowed foreign-born Henry to play a role in its survival.

In *kabuki* and *rakugo*, simplicity of vernacular expression became the catalyst and vehicle for mass entertainment and the efficient transmission of new ideas to mass audiences. Moreover, the new uses to which narrators, orators, playwrights and editors put language under the influence of ideas on Western rhetoric (Tomasi 1999) and fiction represented a radical new understanding of the relationship between language and the individual. After Shakespeare, there was no going back to the tired old forms of dialogue and mannerisms.

Henry Black's role in the preservation and promotion of *rakugo* and *kabuki* illustrates the extent to which foreigners were associated with the quest to utilise the arts in defining a path to modernity. In this regard, *kabuki* is in a small way indebted to Henry Black for its elevation to the status of a high art. The privileging of *kabuki* as a high art has, however, resulted in the marginalisation of *rakugo* in the history of Japan's artistic and intellectual development.

Chapter 14

A question of identity

The 'imported Japanese'

> He is a species of Englishman raised in Edo (Description of Henry Black in the *Ōsaka asahi shinbun* of 7 October 1891)

Henry Black had been born in a British colony and was, therefore, a British citizen. His ability to read English and to adapt works into Japanese for telling on the stage was a major reason for his elevation in 1891 to *shin'uchi* status within the San'yū guild. The combination of British nationality and ability as a stage performer were key components of his evolving identity.

Being British was good for his career as a *rakugoka*. Japan's enthusiasm for things British made Henry an object of intense curiosity in theatres and newspapers. Being British also brought privileges, such as access to British justice and the right to reside in foreign concessions such as Tsukiji. By the early 1890s, Henry was sharing a house with Takamatsu Motokichi in Irifune-chō Kyōbashi Ward, close to Tsukiji. Tsukiji had been opened to foreigners in 1868, so by the time Henry began living nearby, the area had a number of substantial buildings in the European fashion. Missionaries had been there from the early years, so it had a liberal sprinkling of churches, schools and hospitals, including St Luke's hospital, predecessor to the modern St Luke's International Hospital. Just outside the precinct stood Tsukiji Hospital, established by Henry Faulds, the Scottish Presbyterian missionary doctor. A house in Irifune-chō, therefore, offered an ideal combination of proximity to familiar European comforts and easy access to the entertainment districts of Tokyo in which Henry worked.

There was no avoiding the fact that Henry Black was British. Newspapers continually made reference to his nationality. Typical of such references was the *Yamato shinbun* of 24 March 1891 which, when he assumed *shin'uchi* status and took his professional name, Kairakutei Burakku, had described him as 'the Briton Black, promoted as the *rakugoka* with the different coloured hair'. Three months later, the *Tokyo asahi shinbun* of 30 June 1891 described him as 'the *rakugoka* and Briton Black' (*rakugoka eijin Burakku*).

Many papers also gave due recognition to his talent and praised his apparent affinity for Japan. The *Tōkyō asahi shinbun* for 30 June 1891, noting that he was to perform at a number of venues the following month, described him as a 'clever fellow' (*kiyōna otoko*) (Kurata 1981–87:V,108). And the *Hinode shinbun* of 8 August, 1891, in an article announcing his forthcoming performances in Kyoto, described him as 'not only well versed in Japanese affairs, but also no different in his command of the language than a Japanese, and possessed of a fine speaking voice' (Kurata 1981–87:V,114). One of the finest accolades was in the *Ōsaka asahi shinbun* of 7 October 1891, which referred to him as 'a species of Englishman raised in Edo' (*eikoku dane Edo sodachi Burakku*) (Kurata 1981–87:V,126). The newpaper's invocation of Edo ironically made him a reference point for the then accelerating process of selective resurrection of the past.[101] The reference to the old name for Tokyo reflected a nostalgic interest by the 1890s in and selective revival of aspects of pre-Restoration Edo culture. As a sign of the times, two years prior to this newspaper article, ex-shogunal supporters had established the Edo Association in Tokyo to record Edo culture for posterity before it disappeared. This was also their way of salvaging some of the good from the Tokugawa Period. The preservationist nature of the association also reflected the growing push for 'a Japanese path to modernity' (Waswo 1996:94).

The notion that the Australian-born Henry Black was 'raised in Edo' bolstered his credentials as a practitioner of an art form with its roots in the Edo period and emphasised his affinity with Japan. Henry's affiliation with *rakugo*, which relied on the commodification of Edo in its narrations, underscored his association with this resurrection of Edo in support of the modern state. By this stage, nostalgia for old Edo was frequently invoked 'to sell everything from *sake* to liver pills' (Gluck 1998:265). Being 'raised in Edo' was as good as saying that Henry had what it took to be a narrator.

But for an ambitious performer who wanted to reach as many people as possible, Henry soon encountered a major obstacle. Under the terms of Japan's treaty with Britain, although Henry was legally free to move around the three cities of Tokyo, Kyoto and Osaka and the five treaty ports of

---

101 Gluck (1998:272) claims that the association was 'partly preservationist, partly anti-oligarchy' and that it effectively 'filched the most hallowed Meiji claim' (that the Meiji era represented a time of great progress) and applied it to the Edo period, which since the advent of the Meiji period had 'evoked such vile epithets as "feudal" and "antiquated".' See also Gluck (1985:24).

Niigata, Yokohama, Kobe, Nagasaki and Hakodate, he was obliged to seek police permission each time he wanted to travel elsewhere for performances. The restrictions on the movement of a British citizen outside the treaty ports under Japan's unequal treaty with Britain placed limits on his career trajectory. Another obstacle was the government's issuance on 15 August 1890 of Police Order No. 15 stating that special permission was required for *yose* performances by foreigners (Morioka & Sasaki 1990:251–252). Whether or not the regulation was aimed directly at Henry, its immediate outcome was to place *yose* within the government's extended purview with regard to foreign cultural influence. This legislated attempt to restrict foreign influence in the arts represented a further step in the ascendancy by the mid-1890s of those who favoured an indigenous path to modernity in Japan (Waswo 1996:94). So by 1891, Japan's first foreign-born *rakugoka* of British nationality was held back and frustrated by Japanese red tape. The British nationality that so appealed to his mentors as a novel means of attracting audiences had become a major impediment.

While Henry Black's association with the concept of old Edo through *rakugo* helped negotiate a way through the ambiguities related to being a foreign-born *rakugoka,* it was not enough. It did not guarantee him automatic passage out of Tokyo to other parts of Japan. Outside a limited number of cities, Henry's movements were subject to police scrutiny. And the police did not always grant him approval to perform outside Tokyo. As reported in *Tōkyō nichinichi shinbun* of 6 August 1891 the police invoked Police Order No. 15 and refused permission for Henry to travel to Shizuoka Prefecture to give performances (Kurata 1981–87:V,114). Henry, however, soon found a novel solution to the problem.

A very novel solution

In April 1893, at the age of 33, Henry Black underwent a marriage of convenience to a Japanese woman, which gave him access to Japanese citizenship. Reporting the marriage, the *Chūō shinbun* of 24 May 1893 stated that his new wife Ishii Aka was the 18-year old second daughter of Ishii Mine, who sold confectionery at Moto-hatchōbori in Tokyo's Kyōbashi Ward (Kurata 1981–87:V,177–178). It noted that Henry Black was residing at nearby Irifune-chō 8 chōme, 1 banchi also in Kyōbashi Ward. Upon marriage to Aka, Henry was formally adopted into the Ishii family.

Documents related to Henry Black in the ledger of marriages between foreign nationals and Japanese for this period are in the Tokyo Metropolitan Archive. The events they record give ample reason for believing that the union was a marriage of convenience designed to facilitate Henry's career. Since Henry was a British national, the Home Ministry's bureaucratic processes required that the police compile a report on the prospective groom's occupation, age, and moral standing (*hinkō*). A nine-line document, submitted in the name of Kyōbashi Police chief Superintendent Tomisawa Ryō and dated 28 April 1893, gives Henry's occupation as 'storytelling in the Japanese language' and noted that he 'ordinarily likes homosexuality' (*tsune ni nanshoku wo konomu*) and 'very much loves the Tokyo commoner (*heimin*) Takamatsu Motosuke [*sic*]', with whom he was said to be living as 'virtually husband and wife' (*hotondo fūfu*). 'Motosuke', whose date of birth is given as 18 April 1870, is almost certainly a misprint on the part of the police. In May 1891, Henry had written a book on cosmetics and health care with Takamatsu Motokichi. He had also commemorated Motokichi by using his name for one of the central characters in *Shachū no dokubari*. Motokichi would have been 23 at the time of Henry's marriage, making him 12 years younger than Henry. The report concluded that, apart from his relationship with Motokichi, there were 'no other indications of untoward behaviour'.[102]

The police document implied that the relationship between Henry and Motokichi was no impediment to the marriage with Aka. Although forms of male-male sexuality tolerated during the Edo period were increasingly marginalised by the influence of Western psychoanalysis and legal codes as the Meiji period progressed, there is ample evidence that homosexual liaisons were tolerated in the 1890s.[103] Moreover, aspects of Napoleonic law introduced by the French *yatoi*, Gustave Boissonade, had ensured that male–male sexual acts were treated as outside the jurisdiction of the state, so long as they did not involve minors or coercion (Pflugfelder 1999:170).

Subsequent documents show that on 23 May 1893, the Englishman (*eikokujin*), Henry Black, married Ishii Aka, the second daughter of Ishii Mine, in the presence of the Tokyo governor. On 24 May, Henry's name was entered into the Ishii family register as the *muko yōshi* (son-in-law adopted as heir), Ishii Burakku. This information was conveyed to the British Vice-Consul Joseph Longford from the Governor of Tokyo Tomita Tetsunosuke

---

102 Tokyo Metropolitan Archive, *Naigaikokuji kekkonbo*, Meiji 26, Document No. ZBECH0045_00565.

103 Gregory M Pflugfelder (1999:147–148) has concluded that a 'profound reformulation of official discourse surrounding sexuality' occurred during the Meiji period, with the codification of 'civilised' standards of sexual behaviour resulting in the centralised state's promotion of male-female sexuality and monogamous marriage.

in the document dated June 6, 1893.[104] The documentation noted that Henry Black was living at Kyōbashi Ward, Irifune-chō, and that Mrs Ishii was a commoner (*heimin*) living in Asakusa ward.[105] The records thus showed that Australian-born British citizen Henry James Black had become the Japanese citizen Ishii Burakku.

The documents give scant detail about Ishii Aka. There were few subsequent references to Aka in Japanese newspapers; unsubstantiated and unreliable reports in the English-language newspapers suggested that she may have died soon after the marriage. Attempts by researcher Asaoka Kunio to trace Aka through family registers have brought no results. Descendants of Henry's adopted son have also told me they know nothing about her. Full details of the identity of Motokichi also remain a mystery.

Henry Black's marriage, adoption and naturalisation procedures were based on legislation, in effect since 1874, which mandated that a foreigner adopted into the family of a Japanese woman was entitled to Japanese citizenship. It was not until 1899 that the treaty-port system that prompted the marriage completely disappeared.

A Japanese of European descent

Henry took up Japanese citizenship at a time when government and intellectuals were selectively redefining the meaning of the nation predicated on a newly found set of criteria, including race, language, religion, a community of interest and geography. In spite of his Japanese citizenship, Henry Black never completely escaped references to his different cultural and ethnic origins. The *Chūō shinbun* of 24 May 1893, for example, commenting on his marriage to Aka, described him as the 'Briton Black'. But others took note of the change and began to note his hybrid identity as a Japanese of European descent. Several months after the marriage, on the occasion of his appearing at a theatre in Osaka, the *Tokyo nichinichi shinbun* of the 10 August 1893 described Henry, dressed in a *haori*, as 'every bit the perfect Japanese' (Kurata 1981–87:5,187). The article went on to qualify his Japanese credentials by referring to him as 'the imported Japanese Ishii Black' (*hakurai no nihonjin Ishii Burakku*).[106] On 21 January 1894, eight

104 Tokyo Metropolitan Archive, *Naigaikokuji kekkonbo*, Meiji 26, Document No. ZBECH0045-00554.

105 Tokyo Metropolitan Archive, *Naigaikokuji kekkonbo*, Meiji 26, Document No. ZBECH0045_00558.

106 '*Hakurai*' means 'brought in by ship' and was applied to the imported goods one might buy at a department store. Black was indeed an 'imported Japanese', having arrived on a

months after Henry took Japanese citizenship, the *Fusō shinbun* in Nagoya introduced him to its readers when he went to that city to perform, noting that he was so fond of Japan that he had affiliated with the San'yūha and even taken Japanese citizenship and a Japanese name by marrying Ishii Aka. The article said Henry had come to Nagoya as a 'citizen of Tokyo' (Kurata 1981–87:V,199). Two years later, on 2 July 1896, the *Osaka mainichi* signaled its recognition of the 37-year-old Black's status as a member of the *rakugo* fraternity by referring to him as 'that amiable fellow among *rakugoka*, Ishii Black' (*rakugoka chū no aikyō mono Ishii Burakku*) (Kurata 1981–87:VI,87). More than any legal procedure, his demonstrations of loyalty to Japan, together with his continuing involvement with the theatre, assisted in the naturalisation and assimilation of Henry Black in the minds of many over time.

The expressions of praise and admiration in reaction to Henry's taking of Japanese citizenship in 1893 contribute to a more nuanced understanding of the development of Japanese identity at the time. While Meiji Japan was in the process of emulating Western nation-states by redefining Japaneseness on the basis of race, it was still possible for someone like Henry to become Japanese. He was not alone. A few foreign men had acquired Japanese citizenship by marrying Japanese women. Among them was Lafcadio Hearn, the Greek-born son of an Irish surgeon. Hearn had moved to Japan in 1890 to write and teach. Hearn married Koizumi Setsu after moving to her hometown of Matsue in the summer of 1890. Elsewhere, however, racial intolerance in places like Australia and California was finding expression in legislation that denied Japanese citizens access to citizenship. In 1894 and 1895, for example, parliaments in the Australian colonies of South Australia, the place of Henry's birth, and in Queensland voiced misgivings over Japanese interests in the pearling industry in northern Australia. Japanese divers then constituted the largest national group employed in the pearl industry at Queensland's Thursday Island (Frei 1991:74). Whereas it was possible for a South Australian-born British citizen to become a Japanese, California and the Australian colonies were at the same time moving toward defining national identity based on the exclusion of non-white races.

Yose as a neutral zone

In the end, for Henry Black the *yose* stage was a neutral zone where the ability to entertain mattered and sexual identity was not an issue. In spite

ship from Australia and taken Japanese citizenship much later.

of bureaucratic attempts to restrict his activities, Henry's British heritage was an asset that gave him advantages alongside other exotic and strange entertainers – the comedians, jugglers, and musicians who peopled the same *yose* theatres where he performed. As Henry had pointed out in *Eikoku Rondon gekijō miyage*, in his aside about the lowly status of stage entertainers, *yose* were cultural marketplaces where even lowly born performers could rise above their social status and achieve fame and accolades. *Yose* were zones where any accomplished performer could make good and escape their own social origins (Nishiyama 1997:210).

Chapter 15

The uncertain years, 1895–1900

> You red-haired fool! –
>
> (San'yūtei Enshō's jibe in an argument with Henry Black, reported in *Tōkyō asahi shinbun* 5 May 1895)

In the Spring of 1895, Henry Black became involved in a heated argument with his colleague San'yūtei Enshō. Henry had been drinking before he visited Enshō to discuss a pay dispute and took offence when Enshō tried to excuse himself to attend a performance. Enshō would not have wanted to keep his rickshaw-driver and the audience waiting. But when Enshō tried to extricate himself from the argument, Henry flew into a rage and accused him of treating him in an offhand manner because he was a foreigner. The *Tōkyō asahi shinbun* quoted Enshō as having responded with the unfortunate and contemptuous retort: 'You red-haired fool! The colour of your eyes has never changed. You're a fine one with your lame excuses.' The insinuation that Henry's different coloured eyes and hair made him forever a foreigner at heart, in spite of his recently acquired Japanese nationality, would have upset him greatly.

The report in the *Tōkyō asahi shinbun* would have caused considerable embarrassment and consternation among the San'yū guild leadership. On the face of it, the incident involved an argument between Henry and his colleague Enshō, a respected member of the San'yū guild. But the report exposed a high level of bitterness within the guild over Henry's presence in its ranks. In one drunken, visceral moment, mutual resentment had burst to the surface. Henry may well have been aware of the unspoken thoughts of others about his different physical features – his longer nose, paler skin, different coloured hair. He was unavoidably different. On stage, Henry was Kairakutei Burakku. And on documents confirming his marriage and acquisition of Japanese citizenship, he was Ishii Burakku. But no matter what his audiences and colleagues called him, he was a curiosity who had been allowed to affiliate with the guild to revive its flagging fortunes by providing it with a new repertoire of tales liberally adapted from European mystery novels. There was no doubting Henry's skill at adapting these stories, or even at producing entirely original ones. But he had received special treatment. He had not undergone a long and arduous apprenticeship from an early age like his colleagues.

In the aftermath of the incident, since Enshō had *kanji* (manager) status within the San'yūha, his disciples demanded that Henry resign from the guild for showing disrespect. Other members of the guild quickly intervened and the rift was papered over. Nevertheless, the incident indicated the sensitivity Henry nursed over his different appearance and the latent resentment of him among some colleagues.

It is interesting to speculate on the manner in which the details of the incident reached the paper. Was the report a compilation of detail from Enshō's side? If this was the case, it may have been an attempt by Enshō's sympathisers to caution or restrain Henry. Did other witnesses to the incident report it to the press? Henry did very little to ease the ongoing tension between him and his colleagues within the guild. In May 1896, just a year after this altercation, Henry was extensively quoted in the respected daily newspaper *Yomiuri shinbun* openly criticising his colleagues, including Enshō. The article purported to be an interview with Henry on the subject of the survival of *rakugo*. Many of Henry's comments may well have been valid, but it was not politic to air them so publicly. As Henry saw it, the survival of *rakugo* was not a foregone conclusion, but many of his colleagues failed to appreciate this. He complained to the *Yomiuri* that the majority of *rakugoka* merely paid lip service to calls for reform, and protested that despite

> enlightenment of society in every-day life (*yo no naka wa hibi ni hirakete mairiyasu*) ... *rakugo* does not advance one iota. The telegraph, the railway, agriculture and technology all advance on a daily basis, but the reform of drama and society, well, we hear about it, but there is nothing that amounts to reform of *rakugo*. There are none among the majority of the *rakugoka* who do not call for reform, but they do it in name only. They do not get together and discuss the pros and cons.
>
> There might be about 180 *rakugoka* in Tokyo now, but I dare say there is not a single one among the younger generation of them who will become a *shin'uchi*. All of them are good at *hauta* (short songs), *dodoitsu* (love songs), *mai* (dance), and *teodori* (gestures), but these are just

> accomplishments that please the audience when they get onto the stage and they won't last for long at all.
>
> Will Koen'yū succeed to En'yū? Ryūba and Kinba, even though they become *shin'uchi*, they are all-so-rounds, none of them rate enough to make the big time. So who will follow En'yū? When Enshō and Enkyō die, who will follow them? There's not a soul in sight. If things go on like this, then the world of *rakugo* will be in a sorry state (Nyorai 1896:1).

As an example of good practice, Henry cited the detailed and lengthy training to which Enchō subjected apprentices before permitting their first public performance. He complained that 'today's *rakugoka* do not teach', and instead trained apprentices merely by making them clean the house before finally letting them give a *zenza* (curtain-raiser) in a *yose*. Henry said that allowing apprentices merely to mimic their master was treating them no better than 'cows and horses'. 'They are pitiable beings (*aware binzen na mono*)', he said. 'It doesn't serve the apprentices any purpose, and there is no hope that *rakugo* will progress' (Nyorai 1896:1).

Henry also complained of a breakdown in the spirit of mutual obligation among *rakugoka*, a lack of financial support for retired colleagues, and a lack of creative energy among younger *rakugoka* who were failing to show an interest in devising new material. It was at this point that he displayed his most damning criticism of Enshō.

> Enshō and Enkyō are skilled so that in their delivery they are not inferior to Enchō. But Enchō frequently composed narrations. Even though Enshō and Enkyō stick to the old styles, their standard is different because they are not creative. I am not one who is unable to compose stories myself, but perhaps the reason they do not do so is because they lack enthusiasm (Nyorai 1896:1).

Henry Black berated colleagues for not paying proper attention to annotations in the book held backstage for performers to record the titles of stories they had delivered so that performers appearing on stage on the same day would not repeat those stories. Failure to look at the book often meant that audiences were subjected to repeats on the same evening.

> It is good if there are always plenty of customers, but these things are happening and it is a sorry state of affairs for the world of *rakugo* (*rakugokai no tame ni nagekawashii*).

> Then there's the music. I won't mention names, but there are some who do the same song every night. It's terrible when you hear the same narration, but I can't stand it on days when I hear the same song. And what is the intention of the person singing? Among the numerous customers, there are many who come two or three nights in a row, so I can't fathom what's going on in the mind of such a singer who doesn't care. If it were someone special doing it at the wish of the audience, it would be all right, but when that's not the case, I cannot remain silent (Nyorai 1896:1).

Henry had not experienced the lengthy apprenticeships of the colleagues whose names he cited, but he had the gall to criticise them in the *Yomiuri shinbun*. His outspokenness worked against him in future years. It was not always appreciated by his peers, but Henry was able to get away with such criticism at the time because his innovations had earned him the backing of powerful mentors like Enchō.

In the world of *rakugo*, a propensity for publicly discussing the faults of colleagues is not a recipe for continued popularity with one's peers. Publicly aired reports of his ongoing differences with Enshō and other colleagues were a reminder that Henry was not entirely free of blame for any setbacks he experienced at this stage of his life.

That Henry continued to drink heavily did not help him either. His fondness for alcohol was clear from the time of earlier reports of his involvement in an illegal still in Tsukiji. Other evidence comes from his sister Pauline, who claimed that on one occasion, after their mother entrusted Henry with money to refurbish his father's grave in the Yokohama Foreigners' Cemetery, he squandered it all on drink. His heavy drinking goes some way toward explaining his difficult relationship with his family, signs of which surfaced in October of 1895, six months after Henry's drunken showdown with Enshō. Henry's status as a naturalised *yose geinin* caused embarrassment to members of his family who failed to appreciate the contribution he was making to Meiji-era culture.

As far as close family members were concerned, Henry's career choice and behaviour were not the hallmarks of civilised behaviour. The family's dissatisfaction and embarrassment at Henry's lifestyle became public knowledge in a dramatic fashion one evening in October 1895. Henry was on stage performing a narration when his younger brother John stunned the audience by suddenly interrupting and very loudly berating him for demeaning himself by following a career in the low art of *rakugo*. In its report of the incident, the *Tokyo asahi shinbun* of 16 October 1895, displaying its access to backstage gossip, explained that Henry's uncle, who lived in Britain, had threatened to withdraw financial support unless he abandoned a career as a *rakugoka*. Henry's promise to do so had been conveyed to the uncle, but, when the family realised that Henry was not keeping his promise, the younger John angrily interrupted the performance. Henry reportedly responded to his brother's interruption by immediately terminating his narration and leaving the stage (Kurata 1981–87:VI,62). As if to draw a comparison between Henry's Japanese lifestyle and those of other family members, the newspaper article pointedly noted that John was a clerk, while their sister Pauline and mother Elizabeth were teaching English. John was soon to find employment with a foreign company in Kobe.

Henry as media darling

Between 30 April and 4 May of 1896, when Henry Black was 37, the *Yomiuri shinbun* paid the ultimate tribute of running a series of interviews with him. The articles were part of a longer series featuring popular celebrities of the time. The interviews are among the more definitive extant resources about Henry Black. They offer a window onto his past, although some of his statements, such as that he came from London, have to be read in the context of an entertainer wanting to please a public with scant knowledge of or interest in Adelaide or Australia. In the interviews, Henry refers to his father's background in the newspaper industry, the beginnings of his interest in public speaking which he attributes to Hori Ryūta's interest in him, his friends' opposition to his career on the stage, his brief interlude as an English teacher, and his compelling interest in maintaining the standards in *rakugo* as a profession. On reading the interviews I am impressed by Henry's dedication to his art, but at the same time I cannot help feeling that the insights into Japan he gained from his career, together with his lifestyle as head of an extended household that included his adopted son Seikichi and Seikichi's French wife Rosa, may well have contributed to the widening gulf between him and his sister and brother, who led very different lives. His sister Pauline could by this stage boast of having been a tutor to the offspring of Fukuzawa Yukichi and his brother John was on the way to becoming a respected and comfortably married scion of expatriate society in Kobe.

Further illustrating his popularity and fame was the appearance of his name in a series of 30 woodblock prints produced in 1896 depicting the favourite haunts of famous personalities in Tokyo (*Tokyo jiman meibutsu kai*). The print does not depict Henry, but his name is on the print depicting Akasaka Some, a famous *geisha* of the time, and one of Tokyo's top restaurants, *Yaozen*, in Ueno Park. It was effectively an endorsement for the restaurant by two popular entertainers of the time. Henry was then living in Negishi, which is near today's Ueno Station and not far from the restaurant. Negishi was developing into an artistic colony. Earlier, it had been possible to look from Negishi across paddy fields to Yoshiwara. Some of the owners of the great Yoshiwara houses sited their villas in Negishi from which they could hear the sound of the bell at Kan'eiji Temple. The cultured literati of Edo had also built their retreats here, in what had been countryside. Among the better known artists who lived in the area were the poet Masaoka Shiki, the artist Sakai Hōitsu, the woodblock print artist Kitao Shigemasa … and Henry Black.

Artist Henry Black was an ideas man. In October 1896, he is reported as having given a charity performance of hypnotism at Jinbōchō in Kanda. The performance was to raise money for victims of flooding in the city. It was possibly the first instance of a public performance of hypnotism in Japan. It should also be noted that the idea of a charity performance was new at the time. It is an instance of Henry's compassion for the less fortunate, a quality which his siblings failed to notice when they criticised his lifestyle as uncivilised. Henry had used hypnotism to advantage as early as 1891 in the narration *Setsunaru tsumi* (The pitiful sin), a detective story set in Bedford and Liverpool in England. It tells of a woman who poisons her lover's wife but later repents on her deathbed. In the story, a clever lawyer uses novel methods, including hypnotism, to track down the guilty party.

By the late 1890s, Henry Black had become a frequent traveller to country areas to give performances. One of his favourite places was the mountain hot spring resort of Ikaho in present-day Gunma Prefecture. Two pieces of evidence indicate Henry's fondness of Ikaho. One is the passage referring to the resort in his 1886 English language primer; the other is a firsthand account of Jules Adam, First Secretary at the French legation. Adam had a personal interest in Japan's storytellers and in Black because of his foreign origins. He wrote about Henry Black in an account of Japan's storytellers, published first in French and later in English in Tokyo in 1899. Although Adam's view of the Japanese was patronising and condescending, and the section dealing with Henry Black contains several inaccuracies (notably the claim that Henry had children by his Japanese wife), it is worth quoting at length.

> I will conclude this short study of the *hanashika* with a curious fact. This association of artists includes among its members – you would scarcely believe it – an Englishman, Mr. B…; how he came to Japan no-one knows. He is always moving from one important town to another; his name heads the bills of the best *yose*; he has married a woman of the country, by whom he has several children, and has given up entirely his European habits in order to adopt the Japanese mode of life. I imagine that he has almost forgotten his mother tongue and became a naturalized Japanese citizen some years ago. At present he is a man of about forty, who manipulates his adopted language with the ease not only of an accomplished scholar but of a veritable virtuoso, displaying infinite talent.
>
> Moreover, he is an artist, who by remaining in Europe would assuredly have cut an excellent figure there. Only those, who have studied the most difficult of languages – Japanese – who have lifted, however slightly, the veil, which covers its mysterious idiom, can understand how this man must have worked to arrive at such perfection.
>
> Surely the peculiar case of this Englishman must be unique. By what accident, through what vicissitudes of fortune was this European stranded on the shores of Nippon? He has grown up in the midst of this delicate people; an artist himself, he has fallen in love with this artistic race, with this beautiful land; others have been seduced and captivated, while he has been wholly and solely absorbed.
>
> I had been haunted for a long time by a secret longing to become acquainted with this phenomenon, dilettante or outcast – I knew not what to call him – for whom I cherished a strange admiration mingled with sympathy and curiosity. I wished to question him, to study him, to turn over page after page of his life, as one might be a book or a document. What interesting things might be learned from such a man! How much he must know about Japan, so little known yet! Many a time on my travels I had searched for him and was always eluded at the very moment, when I thought to overtake him, for his profession drives him from place to place like a wandering Jew. In the June of last year, I arrived one day at Ikaho, a fashionable summer resort with hot

> springs, situated in a mountain district at a height of 2500 feet. The hotel servant showed me a room, saying:
>
> 'This room, Sir, has just been occupied by a fellow countryman of yours', (to most Japanese, all foreigners are English) 'the celebrated *hanashika*, Mr. B…'
>
> 'And where is he', I cried wildly.
>
> 'He went away, Sir, yesterday.'
>
> I could not ascertain in what direction. Some months afterwards, I happened to be at Kobe, a large town about 375 miles from the capital. After dinner I was strolling through the picturesque and crowded streets of that lively port, when suddenly passing before a *yose*, I caught sight of the portrait of my evasive friend, conspicuous among many others on the enormous poster. He was to recite that evening. Every minute, the crowd at the door grew denser, and more than one was talking loudly of the celebrated foreign *hanashika*. At last, then, I had caught him!
>
> I entered and had the good fortune to hear him for the first time. I was astounded. The room shook with thunders of applause, when he left the platform. I was touched and gratified at the same time, for it almost seemed as though the ovation, coming from Asiatics, was partly meant for me, since I too was European. I hastily left the room anxious to introduce myself and congratulate my friend with all my heart, but he had already gone, to avoid the triumphant reception awaiting him in the street. Leaping into a *jinrikisha*, I drove to his hotel, having fortunately procured his address. Alas! I arrived about as opportunely as Offenback's carbineers: the bird had flown. He had gone by the midnight train to fulfil an engagement in an important town in the South (Adam 1899:18–24).

In 2007, I visited Ikaho with my family to try to find out where Henry might have stayed. The managers of the inns where we imagined he might have stayed were kind enough to listen to our inquiries, even if they must have thought us a little odd, but no-one could assist us. But this was not surprising. We learned that many such buildings had been destroyed in successive fires that had ravaged the town. Ikaho is built on a steep mountainside with inns and shops clustered around a central stairway with narrow laneways zigzagging upwards. Any fire starting at the base of the town would find an easy path up the slope, burning everything in its way. That the town lived off its hot spring was of no real help in the event of a serious conflagration. We also learned that foreigners visiting the town had to record their names in a registry, incomplete copies of which are kept by the town's museum. Henry's name is not in any of the copies. By the time Henry was a regular visitor to Ikaho, he would have been a Japanese citizen and, as such, not obliged to register with authorities. A local historian told us that many of the pages from guest records kept by inns were used to paper over holes in the partitions of sliding doors.

We did learn, however, that an inn called Suigetsu had been popular with *rakugoka* during the Meiji era, but Suigetsu Inn no longer exists. It stood about two-thirds of the way up the slope, not too far from the town's main shrine. In return for entertaining the guests, the owner of the inn offered free accommodation. It is impossible to know for certain if this was the inn where Henry stayed in just before Jules Adam was there. But since Suigetsu means 'drunken moon', and since Henry was fond of a drink, the thought that Henry Black lodged there is an intriguing one. There is one other link to *rakugoka* in the town. Beside the town's central stone stairway, there is a barber shop with several plaques bearing inscriptions dedicated to *rakugoka* in the cursive script known as *yose moji* characteristic of that used in recording the rankings of *rakugoka* and program announcements at *yose*. In Henry's time, this barber shop boasted that it used the health-giving waters of the hot spring to wash customers' hair.

1900 as a turning point

Henry Black suffered a significant personal setback in 1900 when his long-time mentor San'yūtei Enchō died. Enchō's death paved the way for a subtle, but important shift in the power balance within the San'yūha. The long-festering hostility from other members of the school, which surfaced once Henry had lost San'yūtei Enchō's backing, sent 41-year-old Henry's stocks within the San'yūha into a decline from which he was never to recover. A new generation of *rakugoka* had begun to assume control of the guild.

Perhaps one bright spot in Henry's life in these years was the adoption of Seikichi. As Henry was a Japanese citizen with the surname of Ishii at the time of adoption, the boy became Ishii Seikichi. Seikichi later took the stage names of Shōkyokusai Tensa and Hosuko.

Despite the setbacks, his brother's protest, the public feuding within the guild and his distant uncle's threat to withdraw financial backing were not enough to persuade Henry to end his *rakugo* career. When the only other options were to become a clerk in England or an insurance agent in the foreign enclave of Yokohama, the business of telling stories was far too alluring. Henry James Kairakutei Ishii Burakku was too much at home in Japan.

Chapter 16

Saved by new technology

> A Mr. Black was to help us to find artists and arrange their programmes. He was an Englishman married to a Japanese lady, and had lived thirty-five years in Japan. He was almost a professional story teller. Naturally, as he spoke both English and Japanese with equal fluency he was a godsend to us (Gaisberg 1946:68).

As the 19th century drew to a close, Henry Black continued to produce new narrations, but they lacked the creative edge of his earlier adaptations. To make matters worse, Henry's popularity as a teller of stories of European origin waned as audiences developed a more sophisticated understanding of Europe through a flood of more professionally translated European novels. This caused a serious drop in income for Henry and obliged him to reinvent himself as a variety act by incorporating hypnotism and Western-style conjuring into his performances. Meiji-era audiences were as much followers of fashion as audiences today.

Then in 1903, Henry received a welcome injection of funds. The American-born impresario and producer of early disc-shaped records, Fred W Gaisberg was the first person to make gramophone recordings in Europe, where he worked for The Gramophone Company which owned the His Master's Voice label. He had earned a reputation as the person who had persuaded Caruso to sing for his company for what was an extraordinary sum at the time. In the first week of January 1903, Gaisberg walked down the gangplank at Yokohama with his 'business head' Tom Addis and an assistant George Dillnutt with an offer that, under the circumstances, was much too good for Henry to refuse. For Gaisberg, Henry Black was the perfect go-between in his search for talent in Japan. Henry spoke Japanese, was familiar with all the right people in the theatre, and could accompany him to the *kabuki* to explain what was going on. Gaisberg was a white knight with money to boost Henry's bank account.

Gaisberg's arrival could not have come at a more opportune moment. With the decline in demand for his stories of Western origin, Henry had turned more to recitations of humorous short stories. By the late 1890s, he was attempting to offset a fall in popularity by diversifying into other forms of entertainment, including teaming with a *naniwabushi* group, conjuring and hypnotism, and the creation of his own Western-style band.[107] Colleagues and *rakugo* purists saw this as a regrettable departure from the narrative art form, but Henry regarded it as necessary experimentation in new mediums and as a way to supplement his diminishing income. He also resorted more to touring outside Tokyo, which was not uncommon during the summer off-season in Tokyo when many entertainers sought respite in the cooler mountain resorts by trading their talents for reduced rent or free accommodation at inns in resort towns.

Disputed modernity

Henry Black's pursuit of experimentation and diversification was not just attributable to an innovative spirit. By the end of the 19th century, several factors beyond Henry's control were making his life difficult. Henry's mission to modernise and socialise audiences through his narrations was overtaken by the modernising and socialising agendas of the government through its education system. His mission to introduce European culture was also overtaken by the proliferation of other mediums, including the easy availability of translations of canonic European literature. By the late 1890s, audiences were better educated and found their information about European culture from diverse sources including novels, magazines and other modern media, as statistics confirm. In the late 1880s, most of the literature translated into Japanese consisted of British and French novels and Henry's choices of story material from British and French authors reflected this trend. But from the 1890s onward, readers of fiction could avail themselves of a greater variety of foreign sources, as translations from Russian, Scandinavian and other European languages entered the market. By this stage, too, Japanese authors had so completely absorbed the Western story idiom that Japanese literature had become, as Jonathan E Zwicker, puts it, 'simply Western literature in Japanese' (Zwicker

107 An article in *Kainan shinbun*, 10 October 1897 (Kurata 1981–87:VI,121) refers to Black performing hypnotism in Matsuyama. Other references to his hypnotism performances are in *Yamato shinbun*, 8 October 1896 (Shogei 1977:5), and *Hinode shinbun*, 16 August 1898 (Kurata 1981–87:VI,160). For a report of his performance as a hypnotist at the Hakubaitei *yose* in Kanda in April 1905, see Shogei (1977:5).

2006:168). Reflecting this, the figures for book sales show that translations were relegated to the status of a niche market (Zwicker 2006:152). Similar things were happening in the theatres. As newer, more radical forms of Western-style realism in stage drama began to flourish, even *kabuki* had begun to ossify and lose some of its attraction (Minamitani 1990:184–185).

In the late 19th century, governments, as well as writers and intellectuals, had been bent on the task of reinterpreting Japan's history and reinventing its traditions to explain the country's transition from a military state under the *bakufu* to a modern 19th-century nation-state, fashioned after a number of European models. The models they had chosen had constitutions, were run by civilian bureaucracies, possessed elected governments, and industrial infrastructures. Some had monarchies. In the 1880s and 1890s, Henry, Enchō, and other *rakugoka* had joined, on the stage and in print, in the national discourse of the process of redefinition. But by the dawn of the 20th century, Japan's rulers had cemented the process of seeking legitimacy in their rule in a redefined version of the country's history, melding together strands of mythology and reinvented tradition with a mission to gain an empire commensurate with those of other European nation-states. In addition, the rapid increase in the reading public, which was reflected in the merging in the early 20th century of the *ōshinbun* (major newspapers) and the *koshinbun* (minor newspapers), together with the development of a vernacular literature and the growth in other forms of entertainment and information media, sent *rakugo* into a gradual decline. The decline was not helped by an overall downturn in the world economy, when many *yose* closed (Morioka & Sasaki 1987:10). Belt-tightening brought about by imminent war with Russia also had a detrimental impact on ticket sales (Morioka & Sasaki 1983:148).

Further contributing to the decline of *rakugo* was the simultaneous rise in popularity of female performers of *gidayū*, a type of powerful 'narrative chant' of historical and romantic narratives accompanied by a solo three-stringed lute known as the *shamisen* (Japan 1993:454). By the early 1890s, when Henry was at his peak of popularity, female *gidayū* performers had become extremely popular on *yose* programs, posing a challenge to some of the more prominent *rakugoka*. Henry could hold his own, thanks to his novelty value as a foreign-born narrator with original material from Europe. By the mid-1890s, however, the popularity of *gidayū* had risen to the extend that *yose* featuring women's *gidayū* alone were outdoing those specialising in *rakugo*. Consequently, many *yose* were obliged to either include women's *gidayū* in their programs or suffer economic decline. Purists were aghast, but audiences, particularly men, loved the idea of a woman on stage. The female *gidayū* singers of the mid- to late 1890s were the equivalent of today's rock stars. They were so popular that politicians worried publicly that male students were wasting all their precious *yen* at their performances.

The *gidayū* singers were a direct challenge to the rakugoka's supremacy in the *yose*. In 1894, for example, when the highly popular women's *gidayū* performer Takemoto Ayanosuke I performed at the Kotohira Theatre in Shiba, two nearby *yose* countered with programs featuring well-known *rakugoka* from the San'yūha and the other major *rakugo* guild, Yanagiha, but could not compete for patrons (Takahashi 1989:180). Although the unprecedented proliferation of women performers of *gidayū* was one outcome of the social freedoms instituted by the new Meiji government, the government ultimately sought to curtail women's *gidayū*, regarding it as a threat to public morals. When performer numbers peaked in 1900, the government prohibited students from attending the performances at *yose*, 'ostensibly for their own good' (Coaldrake 1997:203–218).

The diversification in the *yose* programming represented by this trend may also partly explain Henry's apparently abrupt cessation of lengthy serialised adaptations of European stories. Ironically, another factor contributing to the demise of *rakugo* may have been the popularity of *sokkibon*. The very success of the *sokkibon* prompted some more unscrupulous *rakugoka* to plagiarise the *sokkibon* of other *rakugoka* and claim them as their own, prompting disputes over income rights just when *yose* revenue for *rakugoka* was diminishing (Miller 1994:49:4:484).

These disputes can be regarded as symptomatic of the difficulties experienced by *rakugoka* in the early 20th century as interest in their art began to fade in the face of multiplying alternatives. In keeping with his temperament and past history of innovation, Henry Black's reaction was to experiment, but his apparent distancing from pure *rakugo* alienated colleagues. And the alienation was exacerbated by his outspokenness, as his dispute with Enshō in 1895 demonstrated. He had long complained that *rakugoka* colleagues were complacent in the face of change and many of these colleagues looked askance at his attempts to diversify. To his detractors, the new forms of entertainment that Henry experimented with had little to do with *rakugo*. They were unwilling to tolerate experimentation in the name of modernity.

Evidence of these emerging differences appeared in a report in the *Miyako shinbun* on 12 January 1902 which, while praising Henry for his love of Japan, his devotion to his art, and his fostering of the careers of younger *rakugoka*, noted that he was losing popularity and touring the provinces performing hypnotism and variety shows (see figure 5). It advised him to stick to *rakugo*. Henry ignored the advice and shortly afterwards, as noted in the *Ōsaka mainichi shinbun* of 1 March 1902, he and his adopted son, now using the stage name of Hosuko, were in the Osaka area, giving performances (Kurata 1981–87:VII,161). These performances undoubtedly included magic, as Henry was encouraging Hosuko to train as a magician. Henry's cooperation with Gaisberg in 1903 was yet another way of leveraging his abilities and contacts.

A modern medium – recorded sound discs

Gaisberg's team arrived from India to make recordings for the London Gramophone Company. Gaisberg needed someone who could speak Japanese and English, as well as enlist Japan's best entertainers and negotiate with them to perform for his microphone. Henry fitted the bill perfectly. It took two weeks for Gaisberg's equipment to pass through customs and arrive at the Metropole Hotel in Tsukiji where, with Henry's assistance, he set about recording a number of musicians and vocal artists.

Gaisberg had sailed from London on 28 September 1902 to record the music and sounds of the Far East. He was to be absent from London until August 1903 (Moore 1977:77–85). While in Asia, he made recording stops in Calcutta, Tokyo, Shanghai, Hong Kong, Singapore, Bangkok and Rangoon. In Tokyo, they worked throughout the cold months of January and February 1903 to complete their assignment, Gaisberg making use of Henry Black's contacts in the entertainment industry to bring together a wide range of talent after 'two weeks visiting theatres and tea-houses and holding auditions'.

Gaisberg described Henry as a 'godsend' (Gaisberg 1946:59). Together, they were to make history by producing the first disc-shaped recordings made in Japan. The Metropole was central and near enough to entertainment quarters frequented by many of the blind musicians, *geisha* and *rakugoka* whom Henry recruited for Gaisberg. The records they cut included a *geisha* band of 'little women with big European band instruments' which Gaisberg described as 'the funniest thing imaginable', and the Imperial Household Band, whose music was 'weird and fascinating indeed' (Moore 1977:82). Gaisberg's diary entry for his first day of recording in Tokyo, 4 February 1903, indicates he did not have much empathy for Japanese music:

> We made some 54 records. Japanese music is simply too horrible, but funny to relate, Europeans who have been long in the country profess to

really enjoy it, and say that there is more in the music and acting than a casual observer would believe (Moore 1977:82).

Perhaps Gaisberg made this observation after talking to Henry, whose opinion on Western and Japanese tastes in music was expressed in his 1891 *Eikoku Rondon gekijō miyage* when he comments on Gātsurudo's first visit to the Adelphi Theatre in London:

> When the Japanese first heard Western music, they found it merely rowdy (*souzoushii*) and could not adjust their ears to it. And when foreigners first hear Japanese instruments, they puzzle over how a human being could find pleasure in such a thing. But if they listen often enough, even foreigners conclude that Danbei's *shamisen* playing is good (Eikokujin 1891:15).

Gaisberg was frequently amused to find that some of the actors whom he auditioned to perform scenes from the *kabuki* would at first insist on donning their makeup and bringing their costumes. He thought they were unused to the idea that it was only their voices he wanted for posterity. He seems to have ignored the possibility that the actors may well have wanted to don their costumes so as to more professionally assume the voice traits of the characters they played. Gaisberg devoted considerable space in his memoirs to a detailed description of a visit to the *kabuki*, but very little to *rakugo*, noting merely that Henry, whom he described as 'almost a professional story teller', performed while seated at a table delivering narrations which lasted 'from thirty to sixty minutes, an amusement of which the Japs were extremely fond' (Gaisberg 1946:59–60). But it is through Gaisberg that we also get some inkling of Henry's tendency to boast. Gaisberg recounts how Henry told him he had once narrated before the Crown Prince, taking 30 minutes to give his first offering. According to Henry, the prince so liked the story that he requested more, so Henry told another story of longer duration. This elicited a further request for more, so that in total Henry claimed to have spent three hours reciting stories for the prince.

A photograph of Henry from this period shows him in one of the tea-house districts of Tokyo standing beside Tom Addis with a tea-house attendant in the background (see figure 1). Doubtless this was on one of the occasions Gaisberg refers to in his diary:

> February 12th, 1903. Tokio: …if one wishes to visit the theatre here, one first goes to a neighbouring tea-house, in order to procure tickets and make arrangements for the supply of food during the long play,

> which usually lasts from 10 a.m. to 10 p.m. During the long intervals between acts one can retire to the tea-house to rest (Gaisberg 1946:60).

On one of these occasions, they dined on 'raw fish, little raw minnows, fish hash, seaweed and croquettes of game, chestnuts, apple sauce, fried fish garnished with plums, custard fish-chowder, *sake*, beer and rice' (Gaisberg 1946:61).

Gaisberg's recordings included narrations by Henry Black. Henry's contribution included a story purported to be a recollection of an incident in which Henry, feeling particularly hungry, enters a restaurant and orders a large number of bowls of noodles. The waitress fails to bring his order despite serving other customers who all eat and leave. Finally Henry hails the waitress again and demands to know why he has not been given his order, whereupon the waitress responds that she had thought that since he ordered so many bowls, he wanted to wait for his friends to arrive before eating.[108]

As these were the first voice recordings made in Japan, foreign-born Henry Black serendipitously made a valuable contribution to the study of the Japanese language as it was spoken at the time. The recordings are proof that Henry spoke Japanese fluently. For linguists, they encapsulate and exemplify the standard Tokyo dialect of the day (Shimizu 1987:14).

By the time Gaisberg's team packed their bags and caught the train west for Kyoto on the Tokaido Line, Gaisberg had recorded 'some six hundred titles covering every variety of the national music' (Gaisberg 1946:59), largely thanks to Henry Black. One of the great ironies of the production of those records was that the new, modern medium of the recording would eventually compete with, and to a large extent replace, the *yose*. But that was not to be for many years, because records were extremely expensive, as were household gramophones, so, for the time being, the theatre remained a cheaper option.

A normal state of disputation

After Gaisberg left, things returned to normal, which for Henry Black meant disputation, possibly fuelled by alcohol. In June 1903, his innovative instinct again caused problems when he clashed with members of the San'yūha over his affiliation with the *naniwabushi* reciter Naniwatei Aizō (1870–1906). Slightly different from *gidayū*, *naniwabushi* are a 'type of narrative ballad

108 The recordings have been reissued as *Zenshū: Nihon fukikomi kotohajime*, TOCF-59061~71, EMI Music Japan.

rhythmically intoned by a solo chanter to the accompaniment of a single *shamisen* player'. (Japan 1993:1047). Henry had begun performing with Aizō in Tokyo in June, a time when many *rakugoka* traditionally escaped the heat of the capital for performances in provincial areas (Kurata 1981–87:VII,229). In July, the *Chūō shinbun* went public with details of the dispute. The newspaper noted that Henry had previously maintained a band of more than ten members together with a number of apprentices. In the days when professional storytellers often kept apprentices in their households, these numbers suggest considerable financial resources would have been required. But the newspaper also berated Henry, who was, the writer said, now consuming two *shō* (3.6 litres) of *sake* a day.[109] Although this could have been the amount consumed by the extended household, it nevertheless hints at a high level of consumption by Henry. The newspaper then went on to note that, although he was fully occupied performing at up to four *yose* each day, he had recently begun joint performances with *naniwabushi* and *gidayū*, with the result that the number of appearances had actually fallen. As many *rakugoka* regarded *gidayū* as undermining the popularity of *rakugo*, Henry's flirtation with *naniwabushi* and *gidayū* was, from their perspective, akin to a betrayal. The newspaper said that his plan to team up with Aizō had been opposed by the younger *shin'uchi*-ranked members of the San'yūha, which is a clear indication that the younger generation did not appreciate his actions.

In the end, Henry called their bluff by threatening to leave the San'yūha (Kurata 1981–87:VII,233–234). His opponents caved in and Henry subsequently appeared with Aizō and others on numerous occasions.[110] But the whole messy incident was indicative of divisions within the ranks.

Hit by a mood of austerity in the anxious lead-up to the Russo-Japanese war, the world of *rakugo* could ill afford such distractions. A pre-war mood of austerity resulted in smaller audiences for the theatres and less employment for *rakugoka*. But with the outbreak of the Russo-Japanese war, which lasted from February 1904 to September 1905, *rakugoka* rallied to the cause. Inventive narrators turned their talents to producing stories related to Russia or the war, resulting in a marked rise in the number of *sokkibon* at this time. J Scott Miller has suggested a number of explanations for this, including that *sokkibon* became an arm of state propaganda during the war and that

---

109 One shō is 1.8 litres.

110 Reports of these performances appeared in *Tōkyō asahi shinbun*, 29 July 1903 (Kurata 1981–87:VII,239), *Yorozu chōhō*, 9 August 1903 (Kurata 1981–87:VII,240–241) and *Ōsaka shinpō*, 31 October 1903 in (Kurata 1981–87:VII,251.)

they 'reflected the jubilation of the populace' at Japan's victory over Russia (Miller 1997:587).

Japanese citizen Henry Black also identified with the cause. In 1904 he publicly offered himself for military service together with a number of other *rakugoka*. He was turned down on the grounds that he too closely resembled a Russian (Kurata 1981–87:VII,281–282). As had happened so often before, his ethnicity was a sticking-point.

Chapter 17

The end of an era, 1908

> Whatever the case, it is a sad state of affairs (*Ōsaka mainichi shinbun* 23 September 1908, commenting on Henry Black's apparent suicide attempt.)

On the evening of 21 August 1908, during a tour of the Kansai district, Henry Black's colleagues found him backstage at the Ebisu Theatre in Nishinomiya writhing in agony. He had not long before finished a performance. The *Ōsaka mainichi shinbun* was unequivocal. It was, it said, an unsuccessful suicide attempt. He had taken arsenic.

The newspaper used the opportunity to take stock of Henry's lifetime accomplishments, and then listed recent setbacks, implying that they must have felt insurmountable. It praised the 'London-born' Henry Black for his devotion to Edo rather than Britain, commended his accomplishments under *kabuki* actor Danjūrō, as well as his dedication to the narrator's art, and noted his decision to abandon his family's British heritage and take Japanese citizenship. It listed his other achievements as gaining *shin'uchi* status under the San'yūha banner, taking a Japanese family name upon marriage to Ishii Aka and presenting detective and other serialised stories.

In the list of setbacks, the newspaper concluded that Henry's popularity, which had at one stage 'attained great heights', had not lasted long and that he had been performing as a hypnotist in Tokyo and Osaka for the past seven or eight years. It noted that Henry was experiencing financial difficulties and had recently combined with his adopted son Hosuko to form a troupe specialising in Western conjuring tricks. The newspaper quoted theatre staff as saying that since beginning performances in Nishinomiya, Henry Black had been 'behaving strangely'. It said he had been depressed about a lump resembling a tumour in his throat and may have been afraid he had cancer. It also speculated that he may have simply been depressed over his fall from former popularity as a *rakugoka*. 'Whatever the case, it is a sad state of affairs', the newspaper concluded (Kurata 1981–87:VIII,175–176).

In its report of the incident, the *Asahi shinbun* noted that, because of financial constraints, Henry had recently had to dissolve his large household and relocate to a smaller house in Tokyo. It stated that he had received financial support from his mother and from General Tōgō Heihachirō (Morioka & Sasaki 1983:150; Shogei 1977:5). Tōgō's interest in Black may have stemmed from Henry's offer to volunteer for military service during the Russo-Japanese War. He may also have been known to the Black family from the time Henry's father had edited newspapers.

The *Yamato shinbun* claimed that Henry Black's motive for the attempt was 'said to have been a general weariness of life rather than any specific reason' (Morioka & Sasaki 1983:149–150; Shogei 1977:5). None of the newspapers recorded what Henry thought of his circumstances. Whatever the real reasons, the list of woes given in the newspapers was lengthy and presumably gathered from those close to him who were willing to talk.

There was, however, an additional family-related factor not mentioned in the newspaper reports. Japanese newspapers would not necessarily have known of an important family event in England that may have contributed to Henry's depression. On 6 August 1908, two weeks before the suicide attempt, Henry's younger brother John had married at the Parish Church, Ewell in Surrey, England. The marriage was reported in Japan three weeks later (*Japan Chronicle* 1908). An announcement of the coming marriage between 'Mr John Reddie Black of Messrs. Samuel Samuel & Co., second son of the late Mr J.R. Black formerly editor of the *Japan Gazette*, Yokohama, and of Mrs Black of Tokyo, to Helen Dorothy, eldest daughter of the late Mr Edward Flint Kilby of Yokohama' had also appeared a month before Henry's suicide attempt in the English-language *Japan Chronicle*. John had met his Japan-born British wife on a ship from Japan to England. John Black was to return to Kobe shortly after the marriage to begin work as an insurance agent and surveyor. In the early 1920s, John was to become president of the bastion of expatriate life in Japan, the Kobe Club. John's hostility toward his elder brother's stage career, his marriage in England and his imminent return to nearby Kobe, may well have served as proof to Henry of irreconcilable differences between Henry's itinerant and homosexual lifestyle and the monogamous norm upon which John had embarked. The differences would have served only to exacerbate Henry's concern over his waning popularity on the stage, his financial insecurity and any worries he had about possible cancer.

Although Henry recovered from the suicide attempt, it was a defining moment in that it was the culmination of a series of woes, some of which were of his own making and others beyond his control. As for the cancer scare, a lump in the throat might simply have been a polyp, common enough among people whose professions require them to project their voices frequently. Polyps sometimes subside or break free with some slight loss of blood, but they are not cancerous tumours.

Whatever the real reasons, the litany of problems given in the newspapers indicated difficulties Henry was experiencing in adjusting to his reputation as an increasingly dated entertainer on the Japanese stage. Foreign birth was no longer the big drawcard it had been. This was clearly signalled by his name dropping to ninth place by 1907 on a public list of rankings of *rakugo* performers (*higashi maegashira yonmaime*) (Shogei 1977:3), similar to those that today list *sumo* wrestlers or tennis players. Underlying his fall in popularity was the fact that many of the conditions that had audience interest in his presentations of European themes as examples of modernity no longer existed. This state of affairs had worsened since the dawn of the 20th century and was beyond Henry's control.

To make matters worse, Henry's relationship with the San'yū guild was not smooth. Support from its members had begun to diminish by the mid-1890s, because of his tendency to be outspoken, which was exacerbated by his drinking habit. The death in 1900 of his mentor Enchō had also ushered a new era into the the guild under a leadership that was not necessarily warm toward Henry. Many younger guild members were indifferent or even hostile.

By the time the newspapers recorded his 'attempted suicide', other forces were at work that were even beyond the control of Henry Black's rivals. As the 20th century arrived, the forces of modernisation extended into the world of entertainment in the form of Gaisberg's sound recordings and the invention of the cinema. The new forms of entertainment steadily eroded the popularity of *rakugo*. Declining *yose* numbers reflect this. By the late 19th century, police surveillance of *yose* had lessened, but *yose* numbers reflected the fortunes of an entertainment industry dependent on political and economic factors. In Tokyo, for example, where there had been 199 *yose* in 1885 and 230 in 1886, the number dropped dramatically to 80 in 1901 (Morioka & Sasaki 1990:251–252). Although the decline was attributed to economic depression and belt-tightening due to imminent war with Russia (Morioka & Sasaki 1983:148), their numbers did not recover once the depression and war had passed. Henry's travels beyond the cities to perform were an attempt to stave off the financial effects of the decline in his own popularity and the popularity of *rakugo* in the cities.

Despite the erosion of his career base and his relative obscurity in his later years, one of his tales from those years persists today as a part of his legacy to his profession. It is the humorous short tale *Tabakozuki* (The heavy smoker), published in 1905. *Tabakozuki* tells of a London merchant Inoue Hatsusaburō who is called to the bedside of his dying friend Mr Itō to help him draw up a will. The dying man's doctor informs the merchant that the man is terminally ill with bubonic plague (*pesuto*). The doctor explains that the symptoms of plague (la peste) are cysts under the arms and a high fever. Upset by the news, the merchant becomes worried, as he rides his horse home, that he might have caught the disease, because he had to get very close to Itō to hear him when he dictated the will. Distracted by these thoughts, Inoue absentmindedly puts an unextinguished pipe in his pocket. The pipe burns through his coat making him sweat and convincing him that he has caught a fever from his friend. It begins to snow, but despite the cold, his right armpit begins to feel hot. He probes the spot through his coat and encounters what feels like a large cyst. Finally he reaches home and, after he complains to his wife that he feels ill, his wife discovers the burning pipe and explains that rather than having *caught* the plague (*pesuto*), he *is* the pest (Kairakutei 1905; Nishūbashi 1905:293–300).[111]

There is a qualitative difference between this story and his other stories set in Europe. In his earlier narrations, Henry had adapted mystery novels and told them over many nights, stringing out the element of suspense to delight his audiences, *Tabakozuki* is brief, probably only seven or eight minutes in length, and it is not episodic. It is too brief to permit of the lengthy and informative digressions characteristic of his adaptations and serialised narrations of the 1880s and 1890s. Henry was no longer a sought-after bearer of civilisation and enlightenment. He had become a one-man comic.

Identity and personal life

Because of his lifestyle, Henry Black had no offspring, but a newspaper report of his attempted suicide indicated that he was accustomed to a large and gregarious household. He lived as a member of an extended household which included his adopted son Seikichi and a variety of persons working in the entertainment world. Members of the Western- style band Henry formed

111 Morioka and Sasaki (1983:149, fn73), citing *Rakugo Jiten*, note that 'the story is no longer presented on the *rakugo* stage today, although there is another story of different content with the same title.'

and trained for theatre performances may also have been accommodated. Together these people constituted a surrogate family for Henry.

Henry also fostered a Japanese boy called Kanō Gunji who spent some years in this household (see figure 4). Gunji was roughly the same age as Seikichi. Gunji's two sons attest to the fact that he was the son of a Buddhist priest whose family name was Kitamura from Saitama Prefecture near Tokyo. There is evidence to suggest that before he entered Henry's household, Gunji's mother had sent him off to Tokyo because he had become difficult to control. Gunji's sons agree that Gunji moved to Tokyo around 1903 or 1904 where he was at first looked after by a couple, living in Asakusa, who ran a small foundry. It appears that Henry offered to foster Gunji when he was not getting along with the couple. It is possible that the connection was made because Henry frequented the area's theatres. One of Gunji's sons has suggested that Gunji was 14 when he entered Henry's household; the other has suggested it was slightly earlier.

At some stage while Gunji and Seikichi were with Henry, the household was situated at Kohinata, Suidōbashi, in present day Otowa. Since we know that at the time of his attempted suicide in 1908, Henry was at an address in Minami Futaba-chō in Honjo Ward, we can safely assume that, since Gunji was in the household for some time, the household moved to Otowa soon after the attempt. The house in Suidōbashi was rented from the famous Hatoyama Kazuo, who was only a couple of years older than Henry. Henry may have known the Hatoyama family through his father's connections as a journalist and editor with prominent figures in Japan's intellectual and political classes or as a result of friendships with former adherents of the pro-democracy movement. Hatoyama Kazuo was a graduate of the prestigious Kaisei Gakkō, later Tokyo University. He went on to study at Columbia and Yale Universities and by 1885 was in the Foreign Ministry, where he helped revise the unequal treaties with Western nations. In 1892, he was elected to the House of Representatives for the Rikken Kaishintō Party. Kazuo's wife, Haruko, was equally renowned as an educator. The Hatoyamas had two sons – Ichirō, who would have been 20 in 1903, and Hideo, who would have been 19. Ichirō became Japan's Prime Minister in 1954.

The Hatoyama house and the one Henry rented from them were near Gokokuji Temple which at that time was one of Tokyo's busiest and most prosperous. There would have been a constant stream of people passing along the main street near Henry's house on most days of the year and certainly on the more auspicious days on the Buddhist calendar.

There were several women in Henry's household during these years[112]. Kanō Hisashi, one of Gunji's sons, suspects that some of these women may have been mistresses to Henry, but could not offer definitive proof. This is an intriguing suggestion, given Henry's earlier affair with Motokichi, who was no longer a part of Henry's household. Henry did not tell Gunji the details about his legal wife Aka, but Gunji's sons always assumed Henry paid Aka and her mother to be adopted into her family so he could acquire Japanese citizenship.

Henry encouraged Gunji to learn the violin and become a member of the Western-style band he trained and maintained. The band used sheet music imported from England, making it a novelty attraction at Henry's performances. Gunji's talents complemented Henry's plans for expanding into forms of entertainment other than storytelling. According to Gunji's elder son, Ichirō, Henry boasted to Gunji that he had once taken the young Emperor Taishō on an incognito visit to the Tamanoi pleasure quarters to buy the services of a prostitute. Henry claimed that he had befriended the Emperor when he was Crown Prince and Henry had delivered his father's newspapers to the palace. It is impossible to know if this was true, but the difference in the ages of the prince and Henry, as well as the fact that the prince was under constant supervision would make it highly unlikely. Henry may have relished the element of truth in the story which was that the Emperor was generally known to be a womaniser. Henry, inveterate teller of tall tales that he was, also told Gunji that his family was descended from an English squire (*jinushi*).

By the time Gunji joined the household, Henry had acquired a dog. He sometimes took Gunji with him when he walked the dog and would use these occasions to teach English to Gunji by telling him English words for objects they passed on the way. According to Kano Hisashi, Gunji told him that Henry's favourite drink in these years was Takara *shōchū*, a brand of distilled liquor that was cheaper than *sake*. Henry was also fond of composing *haiku* poems.

Gunji's younger son, Kanō Hisashi, told me that Gunji smoked cigarettes, but that Henry would at times urge him never to ask others for a cigarette. Henry wanted to teach him to be responsible for his own vices. Once, when Gunji made fun of a beggar, Henry scolded him, saying that it was the beggar's choice to be so and that he should not look down on such people.

---

112 This information was provided by Kanō Hisashi and Kanō Ichirō in an interview with the author on 8 October 1991.

Another member of the gregarious household in Suidōbashi was a woman called Abe Asa. Asa had moved to Tokyo from the Fukushima area as a result of upheavals during the early Meiji years. Her family's earlier political affiliations made her a refugee. This would have appealed to Henry who was also living on the fringes. Asa was a talented player of the stringed instrument known as the *koto*, which made her an asset in Henry's troupe of performers. She was also said to be reasonably competent at speaking English. Asa learned conjuring while in Henry's household. Kanō Ichiro recalled her performing a trick with a small metal bar which she would place in one bag and then seemingly produce from another. One of Henry's special tricks in these years was producing watches belonging to members of the audience from his own pocket.

It is not clear how Asa came to be a member of the household, but Kanō Hisashi has suggested that Gunji was responsible. It appears that, although Asa was about ten years older than Gunji, she and Gunji developed more than a passing liking for each other. According to Hisashi, when Gunji was around 19 years old, probably in 1914, Asa fell pregnant to Gunji during one of Henry's absences to perform outside Tokyo. Henry returned from the tour to find that Gunji had spent money left to maintain the household and had pawned a valuable *kumadori kaogata* (a cloth impression of *kabuki* makeup) from the *kabuki* actor Ichikawa Danjūrō V, as well as several antiques and some valued calligraphy. Cloth impressions such as Henry's were sought after by collectors and this one would have had considerable monetary and sentimental value for Henry. The incident led to a temporary falling-out between Henry and Gunji, which resulted in Gunji leaving the household. But any ill-will that it caused was forgotten when Gunji, who had been working as a violinist accompanying silent movies in cinemas in Hokkaido, visited Henry some years later. He was well received by Henry, who promptly shared a considerable amount of *shōchū* with his prodigal guest.[113] Henry had it within him to forgive.

The fact that the key members of Henry's household, Gunji, Seikichi and Asa, were all cut adrift from their own birth families made it easier for Henry to identify with them. The picture of Henry gained from talking to Gunji's sons and to Seikichi's descendants is of a generous and forgiving benefactor who sometimes boasted of larger-than-life adventures, was

---

113 Gunji's story, as well as Black's claim of friendship with the Emperor, was gleaned from the author's interviews with his two sons, Kanō Hisashi and Kanō Ichirō on 8 October 1991.

careless with money, overly fond of alcohol and, at times, unable to make accurate judgments about the reliability of those he trusted because he had too much faith in human nature.

Gunji and Asa named their son Ichirō after Hatoyama Ichirō, the eldest son of Henry's landlord at the time, Hatoyama Kazuo. Gunji never married Asa, but registered Ichirō's birth and acknowledged him as a *shoshi* (child born out of wedlock). Asa later married an older brother of Gunji and settled in the Tokorozawa area north of Tokyo. One of the more lasting legacies of the relationship between Gunji and Henry is a rare and valuable new-year postcard, which is in the possession of Kanō Hisashi. The card was sent to Henry from an admirer who lived in Kyoto. It shows Henry, probably as Omiwa in *Imoseyama* (see figure 2). He is kneeling beside another unidentified actor who is also dressed for a female role. The card is addressed to Ishii Burakku at an address in Kobe, where he may have been performing at the time (see figure 2). Kanō Hisashi also possesses a seal that belonged to Henry, which shows the intertwined letters HJB, standing for Henry James Black (see figure 3).

Life in Meguro

By the 1920s, Henry was living in a household in Meguro Ward with Seikichi and his wife and children. Henry had a room upstairs in Seikichi's house, which was not far from where Henry's mother and sister lived. Seikichi's wife was a French woman, Julie V Pequignot (1885–1949). She played the *shamisen*, was an accomplished singer of *gidayū* and used the stage name Rosa (Morioka & Sasaki 1986a:183–184). By any standards, it was an odd ménage containing the Australian-born Briton-turned-Japanese, his adopted Japanese son and that son's extraordinary French-born *shamisen*-playing wife Rosa. Rosa was the daughter of a French couple, who had been taken to Japan by her uncle, a diplomat based in Yokohama, after her parents died. She went to a French girls' school in Yokohama and later worked as a tutor in the homes of the wealthy. Possibly because of an earlier interest in acting and the stage, she showed an aptitude for *gidayū*. She appears to have fallen out with her uncle, and there is reason to believe that the falling-out was prompted by Rosa's rebuttal of a marriage proposal. From then on, Rosa survived on money her parents had bequeathed to her. She had an older brother, who died during the First World War. Satō Rennosuke, the owner of Waradana, a *yose* in Ushigome Ward, Tokyo, formally adopted Julie and got the female orator Wakayanagi Enjō to introduce her on stage as Rosa.[114] Seikichi and Rosa first met at the Ushigome theatre owned by Satō.

As foreign-born performers of a traditional Japanese art form, Henry and Rosa embodied the eclectic spirit of the Meiji era. Both shared the stage with Seikichi, giving variety shows featuring Henry's stories and demonstrations of hypnotism and conjuring by Seikichi and Rosa.

Henry Black maintained a sporadic presence on the stage in the final years of his life. In 1910, the journalist Hanazono Kanesada visited Henry and noted that he was 'still full of vim' and that he spoke of his mother as being 90 years old and unwilling to receive visitors (Hanazono 1926:78). In December of that year, about the time of Henry's 52nd birthday, the *Asahi shinbun* columnist Hakumenya wrote a short piece about Henry after witnessing one of his performances in Ryōgoku, Tokyo. It gives a good description of his physical appearance and performance style.

> Around 10 o'clock, Black comes on. This man Black appears in front of a small round table covered with a brown cloth. There is a chair at the table and also a water jug and a glass. He wears a black suit with a vest, a Roosevelt collar and a black tie, everything tightly fitting; he has no whiskers, and the hair on his half-bald head is cut short. His eyes and complexion are those of a foreigner, but his deep and sonorous voice sounds like that of a Japanese (Morioka & Sasaki 1983:150).

Henry Black also maintained a relationship with the expatriate community, occasionally using his insights into Japanese culture to inform and educate. In July 1910, when a *Japan Chronicle* correspondent reported on the annual Gion Festival in Kyoto, Henry wrote to the newspaper pointing out a number of errors in the original story. The correspondent had complained of 'the almost total lack of reverence' displayed toward the *dashi* (large floats) and *yama* (small floats) drawn through the city's streets, and argued that the procession appeared poorly coordinated and lacked any music of interest. The correspondent ended by saying 'it would be interesting to have the Japanese point of view in this matter of celebrations' (*Japan Chronicle* 1910a). Four days later, a letter by Ishii Black offered a studied and well-informed rebuttal of many points made in the newspaper article. The letter stated that the floats were not shrines containing local gods but

114 Information about Rosa is compiled from accounts given to me by her daughter and grandson (3 May 1991) and from Morioka and Sasaki (1986:183–184).

'only decorated cars with historical figures and are not even attended by priests, nor anyone from the temple'. Henry's rebuttal of points made in the story suggest that his letter was indeed a conscientious attempt to put the 'Japanese point of view' (*Japan Chronicle* 1910b). Henry Black's knowledge of Japan made him a popular source of entertainment even among the foreign community. Evidence of this comes from another eyewitness, the American, OE Poole, who wrote an account of him at the request of the Australian businessman Harold S. Williams.

> I can only recall meeting...Ishii Black, the Story Teller, on but one occasion, when he came down from Tokyo to participate in a Smoking Concert in the Public Hall, later 'The Gaiety Theater' at the top of Camp Hill. As you know, he spoke Japanese so perfectly that he had become famous among the Japanese as a Story Teller and was much sought as an entertainer at big functions in the Best Japanese Restaurants. I believe he used Shakespeare's plays as the basis of many of his tales, and held his audiences spell-bound. In fact, it comes back to me now that I heard him once in that role, as I recall the unobtrusive way he magically appeared in the middle of the room, seated beside a small tobacco *hibachi*, with a fan in one hand, talking quietly, as it were, to himself, in the traditional way story-tellers melted into a scene. Suddenly the guests became aware of his presence, voices dropped, a hush fell, and guests slipped back into their places. Imperceptibly his voice became audible and with the utmost grace and composure he floated into his story, taking first one part and then another, with marvelous mimicry. It was complete artistry and at the end, the Japanese swarmed around him with congratulations. It was far beyond my modest knowledge of Japanese to follow his tale but his skill held one spell-bound.
>
> On the occasion of the Smoking Concert, he had chosen to tell us about Japanese Street-Cries. He came onto the stage with hardly more than a handful of props such as a *tenugui*, a blind masseur's flute and staff, a '*timbimbo*' &c. which were enough for him to impersonate his various characters to the life. He had a good voice and his street calls were perfect: the blind masseur's '*Ahhh mahhhh, kami-shimo, Go hyakku mon!*' the fish vendor's brisk '*Iwashiiii, Iwashi-ai!*' and the doleful minor-keyed wail of the pedlars of *rikisha* coolies' night meal '*Tofu, Tofuuuuu*' or '*Sobaaaaaa, soba!*'. Then there were the coolies loading bags of rice onto carts – '*Yassu kora sanyo, YASSU kora sanyo!*' and the chant

> of the pike drivers hammering long pine piles into sandy or swampy foundations…I loved to hear some of the plaintive wails at night. I don't recall what sort of end Ishii Black came to; he was a strangely obscure, almost mythical character, better known in Tokyo than in Yokohama. I don't know anything about his personal life, but have a vague idea that he had a Japanese wife and a flair for drink, but this is a completely unreliable impression of a rather obscure character.[115]

In his final years, Henry retained his affiliation with the San'yūha. Documentary evidence shows that his name stayed on its list of members until at least 1917 (Morioka & Sasaki 1983:150). Occasional newspaper reports attest to Henry giving performances in Osaka, Tokyo and Yokohama between 1911 and 1920.[116]

In 1912, at the age of 53, Henry produced a story that bore some parallels with his own life story. This was *Eikoku yodan* (Story from Britain), in which he told of a poor English soldier who had wanted to be a businessman but promised his mother he would go into the army. The story appeared in the September 1912 edition of *Kōdan Kurabu*. The poor soldier seems destined for a life of poverty when an unexpected encounter at a party at the home of his divisional commander changes his fortune. During the party, one of the guests loses a watch. When the soldier refuses to subject himself to a body search, other guests naturally assume that he is the one who stole the watch. The soldier asks his lieutenant-general if he can speak to him privately in another room. In the room, the soldier shows him his possessions. He has a cheap nickel watch and – most heart-rending of all – a meagre meal of bread and cheese wrapped in newspaper. Touched by the soldier's poverty, but more so by his honesty, the lieutenant-general decides to marry him to his daughter. The soldier's career then takes a different turn and his life improves.

Scholars Morioka Heinz and Sasaki Miyoko identify parallels with Henry's father who abandoned a career in the navy to try his hand, unsuccessfully, at business in Australia. In Henry's story, the soldier's father was the cause of the family's penury, as he had squandered the family fortune. Henry too was constantly in debt. Especially familiar are the lines which Henry gave the soldier's mother: 'Generations of your ancestors have served their country as soldiers. Your father in his grave wouldn't

115 Letter by OM Poole to Harold S Williams, 17 September 1965 (Harold S Williams Collection, National Library of Australia) MS6681/1/11.

116 For example, in *Ōsaka asahi shinbun*, 17 February 1917 (Shogei 1977:5).

countenance you alone being a businessman. Be a soldier no matter how hard it is' (Morioka & Sasaki 1986b:4–5). Was there something of Henry's mother here, admonishing him to at least do what his father might have expected of him and take up some respectable occupation?

While performing in the Kansai area, Henry was able to visit his brother John and his family. There must have been some degree of rapprochement with John, because years later one of John's daughters, who moved to Australia, described for me how Henry had once arrived at the family home in the foothills of Mount Rokko to find her in the front garden. Henry lifted her playfully in the air and carried her into the house. Her memory of her uncle Henry included him asking her father for a handout – he was perpetually short of money.

There is also evidence that Henry worked as a *benshi*,[117] a narrator of intertitles for silent motion pictures. Foreign-made motion pictures were shown in Japan from 1896 and Japanese-made ones from 1899. Seated in darkness to one side of the screen, the *benshi* supplied audiences not only with interpretation and elaboration, but also with dialogue for the characters. Black's great-grandson by adoption, Sudō Mitsuo, has explained that his grandfather, Seikichi, also worked as a *benshi*, having trained under one of the country's more famous *benshi*, Tokugawa Musei. Mr Sudō suggested that Henry Black might have introduced Seikichi to Tokugawa Musei, but this is only conjecture.[118]

Henry joined Seikichi and Rosa on stage in performances of conjuring and hypnotism. One of their performances involved a moving image of a flying dove projected onto a screen following the appearance of a real dove on stage. It was an innovative use of the new technology of the cinema.[119]

In 1916 and 1917, Henry visited China with Rosa and Seikichi to perform for Japanese communities in Shanghai and Hong Kong (Tensa Rōza 1920:1). At the time, China's fortunes were rapidly changing. China had been wracked by the Xinhai Revolution in 1911. The First World War was diverting European attention from Asian colonies and any further European partitioning of China. Japan had absorbed Korea into

---

117 *Benshi* were sometimes known as *katsuben*. Both words were an abbreviation of *katsudō shashin benshi* (narrator of moving pictures) (Katsura 1976:18).

118 Sudō Mitsuo (grandson of Rosa and Seikichi), interview with the author, Shizuoka, 3 May 1991.

119 In an interview on 3 May 1991 with Mrs Ishii Kiyoko, the daughter of Rosa and Seikichi and Black's granddaughter by adoption, I was told of a performance she had seen in which an image of a flying dove was projected onto a screen after a real dove had been on stage. Mrs Ishii thought Black had been involved in devising the performance.

its burgeoning empire and had seized the German holdings in Shantung on the pretext of aiding the Japanese–British alliance. A glance at the English-language and Japanese-language newspapers in Shanghai and Hong Kong at the time reveals a preponderance of stories about the distant conflict in Europe. Patriotic British residents in Hong Kong, for example, were busy raising money to send to Britain for the purchase of fighter planes.

In 1916, Russia was suffering badly in the war and approached the Japanese for military support. In return, the Japanese got a treaty giving Russian support for Japan's position in China. Turmoil in Russia culminated in the Bolsheviks seizing power in November 1917. The circumstances and mood in Japan were ripe for further expansion of Japanese power and control in East Asia. When Allied officers met in 1917 in London to discuss how to further their war effort, the Japanese were asked to supply 500,000 soldiers. Although they did not do so in the end, it is interesting to note that Japan felt justified in demanding in return that it be given the north of Sakhalin, as well as control of the Chinese Eastern Railway as far as Harbin and that the Russian port of Vladivostok be demilitarised. The ordered world that the oligarchs of the Meiji Japanese government had known was crumbling, as the new powers in Japan, particularly the military, engaged in a struggle with the more democratic forces for control of the nation's course. China was to become a key stage on which Japan's army was to play out its dreams of empire.

By 1916, the number of Japanese residents in Shanghai had grown to just over 7,000 – significantly more than the next largest group, the British. The Japanese were particularly active in developing the city's cotton industry. Their residences and businesses were spread widely across the foreign settlement in the city, but were most concentrated in the Hongkew district, which by the 1930s was known as 'Little Tokyo'. The precise length of Henry, Seikichi and Rosa's stay in Shanghai is not known, but Rosa gave birth to their first daughter, Kiyoko in Shanghai on 8 September 1917. As it is unlikely that Rosa would have wanted to travel much in the later months of her pregnancy and as it is known that they were in China from some time in 1916, they were probably in China for the best part of a year. Ishii Kiyoko knows that they travelled across Manchuria in northern China by train, so it is possible that they began their journey by sailing from Japan to a port such as Dairen before taking the train through Manchuria and working their way south via Shanghai and Hong Kong. Mrs Ishii claimed that she had been named by Chinese opera star, Mei Lanfang, who was in Shanghai at the time of her birth and had befriended her parents. She also claims that it was about this time that Henry acquired another pet dog.

By the summer of 1920, Henry Black was said to be living with Seikichi and Rosa 'in retirement, a little forgotten by the world in a comfortable home in Meguro Ward', Tokyo (Tensa Rōza 1920:1). Contradicting this is an article in the *Miyako shinbun* of 1 May 1920 which recorded that Henry Black gave *rakugo* performances in some 16 *yose* in Tokyo in May (Shogei 1977:5). At about this time, writer and artist Okamoto Ippei, writing on life in Tokyo, included a description of Henry attending a public bathhouse one morning near his home in Tokyo. Ippei described Henry as rotund, leading a Pekinese dog, and needing a walking stick. The Pekinese was probably the dog he had acquired in China. An illustration accompanying Ippei's description shows him in the company of a boy, possibly one of Seikichi's children. Ippei was impressed by Henry's presence as a larger-than-life Westerner unabashedly striding through the district dressed in a cool cotton *yukata*. He regarded Henry Black's demeanour as a statement of quiet self-confidence in the fact that he was a *geinin* (performer).

Ippei's description of Henry disrobing to reveal that he wore no underwear and then entering the bathroom while 'scratching the flea bites on his backside and patting his fat body with its flabby midriff resembling that of a celluloid kewpie doll' vividly evokes the foreign-born long-term resident now completely at home in his surrounds. With his eye for detail, Ippei also noted that Henry whistled the tune to a hymn as he entered the bathroom and that he lowered his rotund body into the bath 'with all the caution of a warship entering Tateyama Bay'. Once in the bath, Henry whistled a local tune evoking Fukagawa, a district nostalgically linked to a lifestyle known to residents of the *shitamachi* (low city) region of Edo. The low city is forever associated with the theatres, *sumo* wrestler stables and the old licensed red-light district. The area has supplied much inspiration for stories used by *rakugoka*. Henry then emerged to have his back scrubbed by an attendant. Although Ippei wrote that he enjoyed sharing a bath with Henry Black and hearing his whistling, his references to Henry as 'this disused old, foreign entertainer' (*kono sutareta ijin no rō geinin*) and to Henry's choice of a hymn and a tune identified with Fukagawa, reinforce the impression that, in the minds of many, he had become an irrelevance who merely inspired thoughts of an already bygone era (Okamoto 1929:12–17).

During Henry's later years, while he lived in Meguro Ward, his mother, Elizabeth, and his sister, Pauline, lived together in nearby Shirogane Sankōchō in a substantial house with an imposing gateway. Their house was about 15 minutes walk from where Henry lived, but the animosity between Pauline and Henry never faded. Pauline greatly disliked her brother and did not inform him of their mother's death on 7 October 1922 (Morioka & Sasaki 1983:151). An obituary in *The Japan Chronicle* four days later noted that Henry's mother had died aged 93, at her home 'where she had lived for many years with her daughter' (*Japan Chronicle* 1922). Henry is reported to have cried when he learned of her death. That Pauline had not notified him would have reinforced the sorrow of knowing that his close family members still regarded him as a black sheep. Henry was nine years older than John and 11 years older than Pauline.

When Mrs Ishii Kiyoko described the rift between Henry and his sister in later years, she recalled occasions when Pauline's visits to the Ishii household in Meguro would end in arguments between the two, with Pauline storming out of the house in a huff.[120] Mrs Ishii described Pauline as appearing to the children as a frightening older woman (*kowai obāsan*) whose eccentricities extended to throwing water at the family's dog and at her *bāya-san* (maid).

Mrs Ishii recalled that as a child, her mother occasionally asked her to take a plate of green peas upstairs to Henry to nibble with his beer. It was her impression that Henry's past successes as a popular *rakugoka* had made him at times intractable, a tendency often made worse by bouts of drunkenness when he could be stubborn and demanding, but nevertheless benign. Henry drank gin, *shōchū*, and other strong liquors, including Western ones. According to Mrs Ishii, the house was in one of Meguro's quieter, residential areas. It was a medium-sized house with rooms on the ground floor for Seikichi and Rosa and their two children, as well as the bath, toilet and kitchen. There was a *bāya-san* and a *kozō-san* (houseboy) who presumably lived there as was the custom in those days. By day, children played in the streets until about five o'clock in the afternoon when their mothers called them to bath and dinner. After nightfall, the streets were deserted and quiet, except for husbands trudging home from work late and the sound of barking dogs.

120 Much of the account of Henry Black's years in the Meguro household of Seikichi and Rosa in this and subsequent paragraphs is drawn from the author's interview with Mrs Ishii Kiyoko on 3 May 1991.

Sometimes, by the 1920s, a car would drive along the street and children and curious adults would emerge from their houses to stare and sniff the exhaust fumes. Occasionally Henry's friends would arrive in a car to drive him off to important engagements. Cars also brought guests, one of whom was a prince from the Kitashirakawa-no-miya branch of the imperial family. Henry taught English to the prince in a downstairs room in the house. On these occasions, the prince would drive up to the house in his car and wait while one of his entourage knocked on the door. The arrival of nobility in the street impressed the neighbours, but sometimes Henry was too drunk or hung-over and refused to come down to teach the prince. On those occasions, the prince and his driver would leave disappointed.

Seikichi and Rosa were often away from Tokyo on tour, leaving the children in the house with Henry. At other times, Rosa was lonely, as it seems Seikichi had a fondness for what many Japanese call *dōraku*. The word means entertainment, but can imply profligacy. On these occasions, Rosa took the children to see a film to compensate for the loss of her husband's company.

Henry displayed his stubborn streak on 1 September 1923 when the Great Kantō Earthquake struck. The day dawned hot and muggy. People went about their daily chores until it struck at 11:58 am. Downstairs in the house in Meguro, the dog cowered pathetically. Rosa was outside hanging out the washing when the maid screamed that the roof had fallen in. It hadn't, but Rosa looked up to see the house swaying. The initial, violent upheaval, which scientists later calculated as having a seismic intensity of six and a magnitude of 7.9 in the Kantō region, centred on Tokyo was followed by a series of horizontal tremors approximately every 1.5 seconds. During and immediately after the quake, Henry refused to budge from his room, despite the pleadings of the household *bāya-san* and other family members. To Rosa's pleas for him to leave the house, Henry's response was 'Bakayarō! (Fool!) Of course, it's an earthquake.'

Fortunately, the house escaped serious damage and within moments the two children, who had been playing in the street in front of the house, appeared. Henry stayed in his upstairs room throughout the quake and its aftermath, whereas Rosa and the rest of the household, fearful of aftershocks, camped out in the garden. It was a frightening time; mosquitoes bothered them and ashes from the burning city drifted in. The quake destroyed much of Tokyo and Yokohama, including many of the *yose* where Henry had performed. The lower parts of Tokyo burned, as did tens of thousands of people trapped in the flames, which started from cooking fires and chemical factories. In Ryogoku alone, 38,000 people died in a whirlwind of flames that swept down on them while they were sheltering at the former site of the Army Clothing Warehouse. Ghoulish rumours that Koreans were out to take advantage of the panic by poisoning wells circulated. Martial law was declared on 2 September in a bid by the central government to quell rumours and disturbances.

Soon after the earthquake, on 19 September 1923, Henry Black died in his home. The doctor who signed the death certificate gave the cause of death as 'senile decay'. Without consulting with the household, Pauline had the body taken away for a funeral and burial in the Foreigners' Cemetery in Yokohama in a grave shared with their parents. Henry's descendants by adoption have always assumed that she wanted to prevent attempts to arrange anything other than a Christian burial. An inscription at the foot of the shared grave does not acknowledge Henry's accomplishments as an entertainer: 'Also Henry James, their eldest son, died 1923, aged 66'. As far as Pauline was concerned, Henry had been an embarrassment to her and the less said about his career, the better. Pauline even got her brother's age at death wrong – he was 64 at the time of his death. She may not have had access to his birth certificate, or perhaps Henry had always lied about his age.

On 11 October 1923, an obituary in the *Japan Weekly Chronicle* gave the following account of Henry Black's life:

> There passed away in Tokyo the other day a character as unique as that of any of the migrants from the West who have thrown in their lot with Japan. This was Henry James Black, known as Ishii Black, the eldest son of John R. Black the author of Young Japan and the founder of the first newspaper published in Japan. Many foreigners in the past have not only made Japan their adopted country but have also absorbed Japanese ways of life. We can hardly think of one, however, who so far cast aside his native influence and entered so thoroughly into Japanese life as Ishii Black.

Chapter 18

No different from a Japanese

> Henry James Black (1858–1923)
>
> Australian-born rakugoka storyteller, eldest son of James R. Black. First performance in Yokohama, 1876. Member of Sanyu School. Stage name Kairakutei Black. Became naturalised Japanese in 1891. Performed rakugo and told popular Western stories throughout Japan. 1903/04 recorded rakugo and naniwabushi narrations, the first records ever made in Japan (Inscription on plaque beside Henry Black's grave at Yokohama Foreigners' Cemetery).

Henry Black was born British in Australia, died as a Japanese, but was buried as a foreigner. In burying him in Yokohama Foreigners' Cemetery, Pauline reclaimed what little she could of Henry and pointedly placed him in what will forever be a little patch of foreign soil in Yokohama overlooking the port into which he had sailed in 1865. Henry's Japanese descendants by adoption told me Pauline made her decision to bury him there without consulting their family. They feel that Pauline wanted to reclaim her brother as a foreigner and to give him a Christian burial. The circumstances surrounding his burial highlight lingering ambiguities about Henry's identity among family, audiences, and historians. The fact that his death went virtually unnoticed by the press at the time was also indicative of the disregard in which he was held by the 1920s. Events had so overtaken Henry that his contribution to the modernisation of the country was largely forgotten.

When Henry's immediate family considered Henry's lifestyle, the word 'uncivilised' sprang most readily to mind. Few, including Pauline, could comprehend his contribution to Japan. Pauline was of a generation that considered going native as akin to betraying all that was considered civilised. She had always considered it her God-given duty to bring civilisation and enlightenment to Japan, which certainly didn't entail going on the stage and making a fool of oneself. The possibility of bringing civilisation and enlightenment to audiences through adaptations of European detective and sensation fiction was not entertained by her generation. The re-evaluation of Henry Black's role has been left for later generations.

By the time of his death, the world of *rakugo* had also abandoned Henry to relative obscurity. By 1923 adaptations of European fiction from *rakugo* narrators had lost their appeal. Almost none of Henry's stories remained in the repertoire. What remains in the storytellers' canon are the classics, polished over the years perhaps, but persisting in much the same way as a Beethoven concerto is played again and again to appreciative audiences. Nothing remains of *Eikoku Rondon gekijō miyage*, *Shachū no dokubari* or *Minashigo*. Henry's only lasting impact on the repertoire is the occasional telling of *Eikoku no otoshibanashi*, but for the most part, Japanese audiences are not even aware of its origin.

It took two scholars of humour to resurrected Henry Black's memory more than half a century after he died. Sasaki Miyoko, then of Tokyo's Tsuda University, and German-born naturalised Japanese Morioka Heinz, of Sophia University, began their investigation into his life in the 1980s in the course of their research into Japanese oral storytelling and its links to humour around the world. Their search soon led them to the Black family grave in Yokohama, where at first they were confronted with knee-high weeds and a layer of dirt and gravel obscuring Henry's epitaph, which prompted them to speculate that Pauline had deliberately had it engraved into the lowest possible point on the gravestone.

Shortly after their discovery, these two dedicated linguists published a paper in *Monumenta Nipponica*, the journal of Sophia University, one of Japan's oldest Catholic institutions of higher learning. I bought the journal at a Tokyo bookstore, intending to read another paper by a former colleague, but, as I flipped through it going home on the Ginza subway line that day, I was immediately attracted to a large photograph of Henry on page 143. The photo (see figure 2), which showed Henry dressed for what was probably the female *kabuki* role of Omiwa in *Imoseyama*, featured in a paper entitled 'The blue-eyed storyteller'. The expression on Henry's face fascinated me. It seemed to be one of complete satisfaction with the situation in which he had placed himself. The knowledge that a foreign-born person had been celebrated on the Japanese stage intrigued me. Moreover, Henry had been born in Australia, as I had been. Our similarities also extended to our Scottish ancestry and a fondness for Japan.

The efforts of Morioka Heinz and Sasaki Miyoko later inspired interested parties, including active members of Henry's guild of storytellers, the San'yūha, to collect 90,000 *yen* for a commemorative metal plaque to be placed beside Henry Black's grave. It gives due recognition to his contribution to *rakugo* and proudly includes Henry's professional name, Kairakutei Burakku. Henry's grave is now a key attraction at the cemetery. Were she alive, Pauline might be appalled. But times change. Two of his nieces, the daughters of his younger brother John, were proud to know of his exploits when I contacted them in the 1990s. Both had been raised in Kobe and were living in Australia when I met them. They retained a lifelong fondness for things Japanese.

If you approach Yokohama Foreigners' Cemetery from the bottom entrance, as I did on my first visit to Henry's grave, you are likely to run into a spider's web or two. That first visit was on 23 September 1985, an important date on the calendar for an Australian journalist with a quirky story to write. It was to be the first publicly celebrated anniversary of his death. But I had not known, until I got there, that the cemetery entrance, which I found on the map as conveniently closest to the train station, was the little-used rear entrance at the bottom of a steep slope. In Japan, things always begin at their scheduled time, so my choice of gate made me late for the ceremony. I pushed on the rear gate. Beyond it were trees and glimpses of tall moss-covered Japanese gravestones mixed with the more familiar shaped ones I knew from church graveyards in Australian country towns. But the gate was closed. It crossed my mind that, had I been Japanese, I might have known that the main entrance would be at the top of the hill to afford the dead and their families the best view of the harbour or to allow them ceremonial entry to the graveyard opposite some of the then finest 19th-century Western-style wooden mansions in Yokohama.

Frantically, I pushed on the gate again. It yielded to pressure and I entered a quiet world of green shadows and the smell of moldering leaves. Behind me was the street with its souvenir stalls crammed with cheap trinkets, Hello Kitty key rings and postcards. Past the gate, I entered a world in which the present did not belong. The steepness of the slope rendered the distance to the top so much further than it really was. I was drenched in sweat. In the more than 30-degree heat, the humidity in Japan in late summer can be close to 90 percent. Impelled by the smell of incense, I ran full speed into the spider's web. Finally, at the top, I was relieved to find that I was not the only latecomer. I joined the queue and chose a long-stemmed yellow chrysanthemum from the pile to offer at the grave.

It was a distinguished gathering which included the Australian Ambassador, Sir Neil Currie, sharing a joke with the famous storyteller, San'yūtei Enraku, whom I recognised from television appearances. Enraku represented the San'yū guild to which Henry had belonged. There was the Australian Embassy's cultural attaché, Alison Broinowski, who had helped organise Australian representation at the ceremony. No-one came from the British Embassy, although organisers had contacted the embassy in recognition of Henry's British origins. Descendants of Seikichi and Rosa were also there. And, of course, there were the two academics without whose efforts the ceremony would not have been possible, Morioka Heinz of Sophia University and Sasaki Miyoko of Tsuda University. A centrepiece of the ceremony was the new bronze plaque recording the fact that Henry became a naturalised Japanese, that his first performance was in 1876, and that he was one of the voices on Japan's first disc-shaped recordings.

During the ceremony, I wondered how it was possible for some human beings to be born in one country, but feel so much more at home in another. Henry Black was an example of the human ability to survive. His was a case of self-discovery through birth in one country and fulfilment in another. His life was proof of the power to transform.

That 1985 graveside ceremony was a milestone in the rehabilitation of narratives of Henry Black as a contributor to Japanese culture. Histories of Meiji-era arts have largely ignored or marginalised people like Henry Black for a number of reasons. These include the privileging of *kabuki* and *noh* as representations of traditional Japanese performance arts and academic insistence on teaching canonic works in Japanese literary studies.

Conventional histories of the Meiji era privilege major figures such as key politicians and diplomats. Similarly, social historians documenting the role of foreigners in Meiji Japan have displayed a propensity for illuminating the activities of the *yatoi* class of foreigners. The study of *yatoi* is facilitated by the abundance and accessibility of Japanese, British, and United States government records on the subject.

Another reason for marginalising Henry Black is the acclaim rightly accorded his mentor San'yūtei Enchō in accounts of *rakugo* during the Meiji period. Enchō and Henry adapted stories from foreign sources. But Henry did not have the distinction, as Enchō does, of having created *Botan dōrō* (The peony lantern), the first adapted story published as a *sokkibon*, which had such a conspicuous impact on the movement to standardise the use of the vernacular in modern Japanese literature.

In the teaching of Japanese literature, *rakugo*, it is justifiably argued, was a mere catalyst in the evolution of the modern novel. As the timeline for Meiji-era adapted translations suggests, the Japanese appetite for hybridised settings and characters of the sort found in Henry Black's adaptations lasted for a relatively brief period between the mid-1880s and the late 1890s. This has resulted in a tendency among *rakugo* chroniclers to dismiss his opus as a fleeting aberration. Henry Black's narrations are also too easily dismissed as overly derivative adaptations from European sources and as somehow less important than the more 'purely Japanese' and canonic stories in the repertoire.

Although *rakugo* remained a popular art form for much of the Meiji period, it never received the support of the political elite, as did *kabuki*. At a time when theatre culture itself was declared an object of reform for political purposes, the active participation by Itō Hirobumi and other politicians in the singling out of *kabuki* for reinvention as a mark of a civilised country helped marginalise *rakugo*. This was perhaps not so surprising, as it was the one oral art that had displayed links with the opposition Freedom and People's Rights Movement. The reinvention and repositioning of *kabuki* by Meiji governments as an art form suitable for overseas consumption, together with its visual theatricality, contributed to its enduring appeal among foreigners as one of Japan's representative arts. The elevation of *noh*, a performance art long associated with aristocratic *samurai*, is also related to the prominence of former *samurai* among the ranks of the post-Meiji Restoration governing elite.

The obverse difficulty inherent in translating the mainly oral art of *rakugo* to foreign audiences, together with its history of lack of support from the political establishment, has mitigated against its appeal and study both inside and outside Japan. This problem has been addressed in the past decade through overseas tours by English-speaking *rakugoka* from Japan. These include Ōshima Kimie of Tokyo's Bunkyo Gakuin University, who has taken troupes to Australia, the United States and India. Members of the Rakugo Association (*Rakugo Kyōkai*) have also sponsored *yose* performances, using original Japanese-language narrations with foreign-language subtitles, in Australia, France and elsewhere. These ventures have had a degree of support from the Japan Foundation, suggesting that the Japanese government's cultural arm now appreciates the soft-power potential of Japanese humour and popular culture. Several Japanese publishing houses have also recently released English-language translations of *rakugo* tales.

At the height of his career during the 1880s and 1890s, Henry's status as a foreign-born narrator afforded him opportunities to mediate in that process understood as modernisation. Responses to his contribution to Japanese culture and to his place in history have varied over time, depending on the perspective of the observers. The enthusiastic acceptance of Henry Black by audiences at the height of his career during the 1880s and 1890s contrasts markedly with later, retrospective interpretations of him as an eccentric on the margins of the historical narrative. This suggests that perspectives altered markedly during his lifetime. These changes in perspective, brought on by changed definitions of modernity, led to the privileging of Meiji period protagonists in mainstream high-status arts and of high-profile *yatoi* and diplomats. The absence of Henry and of the popular arts from much historical narrative indicates a subsequent failure to acknowledge the complexities of Meiji cultural history. This absence is only now being righted as more historians begin to show an interest in the activities of ordinary individuals as protagonists in the historical narrative.

Re-evaluating Meiji-era histories

Social historian Irokawa Daikichi once posited the separate formation of thought and culture in modern Japan by two dichotomous entities – the intellectual elite and the ordinary people (Irokawa 1985:5). While such dichotomous entities may well have existed in the minds of citizens and historians, Henry Black's life shows that *rakugo* served to mediate between the two. Henry's stories, replete with hybrid visions of modernity, ensured that *rakugo* served as a crucible for shared discourse at a time when a new generation was forging a new understanding of modernity. Participation, in the person of Henry Black at the creative heart of one of the country's popular narrative arts and in *sokkibon* and newspaper novels facilitated that discourse. This is where the true value of Henry Black's contribution to Japan can be found.

Current debate about the nature of history acknowledges that the privileging of selected sources risks teleological distortions, which fail to take account of the complexity of contemporaneous human reactions to historical events. It also acknowledges the impossibility of creating an accurate account of events that belong to the past. Nevertheless, historians are duty-bound to contribute to the resurrection of the past in as accurate and as inclusive a manner as possible. This challenge has prompted a growing number of scholars to follow Irokawa's lead in acknowledging the place of formerly marginalised forms of Meiji popular culture. In this spirit, such studies must also take fuller account of the place of *rakugo* and *sokkibon*.

Social historians also characteristically credit the development of a common, public, mass culture to such agencies of socialisation as public education and the mass media (Smith 1991:10–11). A historical narrative that includes Henry Black shows that, prior to the development of mass circulation newspapers, the full impact of a new public education system, and legislated government controls over the mass media, *rakugoka* played a key role in propagating mass culture. In the years when Henry Black introduced his longest, most innovative narrations, *rakugo* served as a popular vehicle for the introduction of modernity. But by the early years of the 20th century, Henry's fall in popularity as a *rakugoka* relying on European story material for his inspiration paralleled the fall in popularity of *rakugo*. Kairakutei Black, the *rakugoka*, was overtaken as a moderniser by other mediums of entertainment and information, including Gaisberg's recordings, radio and cinema.

Other factors beyond Henry's control were also at play in his loss of prestige within the world of *rakugo*. Henry's initial popularity depended in part on the fact that he had been of British heritage. At one stage British citizens constituted the largest single group of foreigners living in Japan, comprising the officially invited *yatoi* and others who came seeking adventure or to offer their versions of civilisation and enlightenment. The graves of these people are now scattered over the slope of Yokohama Foreigners' Cemetery. Henry Black's British origins were a key reason why audiences looked to him as an authority on modernity. In interviews, Henry regularly stressed his British ancestry and played down or omitted references to his Australian birth. Newspapers also habitually referred to him as 'the Briton Black'.

But the fascination with all things British inevitably waned in the face of a flood of other European influences, so that by the onset of the 20th century, British culture was no longer the *sine qua non* of modernity. Not even the early interest in that iconic British playwright William Shakespeare survived the diminished interest in British culture. Ironically, whereas *kabuki* had at first accommodated Shakespeare via the strong influence of Tsubouchi's translations which drew inspiration from *kabuki* playwright Chikamatsu Monzaemon (1653–1724), it was ultimately because of this very influence that Shakespeare temporarily faded from the scene in Japan (Minamitani 1990:185). Performances of Shakespeare, including Henry's narrations of the bard, served as examples of modernity for only as long as the short-lived period of experimentation in *kabuki* in the 1880s and 1890s, after which they seemed *passé*. Perceptions of a *kabuki*-esque Shakespeare as modern did not survive the introduction in 1909 of the simpler elocution and use of the vernacular in Ibsen's *A Doll's House* (Minamitani 1990:184). In the end, not even Henry Black's British ancestry could stem the decline in interest in him and the development of newer definitions of modernity.

Henry Black's rise to popularity and subsequent decline into relative obscurity therefore reflect changes in Japanese definitions of modernity throughout his lifetime. His ascendancy lasted only as long as the conditions that sustained audience demand for his talents. His popularity waned once prevailing interpretations of the path to modernity no longer provided fertile ground for his talents to flourish on the *yose* stage. For these reasons, the contribution Henry made to the debate over modernity during the 1880s and 1890s had been largely forgotten by the time of his death. But the adaptations of European detective and sensation fiction that Henry Black brought to audiences in the almost two decades after his first stage appearance are valuable tools in the study of the transfer of ideas from the West into Japan.

From this perspective, we can see that the demand for popular literature created by the *sokkibon* stimulated the printing industry and led to the broadening of the market for books, thus facilitating the dissemination of ideas and serving as a major force in shaping Meiji culture (Sakai 1997:10). Social historians now accept that the study of popular culture, including popular literature, affords us insights into the manner in which messages are spread through a society. It stands to reason that the content and popularity of *sokkibon*, including those of Henry Black, which drew for inspiration from European novels, need to be included in literary chronologies of the introduction of ideas into Japan if a better understanding of the Meiji period is to be achieved.

Since the lists of translated foreign-language literature introduced to Japanese readers in the Meiji era usually focus on literal translations of canonic works, reliance on these lists as a basis for any chronology of the introduction of ideas can give rise to misunderstanding and misinterpretation. For a true understanding of the hermeneutics of ideas in this era, we need to include *sokkibon* and adaptive translations in the literary spectrum. Their inclusion is predicated on going beyond characterisations of Henry Black as an eccentric teller of detective fiction to an acceptance of the legitimacy of his role as a uniquely placed mediator and agent of modernity, particularly during the 1880s and 1890s. Henry Black's presence on the stage at this time substantiates findings that these years were indeed more complicated than conventional histories have suggested (Gluck 1978:27–50). Henry's career shows, for example, that the debate over reform during those years was not the sole preserve of government ideologues, foreign diplomats and officially recognised *yatoi*. His narrations show that the debate, begun in the 1870s by the adherents of the Freedom and People's Rights Movement, had a trickle-down effect, with elements of the pro-democracy message filtering through to people via *yose*, newspapers and lending libraries well into the 1890s.

The great Meiji-era experiment in reform was broad and extended into the arts. And as the experience of the *rakugoka* proves, the push for reform within the arts came as much from those involved in bringing democracy to Japan as from those who had the encouragement and approval of the political elite. As developments in *kabuki* showed during its own age of experimentation, reform in the arts was not a matter simply of taking over a Western tradition. It required an extended process of trial-and-error experimentation involving actors and audiences and it was in this process that Henry Black's narrations are invaluable. They represent part of the initial stage of incorporation of modes of thought into the popular culture. Henry Black and his mentor Enchō, as the two great adaptors of foreign novels, helped redefine the thematic boundaries of *rakugo* during this era. Henry, in particular, took *rakugo* beyond the repetition of Edo-related themes to incorporate elements of modernity as he perceived it. These achievements deserve celebration as an important stage in the literary and intellectual development of Japan.

Henry Black's most important adapted stories reflected a variety of contemporary responses to modernity. These include the intrusion of the evils of the 19th-century metropolis upon the old and decaying feudal order as seen in *Kusaba no tsuyu*, which can be interpreted as an initial positive reaction to modernity through the prism of a gothic novel. They also include the many examples of cultural, topographical and psychological hybridity in *Shachū no dokubari*, *Eikoku Rondon gekijō miyage* and *Iwade ginkō chishio no tegata*. And they include the more buoyant and optimistic message at the end of *Minashigo* that the evils of the new city could be overcome. The many warnings about the evils of modernisation and industrialisation in Henry Black's narrations also situate them as part of a growing reaction during the 1880s and 1890s against wholesale Westernisation. They reflect uncertainty over the choices the Japanese people had made on the road to modernity.

These stories also reflect ordinary people's contempt for the excesses of a new bureaucracy and its modernising agenda. They reveal an awareness of the changing roles of men and women under the impact of industrialisation and the increasing influence of government policy on the role of the family. They show an awareness of the impact of more efficient means of travel and communication upon human relationships and of the manner in which these new modes of travel and communication abetted the development of the centralised 19th-century nation-state. They display a fascination for the spirit of scientific investigation which supported the Industrial Revolution. They also show a sense of social justice, warning of the exploitation of women and children by capitalist enterprise and informing audiences of the need for a new and nondiscriminatory rule of law. They display an awareness of the urbanisation of the population as a reflection of the drift from the countryside into industrialised urban areas.

The stories reflect discourses about changes in social relations, which had been based on rigid, feudal, and hierarchical structures, as the newly liberated Meiji-era citizen adjusted to the notion that education and individual endeavour could bring personal success. Such new relations were governed by the burgeoning capitalist market economy in which the price of a person's labour was the basis for his or her wellbeing and status. This reflected a shift from a largely agrarian economy to one that offered the prospect of prosperity through industrial capitalism, with its opportunities for geographic and social mobility of the kind demonstrated by Onobu's move from Italy to Paris in *Shachū no dokubari* and Seikichi's flight to London in *Minashigo*.

The originator of these stories was a single human being who had faith in Japan. But cultural hybrids do not fit neatly into set categories. Having crossed over to Japan, Henry was neither wholly Japanese nor wholly British. As cultural anthropologist Richard Swiderski has suggested, people like Henry were considered by their 19th-century European peers as 'renegade' and morally depraved 'turncoats, abandoning the proper way of life for an escape into savagery' (Swiderski 1991:1). Depending on the position of the observer, the direction of such a crossing was 'invariably judged as having moral qualities: away from the center (civilisation, the good, the true) it is the movement of a renegade; toward the center (and away from the foreign, the barbarous, criminal and false) it is the movement of one becoming civilised' (Swiderski 1991:2). Henry's awareness of his family's dislike of him for his cultural crossing may even have been a contributing factor in his attempted suicide in 1908.

One of the more obvious trappings of Henry's lifestyle was his wearing of the loose fitting cotton *yukata*, which Okamoto Ippei and others praised as symbolic of conformity with the host culture. Such acts of identification rendered Henry more approachable to the Japanese with whom he identified (Swiderski 1991:54). There were other crossings into Japanese culture by Western expatriates during the Meiji years, of which the most prominent example is perhaps that of the Greek-Anglo-Irish vagabond journalist, author and Tokyo Imperial University teacher Lafcadio Hearn. There were a number similarities between the two. Both had settled in Japan and come to regard it as their spiritual home and both had attained Japanese citizenship by marrying a Japanese woman. And both were storytellers who interpreted one culture to another. Hearn is fondly remembered in Japan today because of the role he played in introducing an idealised version of Japan to the West through his writings. In Henry's case, his fondness for Japan found an outlet in catering via the stage to the Japanese hunger for information from the West. Like Hearn, Henry Black showed his strong identification with Japan through his lifestyle. In addition to his fondness for wearing a *yukata*, he enjoyed the Japanese style of bathing. His interest in Japan extended beyond the superficial to include links to the Freedom and People's Rights Movement, his apparent love of Motokichi, his adoption of Japanese citizenship and an interest in tea ceremony and Japanese painting. As Gaisberg's account of his visit to Japan suggests, Henry also took pleasure in educating foreign visitors about his adopted country.

Nevertheless, as the frequent use of the term 'the Briton Black' in newspaper reports indicates, many Japanese regarded Henry Black as a representative of Western civilisation in much the same way as the *yatoi* were. Henry contributed to this perception by playing up this aspect of his heritage in his narrations and in newspaper interviews. But among the generation who forged a new, hybrid culture in the 1880s and 1890s, his later status as a naturalised Japanese was as a 'true son of Edo' who had crossed toward a newly legitimised centre. Although this crossing over to Edo did not redeem Henry in the eyes of his own family members, who regarded him as 'uncivilised', others in the foreign community perceived him differently and wrote appreciatively of what he did. Frenchman Jules Adam and Scottish traveller Francis McCullagh, for example, wrote in honest praise and admiration of his attempts to master what they perceived as a difficult art. But these more positive representations by expatriate colleagues were few and did not entirely abandon the perception that he was an eccentric. In the Japanese newspapers that chronicled his career, comment about him reflects a transition from initial fascination with him as a foreigner on the *yose* stage, through praise and admiration for the feats he accomplished, to ultimate dismissal as irrelevant.

Any dismissal of Henry Black as a mere eccentric represents a failure to appreciate that during the 1880s and 1890s many Japanese aspired to the kind of hybridity Henry portrayed in his narrations. An appreciation of Henry Black's life and contribution to modernity in Japan demands a dispassionate assessment of the cultural crossing that he achieved and of the examples of cultural crossing he portrayed in his stories. Although the direction of the crossing Henry achieved differed from that of his *yose* audiences and the readers of his *sokkibon*, the hybrid outcome was not, in essence, different. Henry's lifestyle and the narrated landscapes he portrayed were timely prototypes for his audiences.

By the beginning of the 20th century, an increase in the number of alternative sources of information and entertainment had ultimately devalued Henry's role as a conduit for information about the West. The earliest intimation that Henry's problems would multiply came with the downturn in the economy during the Russo-Japanese War, which caused a fall in audience numbers. Matters were not helped by his own attempts to diversify into hypnotism and conjuring, which his *rakugoka* colleagues perceived as a departure from the narrator's art. By the time he died in 1923, Henry Black had been largely forgotten. The cinema and disc recordings, ironically two forms of entertainment to which he had contributed, had put paid to the popularity of his art as a form of live entertainment, sowing the seeds for his relegation to the kind of obscurity documented by Okamoto Ippei in his account of Henry's visit to the bathhouse.

If the example of Henry Black can put the case for allowing more space in histories of the Meiji era for eccentric, but dedicated, foreigners and artists, it will have succeeded in showing that the standard picture of events in those years must alter. At the very least, Henry Black's life exemplifies a very human side of the Meiji years in Japan.

In 1891, at the height of his career, Henry issued an appeal to audiences for tolerance and understanding. It is contained in his story *Eikoku Rondon gekijō miyage*. The language of the appeal reflects the historical realities of the Meiji era, but its spirit is timeless.

> Human love and affection do not vary from one country to another. Sail out of the harbour on a mail company steam ship to China, leaving with the smoke behind you, and when you see a Chinaman he will have some sort of pigtail at the back and baggy clothes. He will seem preposterous, with a ridiculous face. But if you look again, this is an ordinary human being with intelligence and love and affection. On the surface, he looks as if he is barbaric and uncultured. But when you look in his heart, you see that of course he is no different from a Japanese.

Henry went on to cite the example of 'the dark people of India, people as black as charcoal'.

> Of course the black colour is only on the surface and, if you cut the skin, you get red blood and, if you see into their hearts, they have human feelings and affection. And what's more, if you visit the white races of Europe, unlike the black people, some of them are so eerily light-skinned that you might imagine they look like ghosts under a willow in the light of the moon. But their human feelings and affection are the same as the Japanese. Even if the language, the clothing, the eye colour or the hair colour are different, everyone has the same sentiments when it comes to human feelings (Eikokujin 1891:41).

If there were more room on the plaque by Henry's grave, surely that last sentence is what he would have chosen to have in the inscription.

Bibliography

Works by Henry Black are listed under different names: Black, Henry; Eikokujin Burakku; Burakku, Henrī Zeemusu; Ishii Burakku; Kairakutei Burakku.

Adam, Jules 1899, *Japanese Story-Tellers,* T Hasegawa, Tokyo.

Adelaide Times, The 1854, 30 October.

Arahata Kanson 1965, *Kanson jiden*, vol. 1, Chikuma Shobō, Tokyo.

Asaoka Kunio 1986, 'Kairakutei Burakku to Miyatake Gaikotsu', *Kairakutei Burakku kenkyū* 1.

Asaoka Kunio 1987, 'Henrī J. Burakku no rainichi jiki', *Kairakutei Burakku kenkyū* 2.

Asaoka Kunio 1988, 'Burakku hen "danjo seibi" keshōhō ni tsuite', *Kairakutei Burakku kenkyū* 3.

Asaoka Kunio 1989, 'Nihon ni okeru J.R. Burakku no Katsudō', *Yokohama Archives of History*, 25 March.

Asaoka Kunio 1992, 'Kairakutei Burakku no "Kekkon/Kika" mondai kō', *Kairakutei Burakku kenkyū* 6.

Balkenhol, Heinz and Sasaki Miyoko 1979, 'Rakugo: Fascination for and Popularity of One of the Classical Japanese Arts of Narration', *Journal of Popular Culture* 13(1).

Barr, Pat 1988, *The Deer Cry Pavilion*, Penguin Books, London.

Beasley, WG 1989, 'Meiji Political Institutions' in Jansen, Marius B. ed., in *The Cambridge History of Japan,* Vol. 5, Cambridge University Press, Cambridge.

Beauchamp, Edward R, and Akira Iriye, eds, 1990, *Foreign Employees in Nineteenth-Century Japan*, Westview Press, Boulder, Co.

Bird, Isabella 1984, *Unbeaten Tracks in Japan,* Pat Barr, ed., Virago, London.

Black, Henry 1905, *Tabakozuki*, *Bungei Kurabu* 11(14).

Black, John Reddie 1883, *Young Japan*, Trubner, London, 2 vols. (Oxford University Press reprint, 1968).

Bond, Chris 1947, 'Freemasonry in Japan', *The Ashlar* 1(4).

Bowen, Roger W 1980, *Rebellion and Democracy in Meiji Japan*, University of California Press, Berkeley, CA.

Braddon, Mary Elizabeth 1877, 'Her Last Appearance' in *Weavers and Weft, and Other Tales*, vol. 3, John and Robert Maxwell, London.

Braddon, Mary Elizabeth 1884, *Flower and Weed, and Other Tales*, John and Robert Maxwell, London.

Brinkley, Francis 1904, *Japan: Its History, Arts and Literature*, TC & EC Jack, London.

Brooke, JH 1880, 'Obituary' [of JR Black], *Japan Herald*, 11 June. (Extract in Harold S Williams Collection, National Library of Australia, MS6681/1/1).

Buradon 1886, *Kusaba no tsuyu* [Dew by the Graveside], Nisshūsha, Tokyo.

Burakku, Henrī Zeemusu, ed. 1886, *Yōi dokushū eiwa kaiwa hen = Easy Conversations in English Written Especially for Japanese Wishing to Learn English*, Chūgaidō, Tokyo (Second edition published 1887).

Burakku and Takamatsu Motokichi 1891, *Keshōhō: danjo seibi* [Beauty and Makeup Methods for Men and Women], Tokyo.

Burks, Ardath W, ed. 1985, *The Modernizers: Overseas Students, Foreign Employees, and Meiji Japan*, Westview Press, Boulder, Co.

Campbell, John Francis 1876, *My Circular Notes: Extracts from Journals, Letters Sent Home, Geological and Other Notes, Written while Traveling Westwards round the World, from July 6, 1874, to July 6, 1875*, 2 vols, Macmillan and Co., London.

Chamberlain, Basil Hall 1984, *Japanese Things*, Charles E Tuttle, Rutland VT and Tokyo. (Reprint of *Things Japanese,* 5th revised edition, John Murray, London, 1905).

Chōya shinbun 1886, January 26 and 29.

Coaldrake, A Kimi 1997, 'Women in *gidayū* during Meiji', in Hardacre, Helen, with Adam L Kern, eds, *New Directions in the Study of Meiji Japan*, Brill, Leiden.

Crow, Arthur H 1883, *Highways and Byeways in Japan: The Experiences of Two Pedestrian Tourists*, Sampson Low, Marston, Searle, and Rivington, London.

Dai jinmei jiten 1953–56, Heibonsha, Tokyo.

Dore, Ronald Philip 1965, *Education in Tokugawa Japan*, Routledge & Kegan Paul, London.

Duus, Peter 1976, *The Rise of Modern Japan*, Houghton Mifflin, Boston, Mass.

Eikokujin Burakku 1891, *Eikoku Rondon gekijō miyage* [Story from a London Theatre], Nomura Ginzaburō, Tokyo.

Endō Masako 1985, *Nazo no ikokusen*, Sanshūsha, Tokyo.

Faulds, Henry 1880, 'On the Skin-Furrows of the Hand', *Nature* 22 (574).

Freeman, Laurie Anne 2000, *Closing the Shop: Information Cartels and Japan's Mass Media*, Princeton University Press, Princeton, NJ.

Frei, Henry P 1991, *Japan's Southward Advance and Australia*, Melbourne University Press, Melbourne.

Fujitani, Takashi 1996, *Splendid Monarchy: Power and Pageantry in Modern Japan*, University of California Press, Berkeley, CA.

Gaisberg, Frederick W 1946, *Music on Record*, Robert Hale, London.

Garon, Sheldon M 1987, *The State and Labor in Modern Japan*, University of California Press, Berkeley, CA.

Garon, Sheldon M 1997, 'The World's Oldest Debate? Regulating Prostitution and Illicit Sexuality', in *Molding Japanese Minds*, Princeton University Press, Princeton, NJ.

Gluck, Carol 1978, 'The People in History: Recent Trends in Japanese Historiography', *Journal of Asian Studies* 38(1).

Gluck, Carol 1985, *Japan's Modern Myths*, Princeton University Press, Princeton, NJ.

Gluck, Carol 1998, 'The Invention of Edo', in Vlastos, Stephen, ed., *Mirror of Modernity*, University of California Press, Berkeley and Los Angeles, CA.

Haley, JO 1991, *Authority without Power: Law and the Japanese Paradox*, Oxford University Press, Oxford.

Halford, S Aubrey & Giovanna M 1990, *The Kabuki Handbook*, Tut Books, Tokyo.

Hall, John W 1983, 'The Problem: When Did Modern Japanese History Begin?, in Wray, Harry, and Hilary Conroy, eds, *Japan Examined: Perspectives on Modern Japanese History*, University of Hawaii Press, Honolulu.

Hanazono Kanesada 1926, 'J.R. Black' in *Journalism in Japan and its Early Pioneers*, Ōsaka shuppansha, Ōsaka.

Hane, Mikiso 1983, 'The Movement for Liberty and Popular Rights', in Wray, Hillary, and H Conroy, eds, *Japan Examined: Perspectives on Modern Japanese History*, University of Hawaii Press, Honolulu.

Hayashiya Reiji, Ishii Shiro and Aoyama Yoshimitsu 1998, *Zusetsu: hanketsu genbon no isan* [literally, Illustrated Book: Legacy of the Original Book of Rulings] (What the Civil Judgement Files Tell Us: Selected Cases from the Meiji Restoration to World War II), Shinzansha, Tokyo.

Hibbert, Christopher 1988, *The English: A Social History, 1066–1945*, Paladin Grafton Books, London.

Hisamatsu Sen'ichi 1976, *Biographical Dictionary of Japanese Literature*, Kodansha International, Tokyo.

Hoare, JE 1994, *Japan's Treaty Ports and Foreign Settlements: The Uninvited Guests, 1858–1899*, Japan Library, Folkestone.

Holroyd, Michael 1988, *Bernard Shaw: A Biography*, vol. 1, Random House, New York, NY.

Houghton, Walter E 1957, *The Victorian Frame of Mind, 1830–1870*, Yale University Press for Wellesley College, New Haven NJ.

Huffman, James L 1997, *Creating a Public: People and Press in Meiji Japan*, University of Hawaii Press, Honolulu.

Irokawa Daikichi 1976, 'Freedom and the Concept of People's Rights', *Japan Quarterly* 14(2).

Irokawa Daikichi 1985, *The Culture of the Meiji Period*, Marius B Jansen, trans. Princeton University Press, Princeton, NJ.

Ishii Burakku 1896, *Eikoku jitsuwa: Minashigo* [A True Tale from England: The Orphan]. Kin'ōdō, Tokyo.

Ishizuki Minoru 1985, 'Overseas Study by Japanese in the Early Meiji Period', in Burks, Ardath W, ed., *The Modernizers: Overseas Students, Foreign Employees, and Meiji Japan*, Westview Press, Boulder, Co.

Itō Hideo 2002, *Meiji no tantei shōsetsu*, Futaba bunkō, Tokyo.

Jansen, Marius B 1989, 'Introduction', in Jansen, Marius B, ed., *The Cambridge History of Japan,* vol. 5, Cambridge University Press, Cambridge and New York, NY.

Jansen, Marius B 1995, 'The Meiji Restoration', in Jansen, Marius B, ed., *The Emergence of Meiji Japan*, Cambridge University Press, Cambridge.

Japan: An Illustrated Encyclopedia 1993, Kodansha, Tokyo.

Japan Chronicle 1908, 28 August (Extract in Harold S Williams Collection, National Library of Australia MS6681/1/1) .

Japan Chronicle 1910a, 20 July (Extract in Harold S Williams Collection, National Library of Australia MS6681/1/1).

Japan Chronicle 1910b, 24 July (Extract in Harold S Williams Collection, National Library of Australia MS6681/1/1).

Japan Chronicle 1922, 11 October (Extract in Harold S Williams Collection, National Library of Australia MS6681/1/1).

Japan Weekly Chronicle 1923, 11 October (Extract in Harold S Williams Collection, National Library of Australia MS6681/1/1).

Japan Weekly Mail 1880, 10 April.

Japan Weekly Mail 1885, 30 May.

Japan Weekly Mail 1892, 3 September (Extract in Harold S Williams Collection, National Library of Australia MS6681/1/1).

Jones, Hazel J 1980, *Live Machines: Hired Foreigners and Meiji Japan*, University of British Columbia Press, Vancouver.

Jones, Hazel J 1985, 'The Griffis Thesis and Meiji Policy toward Hired Foreigners', in Burks, Ardath W, ed., *The Modernizers: Overseas Students, Foreign Employees, and Meiji Japan*, Westview Press, Boulder, Co.

Jordan, Brenda 1997, 'Flowers in the Dawn: Kawanabe Kyōsai and the search for modernity', in Hardacre, Helen, with Adam L Kern, eds, *New Directions in the Study of Meiji Japan*, Brill, Leiden.

Kairakutei Burakku 1891a, *Eikoku no otoshibanashi* [The beer-drinking contest], *Hyakkaen* 45(1).

Kairakutei Burakku 1891b, *Shachū no dokubari* [The Poisoned Pin in the Coach], Suzuki Kinho, Tokyo.

Kairakutei Burakku 1893, *Iwade ginkō chishio no tegata* [The Bloodstained Handprint at the Iwade Bank], Azuma nishiki, Tokyo.

Kairakutei Burakku 1895, *Tsurugi no hawatari* [The Sword's Blade]. Bunkindō, Tokyo.

Kairakutei Burakku 1900, *Kanda Taketarō*, Imamura Jirō, ed., Uedaya, Tokyo.

Kairakutei Burakku 1904, 'Bīru no kakenomi', *Bungei kurabu* 10(15).

Kairakutei Burakku 1905, *Tabakozuki*, *Bungei kurabu* 11(14).

Kamei Hideo 2002, *Transformations of Sensibility: The Phenomenology of Meiji Literature*, translated, edited and with an introduction by Michael Bourdaghs, Center for Japanese Studies, University of Michigan, Ann Arbor, MI.

Karatani Kōjin, 1993, *Origins of Modern Japanese Literature*, Brett de Bary, trans., ed., Duke University Press, Durham, NC.

Katsura Beichō 1976, *Rakugo to watashi*, Popurasha, Tokyo.

Kawamura Megumi 1989, *Koten rakugo*, Cross Roads, Tokyo.

Keene, Donald 2002, *Emperor of Japan: Meiji and His World, 1852–1912*, Columbia University Press, New York, NY.

Kido Takayoshi 1986, *The Diary of Kido Takayoshi*, vol. 1: 1868–1871, Sidney Devere Brown and Akiko Hirota, trans., University of Tokyo Press, Tokyo.

Kinji hyōron, translation in *Japan Daily Herald*, 28 April 1880 (Extract in Harold S Williams Collection, National Library of Australia MS6681/1/1).

Kobe Weekly Chronicle, The 1901, 24 December (Extract in Harold S Williams Collection, National Library of Australia MS6681/1/1).

'Kōdan yose no kairyō wo nozomu' 1897, *Kōdan zasshi*, 5 March.

Kojima Teijin 1988, '"Kairakutei" no yurai?', *Kairakutei Burakku kenkyū* 3.

Komiya Toyotaka, ed., 1969, *Japanese Culture in the Meiji Era*, Donald Keene, trans, adapt., The Toyo Bunko, Tokyo. (Reprint of an 1856 edition.)

Kornicki, Peter 1982, *The Reform of Fiction in Meiji Japan*, Ithaca Press, London.

Kurata Yoshihiro 1980, *Meiji Taishō minshū goraku,* Iwanami shoten, Tokyo.

Kurata Yoshihiro, ed., 1981–87, *Meiji no engei*, vols 1–7, Kokuritsu gekijō chōsa ikuseibu geinō chōsa shitsu, Tokyo.

Kurita, Kyoko 1997, 'The Romantic Triangle', in Hardacre, Helen, with Adam L Kern, eds, *New Directions in the Study of Meiji Japan*, Brill, Leiden.

Lehan, Richard 1998, *The City in Literature: An Intellectual and Cultural History*, University of California Press, Berkeley and Los Angeles, CA.

Lehmann, Jean-Pierre 1982, *The Roots of Modern Japan*, Macmillan Press, London.

Leiter, Samuel L 1979, *New Kabuki Encyclopedia*, Greenwood Press, Westport, CT.

Li Takanori 1996, *Hyōshō kūkan no gendai*, Shin'yōsha, Tokyo.

Macfarlane, Alan 1998, 'The Mystery of Property in England and Japan', in Hann, CM, ed., *Property Relations: Renewing the Anthropological Tradition*, Cambridge University Press, Cambridge.

Mainichi shinbun 1880, Translation in *Japan Daily Herald*, 12 April. (Extract in Harold S Williams Collection, National Library of Australia.)

Matsuō Shōichi 1990, *Jiyū minken shisō kenkyū*, Nihon keizai hyōronsha, Tokyo.

McArthur, Ian, 1992, *Kairakutei Burakku: wasurerareta Nippon saikō no gaijin tarento*, Kodansha International, Tokyo.

McArthur, Ian, 2007, 'Why Sonoe Rebuffed Baron Tokiwa: How a Mary Braddon Penny Dreadful Reached the Kabuki Stage', *International Journal of Diversity in Organisations, Communities and Nations* 7(2).

McArthur, Ian 2008, 'Narrating the Law: *Rakugo* in the Meiji Law Reform Debate', *Electronic Journal of Contemporary Japanese Studies*, 15 August, http://www.japanesestudies.org.uk/articles/2008/McArthur.html

McArthur, Ian and Mio Bryce 2007, 'Names and Perspectives in *Sute obune*, a Meiji-Era Adaptive Translation of the Mary Braddon Mystery Novel, *Diavola*', *International Journal of the Humanities* 5.

McCullagh, Francis 1902, 'The Story-Teller in Japan', *The East of Asia Magazine* 1.

McLaren, WW, ed., 1979, *Japanese Government Documents* vol. II, Asiatic Society of Japan, Tokyo.

Meaney, Neville 1999, *Towards a New Vision*, Kangaroo Press, Sydney.

Meiji bungaku zenshū 1965–1967, vols. 10, 13 and 36, Chikuma shobō, Tokyo.

Meiji ishin jinmei jiten 1981, Nihon Rekishi Gakkai, Tokyo.

'*Meiji: kindai biyō no akebono*' 1986, in *Modan: keshō shi, yosooi no 80 nen*, Pōra Bunka kenkyūjo, Tokyo.

Meiroku zasshi: Journal of the Japanese Enlightenment 1976. Translated with introduction by William Reynolds Braisted, Harvard University Press, Cambridge, Mass.

'Merchants, Professions, Trades etc.' 1866, in *Chronicle and Directory for China, Japan, and The Philippines*, The Daily Press, Shanghai.

Mertz, John Pierre 2003, *Novel Japan: Spaces of Nationhood in Early Meiji Narrative, 1870–88*, Center for Japanese Studies, The University of Michigan, Ann Arbor, MI.

Miller, J Scott 1994, 'Japanese Shorthand and *Sokkibon*', *Monumenta Nipponica*, vol. 49(4).

Miller, J Scott 1997, 'Tale as Text: *Sokkibon* in the Diet Library Collection', in Hardacre, Helen, with Adam L Kern, eds, *New Directions in the Study of Meiji Japan*, Brill, Leiden.

Miller, J Scott 2001, *Adaptations of Western Literature in Meiji Japan*, Palgrave, New York, NY.

Mills, Douglas E 1970, *A Collection of Tales from Uji: A Study and Translation of Uji shūi monogatari*, Cambridge University Press, Cambridge.

Minamitani, Akimasa 1990, 'Hamlet in Japan', *Japan Quarterly* 37(2).

Mitchell, Richard 1983, *Censorship in Imperial Japan*, Princeton University Press, Princeton, NJ.

Miyoshi Masao 1974, *Accomplices of Silence: The Modern Japanese Novel*, University of California Press, Berkeley, CA.

Moore, Jerrold Northrop 1977, *A Matter of Records*, Taplinger Publishing, New York, NY.

Moretti, Franco 1998, *Atlas of the European Novel 1800–1900*, Verso, London, New York, NY.

Morioka Heinz and Sasaki Miyoko 1981, '*Rakugo*: Popular Art of the Grotesque', *Harvard Journal of Asiatic Studies* 41(2).

Morioka Heinz and Sasaki Miyoko 1983, 'The Blue-Eyed Storyteller: Henry Black and his *Rakugo* Career', *Monumenta Nipponica* 38(2).

Morioka Heinz and Sasaki Miyoko 1986a, *Kairakutei Burakku no Nippon*, PHP, Tokyo.

Morioka Heinz and Sasaki Miyoko 1986b, 'Tokei no baikai', *Kairakutei Burakku kenkyū* 2, 19 September.

Morioka Heinz and Sasaki Miyoko 1987, 'Burakku to naniwabushi', *Kairakutei Burakku kenkyū* 2, 19 September.

Morioka Heinz and Sasaki Miyoko 1990, *Rakugo, the Popular Narrative Art of Japan*, Council on East Asian Studies, Harvard University, Cambridge, Mass.

Morris-Suzuki, Tessa 1994, *The Technological Transformation of Japan*, Cambridge University Press, Cambridge.

Nakagomi Shigeaki 1998, 'Rakugo "furoshiki" saikō', *Bulletin of Graduate Studies* 40, Hōsei University, Tokyo,

Nakajima Kawatarō 1964, *Nihon suiri shōsetsu shi* 1, Tōgensha, Tokyo.

Nakamura, Kyoko Motomochi, trans., 1973, *Miraculous Stories from the Japanese Buddhist Tradition: The Nihon Ryōiki of the Monk Kyōkai*, Harvard University Press, Cambridge, Mass.

Neilan, Edward 1993, 'Yokohama: Cradle of Journalism' *No. 1 Shinbun*, 15 September.

Niimura Izuru, ed., 1992, *Kōjien*, Iwanami shoten, Tokyo.

Nishiyama Matsunosuke 1997, *Edo Culture: Daily Life and Diversions in Urban Japan, 1600–1868*, University of Hawaii Press, Honolulu.

Nishūbashi Sei 1905, 'Kairakutei Burakku', *Bungei kurabu* 11(14).

Nobuhiro, Shinji 1986, *Rakugo wa ikani shite keisei saretaka*, Heibonsha, Tokyo.

Noda Yoshiyuki 1976, *Introduction to Japanese Law*, Anthony H Angelo, trans., ed., University of Tokyo Press, Tokyo.

Nolte, Sharon H and Sally Ann Hastings 1991, 'The Meiji State's Policy towards Women', in Bernstein, Gail Lee, ed., *Recreating Japanese Women 1600–1945*, University of California, Berkeley, CA.

Novograd, Paul 1974, '*Rakugo*: The Storyteller's Art', *Japan Quarterly* 21(2).

Nyorai An 1896, 'Shunpū Kanwa: Kairakutei Burakku' [Idle chat on the spring wind: Kairakutei Black], *Yomiuri shinbun*, 30 April – 4 May.

Ōdawara, A 1930, 'Burakku', in Kubota, T, *Nijūichi senkaku kisha den*, Mainichi shinbunsha, Osaka.

Ogasawara Mikio 1992, 'Shinbun shōsetsu no gekika ni tsuite', *Yokohama Archives of History Review* 10, March.

Ogi Shinzō et al, eds, 1987, *Edo Tōkyō gaku jiten*, Sanseidō, Tokyo.

Oikawa Shigeru et al (text); Martha J. McClintock et al, trans. 1996, Kyōsai no giga, kyōga [Kawanabe Kyōsai's comic paintings and prints], *Comic Genius: Kawanabe Kyōsai*, The Tokyo shinbun, Tokyo.

Oizuru Yoshiya 1986, 'Chōya shinbun: kōkoku ran ni miru Burakku', *Kairakutei kenkyū* 1.

Okamoto Ippei 1929, 'Hebo kyūri', in *Ippei zenshū*, vol. 3, Senshinsha, Tokyo.

Okitsu Kaname 1979, 'Natsume Sōseki to rakugo', in *Rakugo: Edo kara kindai e*, Ōfūsha, Tokyo.

Okitsu Kaname 1997, *Meiji shinbun koto hajime*, Taishūkan shoten, Tokyo.

Ōta Hiroshi 1998, *Rakugo to kabuki: ikina naka,* Heibonsha, Tokyo.

Ousby, Ian 1976, *Bloodhounds of Heaven*, Harvard University Press, Cambridge, Mass.

Pflugfelder, Gregory M 1999, *Cartographies of Desire: Male–Male Sexuality in Japanese Discourse, 1600–1950*, University of California Press, Berkeley, CA.

Pykett, Lyn 1994, *The Sensation Novel: From* The Woman in White *to* The Moonstone, Northcote House, Plymouth.

Pyle, Kenneth B 1969, *The New Generation in Meiji Japan: Problems of Cultural Identity, 1885–1895*, Stanford University Press, Stanford, CA.

Ricoeur, Paul 1973, 'The Model of the Text: Meaningful Action Considered as a Text', *New Literary History* 5(1).

Rozman, Gilbert 1974, 'Edo's Importance in the Changing Tokugawa Society', *Journal of Japanese Studies* 1(1).

Rubinger, Richard 1986, 'Education: From One Room to One System', in Jansen, Marius B and Gilbert Rozman, eds, *Japan in Transition: From Tokugawa to Meiji*, Princeton University Press, Princeton, NJ.

Sakai, Anne 1992, *La Parole comme Art: Le Rakugo Japonais*, L'Harmattan, Paris.

Sakai, Cécile 1997, *Nihon no taishūbungaku*, Heibonsha, Tokyo.

Sanches, Mary 1975, 'Falling Words: An Analysis of a Japanese *Rakugo* Performance', in Sanches, Mary, and Ben G Blount, eds, *Sociocultural Dimensions of Language Use*, Academic Press, New York, NY.

Satō, Kō 1989, 'Meiji shoki shinbun seisaku shi no ikkō sai: sain to J.R. Burakku to no kankei wo chūshin ni', *Yokohama Archives of History Review* 7.

Seaman, Amanda C 2004, *Bodies of Evidence: Women, Society, and Detective Fiction in 1990s Japan*, University of Hawaii Press, Honolulu.

Seidensticker, Edward 1983, *Low City, High City*, Alfred Knopf, New York, NY.

Shimizu Yasuyuki 1987, 'Rekōdo ni kiku Kairakutei Burakku', *Kairakutei Burakku kenkyū* 2, 19 September.

Shively, Donald H 1971, 'The Japanization of the Middle Meiji', in Shively, Donald H, ed., *Tradition and Modernization in Japanese Culture*, Princeton University Press, Princeton, NJ.

Shogei Konwakai, ed., 1977, *Kairakutei Burakku kankei bunken mokuroku*, Shogei Konwakai, Yokohama

Shokkō jijō 1998, revised by Inumaru Giichi, vol. 1, Iwanami bunko, Tokyo.

Sievers, Sharon L (1983), *Flowers in Salt: the Beginnings of Feminist Consciousness in Modern Japan*, Stanford University Press, Stanford, CA.

Silver, Mark 2003, 'Putting the Court on Trial: Cultural Borrowing and the Translated Crime Novel in Nineteenth-Century Japan', *Journal of Popular Culture* 36(4).

Sissons, DCS 1978, *Australian-Japanese Relations: The First Phase, 1859–91*, 3rd ed. Canberra (mimeograph supplied by the author).

Smith, Anthony 1991, *National Identity*, Penguin, New York, NY.

Smith, Henry D 1978, 'Tokyo as an Idea: An Exploration of Japanese Urban Thought until 1945', *Journal of Japanese Studies* 1(1).

Steenstrup, Carl 1996, *A History of Law in Japan until 1868*, E.J. Brill, Leiden.

Storey, John 1996, *Cultural Studies and the Study of Popular Culture: Theories and Methods*, Edinburgh University Press, Edinburgh.

Suzuki, Keiko 1997, 'Yokohama-e and Kaika-e Prints: Japanese Interpretations of Self and Other from 1860 through the 1880s', in Hardacre, Helen, with Adam L Kern, eds, *New Directions in the Study of Meiji Japan*, Brill, Leiden.

Swiderski, Richard 1991, *Lives between Cultures: A Study of Human Nature, Identity and Culture*, Denali Press, Juneau, AK.

Takahashi Yasuo 1989, *Monogatari Yorozu chōhō*, Nihon keizai shinbunsha, Tokyo.

Tamura Nariyoshi 1922, *Zokuzoku kabuki nendai ki*, Tokyo ichimuraza, Tokyo.

'Tensa Rōza Koi Monogatari' 1920, *Miyako shinbun*, 30 July.

Teruoka Yasutaka 1978, *Rakugo no nenrin*, Kōdansha, Tokyo.

Thomas, RR 1999, *Detective Fiction and the Rise of Forensic Science*, Cambridge University Press, Cambridge.

Tomasi, Massimiliano 1999, 'Quest for a New Written Language: Western Rhetoric and the *Genbun itchi* Movement', *Monumenta Nipponica* 54(3).

Tomio Kentaro 1997, 'Expositions and Museums in Meiji Japan', in Hardacre, Helen, with Adam L Kern, eds, *New Directions in the Study of Meiji Japan*, Brill, Leiden.

Tsuda Mamichi 1874, 'In Opposition to Protective Tariffs', *Meiroku zasshi* 5.

Tsuda Mamichi 1875 'On Destroying Prostitution', *Meiroku zasshi* 42.

Tsurumi, E Patricia 1990, *Factory Girls*, Princeton University Press, Princeton, NJ.

Twine, Nanette 1991, *Language and the Modern State: The Reform of Written Japanese*, Routledge, London.

Uchida Yūzō 1987, 'Suramu', in Ogi Shinzō et al, eds, *Edo Tōkyō gaku jiten*, Sanseidō, Tokyo.

Umemori Naoyuki 1997, 'Spatial Configuration and Subject Formation: The Establishment of the Modern Penitentiary System in Meiji Japan', in Hardacre, Helen, with Adam L Kern, eds, *New Directions in the Study of Meiji Japan*, Brill, Leiden.

Vlastos, Stephen 1995, 'Opposition Movements in Early Meiji, 1868–1885', in Jansen, Marius B, ed., *The Emergence of Meiji Japan*, Cambridge University Press, Cambridge.

Waley, Paul 1984, *Tokyo Now and Then: An Explorer's Guide*, Weatherhill, New York and Tokyo.

Waswo, A 1996, *Modern Japanese Society, 1868–1994*, Oxford University Press, Oxford.

Wells, Marguerite 1997, *Japanese Humour*, Macmillan Press, Basingstoke.

Whitney, Clara 1979, *Clara's Diary: An American Girl in Meiji Japan*, M William Steele and Tamiko Ichimata, eds, Kodansha International, Tokyo.

Williams, Harold S 1958, *Tales of the Foreign Settlements in Japan*, Charles E Tuttle, Tokyo and Rutland, Vt.

Williams, Harold S 1963, *Foreigners in Mikadoland*, Charles E Tuttle, Rutland, VT and Tokyo.

Wolff, Robert Lee 1979, *Sensational Victorian: The Life and Fiction of Mary Elizabeth Braddon*, Garland, New York and London.

Yamamoto Shōgetsu 1936, 'Hana peko no yaegaki hime', *Meiji sesō hyakuwa*, Dai-ichi shobō, Tokyo.

Yanagida Izumi 1935, *Meiji shoki no hon'yaku bungaku*, Shōhakukan, Tokyo.

Yanagida Izumi 1966, *Meiji bungaku kenkyū Dai 5 maku – Meiji shoki hon'yaku bungaku no kenkyū*, 2nd ed, Shunjūsha, Tokyo.

Yano Seiichi 1999, *San'yūtei Enchō no meiji*, Bungei shunju, Tokyo.
Yazaki Takeo 1968, *Social Change and the City in Japan: From Earliest Times through the Industrial Revolution*, Japan Publications, Tokyo.
Yokohama shi shikō: fūzoku hen (Dai 5 sō, dai 2 setsu, yose 2) 1973, Yokohama Shiyakusho, Meicho shuppan, Tokyo.
Yokoyama Toshio 1987, *Japan in the Victorian Mind*, Macmillan, Basingstoke and London.
Yomiuri shinbun 1896, 'Shunpū Kanwa', 30 April.
Yoshizawa Hideaki, ed., 1976, *Kōdan kankei bunken mokuroku: Meiji-Taishōhen*, Yoshizawa Hideaki, Tokyo.
Yoshizawa Hideaki 1981, *Taishū geinō shiryō shūsei 5*, Sanjū-ichi shobō, Tokyo.
Young, Michael, and Constance Hamilton 2001, 'Historical Introduction to the Japanese Legal System', in Milhaupt, Curtis, J, et al, eds, *Japanese Law in Context: Readings in Society, the Economy, and Politics*, Harvard University Asia Center, Harvard University Press, Cambridge, Mass.
Zwicker, Jonathan E 2006, *Practices of the Sentimental Imagination*, Harvard University Press, Cambridge, Mass.

Index

References to individual people are printed in bold-face type.